Portland Community College

D0687615

NANCY REAGAN

MODERN FIRST LADIES

Lewis L. Gould, Editor

NANCY REAGAN

ON THE WHITE HOUSE STAGE

JAMES G. BENZE, JR.

UNIVERSITY PRESS OF KANSAS

The photographs in this book are courtesy of
Ronald Reagan Library.

© 2005 by the University Press of Kansas
All rights reserved
Published by the University Press of Kansas
(Lawrence, Kansas 66049), which was organized by
the Kansas Board of Regents and is operated and
funded by Emporia State University, Fort Hays State
University, Kansas State University, Pittsburg State
University, the University of Kansas, and Wichita
State University

Library of Congress Cataloging-in-Publication Data

Benze, James G.
Nancy Reagan : on the White House stage / James G.
Benze, Jr.
p.   cm. — (Modern first ladies)
Includes bibliographical references and index.
ISBN 0-7006-1401-x (cloth : alk. paper)
1. Reagan, Nancy, 1923– 2. Presidents' spouses—
United States — Biography. 3. Reagan, Nancy, 1923–
Marriage. 4. Actresses—United States—Political
activity—Case studies. 5. Acting—Political aspects—
United States—Case studies.
I. Title. II. Series.
E878.R43B46 2005
973.927'092—DC22   2005008586
British Library Cataloguing-in-Publication Data is available.
Printed in the United States of America
10 9 8 7 6 5 4 3 2 1

For my wife, Pam, and my son, Jay

CONTENTS

Nancy Reagan was a controversial first lady before her husband assumed the presidency in January 1981, and she has remained so to the present time. From her hints that Jimmy Carter and his wife should move out of the White House early to her current advocacy of stem cell research, Mrs. Reagan has been an outspoken public figure and a target for criticism. During her tenure in Washington, she was labeled "Queen Nancy" for her opulent lifestyle and a "Dragon Lady" for exercising too much influence on her husband during the Iran-Contra scandal. The "Just Say No" antidrug program stirred ambivalent feelings about her commitment to dealing with this recurring social problem.

Most of the historical literature on Nancy Reagan's time in Washington has been negative and polemical. During the 1980s polls of scholars rated her at the bottom among all presidential wives. Subsequent surveys have seen her move up from that poor evaluation, but she seems unlikely ever to ascend to the level of an Eleanor Roosevelt or a Lady Bird Johnson. Nevertheless, Mrs. Reagan deserves more than the heated rhetoric that has followed her even after she and President Reagan returned to California in 1989.

James G. Benze's study of Nancy Reagan in the White House is an important step toward our having a better understanding of where she fits in the continuum of presidential wives. Seeing Nancy Reagan's life in the theater and films as a key to understanding how she approached her duties as first lady, Benze has constructed a careful and informed narrative of what Mrs. Reagan did and her impact on her husband's presidency. The result is a book notable for its balance and insights into what she meant to accomplish. Benze is critical where appropriate; he is not a partisan defender or attacker. His goal is to see where Nancy Reagan drew on the tradition of other first ladies and where she made new contributions to the institution. He succeeds in that task. After finishing Benze's narrative of Nancy

Reagan's eight years in the White House, the reader will understand her importance, the strong feelings she evoked, and the lasting legacy she has imparted to her successors. Nancy Reagan was and is a woman whose performance has stirred passionate defenders and acerbic critics. In Jim Benze, she has been the beneficiary of a sympathetic and astute biographer who provides historical context and perspective of a high order.

Lewis L. Gould

ACKNOWLEDGMENTS

There are a number of people to whom I owe a debt of gratitude. The employees of the Reagan Library were patient in explaining exactly what was and was not available at any particular moment and helped me acquire copies of relevant primary material. Lewis Gould, the series editor, read numerous chapter drafts and critiqued them in positive and careful ways. He was always willing to share his own expertise, and was extremely patient with the many obstacles that arose in the completion of the text. The same can be said of Fred M. Woodward of the University Press of Kansas. I thank them both for the opportunity they have afforded me.

I appreciate the support of Washington and Jefferson College in providing release time from my teaching schedule in order to finish the writing of the manuscript and financial support in obtaining materials for it. I am also extremely lucky to have my own personal editor in my wife, Pamela, who took the time from her busy schedule to help in the many revisions of the text. Final responsibility for the contents of this book is, of course, my own.

NANCY REAGAN

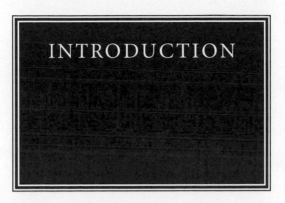

INTRODUCTION

This book grows out of several essays I have written on first ladies, the most notable being a bibliographic essay on Nancy Reagan published in Lewis L. Gould's *American First Ladies* (New York: Routledge, 2001). While this book draws upon these previous writings, it differs from them in several important ways.

The most obvious differences are length and focus: my earlier writings on Nancy Reagan were essays, part of larger works, and sought to place Nancy Reagan in the context of her predecessors; the present work is a book devoted entirely to Mrs. Reagan, and focuses on her influence on her husband's political career and in particular his presidency. While Ronald Reagan was in the White House, Mrs. Reagan had much to do not only with the president's schedule, but also with his appointments and even specific policy issues. However, Mrs. Reagan had no grand political agenda of her own. Her involvement in policy stemmed from her desire to make her husband's presidency a success.

In these pages, I argue that Mrs. Reagan's training as an actor affected the way in which she influenced her husband's presidency. Ronald Reagan has often been quoted as saying, "How can a president not be an actor?" The same can be said of the first lady. Yet up to now, Mrs. Reagan's long experience with the theater and the movies have generally not been considered in examining her role as first lady.[1]

Nancy Reagan had a long association with show business. Her mother, Edith Luckett, was a stage actress, and Nancy caught the acting bug from her. Edith once bought Nancy a Mary Pickford wig complete with long blonde curls. Nancy loved to march around the house wearing the wig, proclaiming that she would grow up to be an actress. From her earliest days, Nancy was indeed an actress, having to be virtually three different people depending on where she found herself. She would act one way when she was staying with her mother's sister in Bethesda, Maryland, another when she was with her father in New Jersey, and still another when she was away at school.[2]

Nancy went on to star in her high school's production of the play *First Lady,* and while attending Smith College she majored in drama. After graduation, she appeared in stage plays, often with actress ZaSu Pitts, a family friend; she later went to Hollywood, looking for a break in feature films. In fact, Mrs. Reagan's ties to the theater and movies were far more varied than her husband's. While he was struggling in Hollywood B movies, she was appearing in off-Broadway plays and even dabbling in television. Her mother was an extremely well-connected actress, and through her mother, Nancy met a variety of actors and had a wide range of theatrical experiences.

Of course, Mrs. Reagan is a complex person not driven solely by her acting experiences. Many other important factors, including her personality, the impact of her family background, the prevailing perceptions of marriage and motherhood, and her obvious love for her husband have been identified in other biographies of the first lady. This biography seeks to add Mrs. Reagan's acting experience to the list of factors that affected her perception of her role as first lady.

Unlike her husband, Mrs. Reagan was usually the supporting actor, not the lead. Though she appeared in big-budget movies, she was most commonly cast in smaller roles, often as a pregnant mother. Mrs. Reagan became a member of her movies' troupe of actors—those whose job it is to flatter and praise the star's efforts, feed the star lines he or she has forgotten, or perhaps help create the environment the star needs to give the performance of a lifetime.

As first lady, Mrs. Reagan did all of this and more for her husband. She occasionally supplied the president with a missing line (as she did at the Bitburg ceremony). She flattered and praised him (and encouraged those around him to do the same) in order to get him "up" for his performance (as she did for the second debate of the 1984 election). She created a working environment free of stress by manipulating his schedule and using her influence to remove aides who she felt were not supportive of her husband (such as Donald Regan). Mrs. Reagan gave the president advice on policy issues such as abortion and arms control—not to push her own agenda, but to ensure a successful legacy for her husband's administration.

Nancy Reagan successfully transferred skills she had acquired during several decades of acting to her role of political spouse. During her acting career, Mrs. Reagan mastered a number of facial expressions that would prove useful to her role as first lady—delight, rapt attention, sympathy, and so on. Of course such expressions are not in themselves unusual. What was unusual was Mrs. Reagan's ability to summon such expressions at a moment's notice and hold them for extended periods of time. Garry Wills notes:

> Though Nancy Reagan never became a Hollywood star, she did not waste the eight years she spent trying. She learned a thing or two about the Look. She practices a severe economy of expression that makes three or four compositions of the features cover all necessary social tasks—the smile of delighted surprise at the top of the airplane stairs, the concerned gaze at redeemable druggies, and—most of all—the upward stare at her husband. In photograph after photograph, one finds the same expression, not varied by a centimeter.[3]

Nancy's typical character parts of a nurse or a young mother helped her convey the empathy a first lady must show to those in distress. Her best physical assets as an actor were her large, expressive eyes—eyes that projected a feeling of empathy. Mrs. Reagan was aware of the effect of her doelike eyes, and often used this feature to her best advantage.

Her Hollywood background also taught Mrs. Reagan the importance of physical appearance. She made sure that her husband was always seen in crisp suits, and cut back dramatically on his use of hair color. Of course Mrs. Reagan was extremely conscious of her own appearance. She was always stylishly coiffed, she made sure to pose for pictures in a way that showed her best profile, and as a spectator she always was careful to appear to be paying full attention.

All the knowledge she had learned in her own career she used to further her husband's, advancing those individuals and programs she felt would lead to his success, not hers. Mrs. Reagan never advanced her own policy agenda, not even when it came to funding for drug abuse prevention, her own pet project. Mrs. Reagan knew her role both within her marriage and within the Reagan presidency.

In short, Mrs. Reagan approached her role as first lady in much the same way she approached her Hollywood roles—as a supporting actor. She helped her husband (the star) through his public performances and enabled him to face political crises. Mrs. Reagan was as much an acting first lady as her husband was the star performer of his presidency. If her role required glamour and glitz, she knew how to obtain designer gowns at minimal cost. If she needed to mock her public image by dressing in dowdy clothes and singing "Second Hand Rose" at a press club dinner, she could do it. If her husband's success required her to tangle with Chief of Staff Donald Regan, she could do that, too.

Like any good supporting actress, Mrs. Reagan exerted her influence in ways the audience never noticed. Consequently, she was not popular with some feminists, who would have preferred a more activist first lady, one with her own ideas and agenda. Later, toward the end of her husband's administration, as her influence became more public, Mrs. Reagan lost popularity with those who thought that a first lady should not be involved with substantive issues. As a result, she annoyed as many as she pleased, and her image suffered among political activists of both the left and the right. In addition, some young feminist writers felt that Mrs. Reagan appeared always to be playing a role, and therefore seemed not as authentic as they thought modern women should be.

Of course, people play many roles in their lives, and Nancy Reagan is no different. Acting is an important aspect of her life, but it is not the only one. She was also an extremely devoted wife. As with many women of her generation, Mrs. Reagan considered marriage to be an essential ingredient to a full and happy life. Like her mother, she married relatively late in life, and gave up her acting career to find fulfillment in her marriage. In making this decision, Mrs. Reagan not only had the example of her mother, but also the support of educators, psychologists, and women's magazines, which all gave the same message: that a woman's primary responsibility was to her husband and her family.⁴ Mrs. Reagan has said many times that her life began when she married Ronald Reagan. Her actions as first lady suggest she meant what she said. Mrs. Reagan's motivation for everything that she did as first lady was to help her husband.

Nancy Reagan's actions often angered feminist critics, but so did her words. As Mrs. Reagan wrote in her first book, *Nancy,* "What I really wanted out of life was to be a wife to the man I loved and mother to our children . . . I always wanted someone to take care of me, someone I could take care of."⁵ Women who regarded marriage as part of a patriarchal system created to dominate and exploit women read her book and saw Mrs. Reagan as an opponent of their cause.

Throughout Nancy Reagan's life her roles as supporting actress and loving wife reinforced each other. Just as supporting actors submerge their own egos for the good of the production, wives often submerged their own needs on behalf of their husband's career and their marriage. Many women of Mrs. Reagan's generation, like those in generations after hers, saw marriage as a partnership requiring both members' efforts to succeed. In Nancy Reagan's generation, however, it was expected that the wife's responsibility in this partnership was not only to tend to the home, but also to support her husband in his profession. In many ways, Nancy Reagan's partnership with her husband was typical of her generation, but it was also unique in how perfectly the two complemented the other and minimized the other's weaknesses.

All modern first ladies must be concerned about their image, but they must also develop their own interests, embracing specific issues and problems in their husband's administration, and Mrs. Reagan followed suit, creating the "Just Say No" antidrug program. Though many skeptics saw the program as primarily public relations, the extent of the first lady's efforts on behalf of "Just Say No" was strong evidence of her commitment to the program. Mrs. Reagan traveled thousands of miles and spoke to hundreds of groups with a simple but seemingly powerful message—that children in particular should "just say no" to drugs.

During her years in the White House, Mrs. Reagan faced more than her share of trauma. She was diagnosed and treated for breast cancer in front of a national audience, some of whom criticized her choice of treatment. She also suffered through the attempt on her husband's life and watched him undergo several major operations. During these years she also had to deal with the loss of both her stepfather, Dr. Loyal Davis, and her beloved mother, Edith. Through all these crises, Mrs. Reagan was pursued by an ever more intrusive press.

Living in the White House can place a great strain on family relations. The Reagan family's being on a public stage exacerbated existing tensions. Although Ronald and Nancy Reagan's relationship with their children was flawed well before their move to Washington, things went from bad to worse during the eight years of the Reagan presidency.

Of course, any biography of Nancy Reagan must include her post–White House days. The Reagans' departure from Washington began with great promise. President Reagan returned to the speech-making circuit, while Mrs. Reagan continued her involvement with the "Just Say No" program. When it seemed that they would finally have the freedom and time to enjoy each other's company, the former president was diagnosed with Alzheimer's disease. During the years of her husband's illness and subsequent death, Mrs. Reagan adopted the role of caregiver and began to speak out on a number of issues related to her husband's illness.

CHAPTER 1

A SUPPORTING ACTOR COMES OF AGE

Nancy Reagan's career as first lady has been evaluated from a number of perspectives—her role as advisor to her husband, her sponsorship of the "Just Say No" campaign against drug abuse, her use of astrology in shaping the president's schedule, and her impact on White House personnel. While most biographical accounts mention her years as a film actress, none has done justice to the influence of Nancy Reagan's acting career on her later life. Her many roles as a supporting actress on the stage and in movies provided her with many of the skills she would need as the wife of Ronald Reagan.

During her acting career, Mrs. Reagan was so often cast as a young mother (usually pregnant) that she became more of a character actor than a leading lady. Character actors serve a number of useful purposes in drama.[1] Their main function is to support the leading players, giving them room to exercise their talents. A Hollywood observer notes the importance of supporting, or character, actor in this capacity: "If it weren't for the career character actors—the supporting cast lifers—Hollywood movies would be even more bombastic and exhausting to watch than they already are. Imagine a picture cast entirely with stars, ex-stars, and star wannabes, dozens of needy egos competing for our attention: that giant sucking sound is the air going out of the room at the beginning of every scene."[2] Nancy Reagan was a supporting player for her star husband. She saw to his needs for attention and support. At times she went beyond the role of a supporting actor, to help clear the stage of members of his administration who got in the way in order to create the space he needed to be the star.

Supporting, or character, actors also supply color in their brief movie appearances; they bring the film to life. They often provide a temporary, but necessary, distraction from the main plot of the movie. While these players are usually fine actors in their own right, they rarely become stars. However, most supporting actors seem untroubled by the lack of recognition, as long as they continue to work.[3] Although Nancy Reagan was a legitimate stage and screen actor, she never obtained star status. Lacking the physical attributes or screen presence of some of her contemporaries, her Hollywood career consisted mostly of small parts. As a result, she became accustomed to being part of the cast rather than the star—performing her role with little notice from most of the moviegoing public.

While Mrs. Reagan was certainly not invisible during the Reagan presidency, she generally wielded her influence behind the scenes. Cabinet seats, press conferences, and presidential task forces were not for her. Instead, she whispered her thoughts in her husband's ear or quietly built coalitions with other moderates within the administration. Yet she greatly influenced the makeup of her husband's staff and the direction of the administration's policies.

Much of what Mrs. Reagan knew about acting and supporting her husband came through the influence of her mother, Edith, also an actress. Nancy, whose given name was Anne Frances, was born on 6 July 1921.[4] She was the only child of the unstable marriage of Kenneth Robbins and Edith Luckett Robbins. Kenneth was an automobile mechanic; Edith was a moderately successful and well-connected actress, who often spoke in an elaborate Southern drawl and told dramatic stories of a childhood amid Virginia plantations, even though she was born in the depressed inner city of Washington, D.C. During her career, she appeared on Broadway with many well-known actors, including George M. Cohan and Spencer Tracy. Kenneth and Edith were wed in 1917, but their marriage seemed doomed from the start. Temperamental differences and Edith's desire for a stage career led to a separation, and ultimately an uncontested divorce on grounds of desertion in 1928. Although Nancy visited both her father and her paternal grandmother during her childhood, in her autobiography, *Nancy*, she makes it clear she never really bonded with her father. She writes, "I visited him only a few times over the years before he died in the 1960s. He was my father, but I somehow could never think of him that way, because there had never been any relationship of any kind."[5]

Nancy's early years were characterized by separation from her mother. Edith had never given up her stage aspirations and needed money to support her daughter, so she returned to acting. Edith, or "Dee Dee" as she liked to be called, initially took Nancy on tour with her. After two years of having Nancy sleep in dresser drawers and accompany her to theatrical parties, Edith decided that her daughter needed a more stable life. As a result, Edith placed Nancy in the care of her older sister, Virginia, and her husband, C. Audley Galbraith. They lived in Bethesda, Maryland, and were better able to provide the child with a comfortable (if less exciting) home environment. Although Nancy was well cared for at her aunt and uncle's, she missed her mother a great deal and often cried herself to sleep.[6] The lack of a firm relationship with her parents in part explains the emotional importance she would later place on her own marriage.

For the next five years, Nancy would see her mother only sporadically, usually when Edith was home from tour or in a New York stage production. Then Nancy would travel to New York to be with her mother—trips that Mrs. Reagan recalls as among her favorite memories. While Nancy was visiting, Edith often took her to see plays in which Edith performed. Nancy was captivated not only by her mother's performance, but also by the costumes, the music, and the drama of the theater. She would later write that she loved "the special feel and musty smell of the backstage."[7]

Nancy was thrilled to spend time with her mother, and she was enchanted by the dramatic life her mother led. When Edith came to visit in Bethesda, she would captivate her daughter by acting out scenes from her most recent play. Although Edith's roles were never very large, in her daughter's eyes, she was the star of every performance.

On one of Nancy's visits to New York to watch her mother perform, she saw Edith's character being badly mistreated on stage. Thinking that her mother was really suffering, Nancy became hysterical, and when she went backstage after the play she would not speak to any of the performers she thought had mistreated her mother.[8] Despite the upheaval that Edith's career caused, Nancy longed to follow in her mother's footsteps. From the moment she saw her mother on stage, she knew that she too wanted to be an actress. On her visits, Nancy would spend time backstage, dreaming of being a star. In her own words, "I loved to dress up in her stage clothes, put on makeup, and pretend I was playing her parts. I would have given anything to have long blond curls, and when mother bought me a Mary Pickford wig I was in heaven."[9] Even when Nancy went back to Bethesda, she made up skits and recruited other children to perform in her productions.

The Galbraiths made every effort to bring Nancy into their family and treat her like their daughter. They sent her to the Sidwell Friends School, one of the most prestigious in the Washington area. Nancy liked the Galbraiths, but being separated from her mother made the time spent with her aunt and uncle difficult. She did, however, become quite attached to her cousin Charlotte. Even though she was only three and a half years older than Nancy, Charlotte became her protector, looking out for her and providing some of the security she was missing.

Then, in 1928, Nancy's life underwent a dramatic change. She met her mother's new beau, prominent Chicago neurosurgeon Loyal Davis. Soon after, Edith asked Nancy for her permission to marry Dr. Davis. As an extra enticement, she promised that she would leave the stage so they could all live together in Chicago. Nancy quickly gave her consent, and on 21 May 1929 Edith and Dr. Davis were married. Nancy not only gained a stepfather, but also a stepbrother, Richard. The timing of the marriage was fortunate, as the Galbraiths soon moved to Atlanta and would have been unable to continue to care for Nancy.[10]

The Davises' marriage was an interesting mix of opposites. Edith, a Democrat, was a gregarious, fun-loving, and outspoken woman who liked (and told) a good story—and liked it even better if it was a little off-color. Dr. Davis, a conservative, soft-spoken Republican, was very strict and well known among his interns for his insistence on punctuality. He also loved the theater and, though not particularly talented, at one time had acting aspirations of his own.[11] Dr. Davis enjoyed reading roles with Walter Huston and other actors while vacationing at Lake Arrowhead, California, which had become a summer retreat for many film stars. Some of their acting friends even became his patients as well as houseguests when they performed in Chicago theaters.[12]

Her mother's marriage significantly altered Nancy's life. She went from a lower-middle-class household in Bethesda, Maryland, to an affluent family living on Lake Shore Drive in Chicago. For the first time, she was living with both her mother and her mother's husband, and there is no doubt that Nancy needed to adjust to Dr. Davis. With his reserved bearing and belief in discipline, he didn't shower Nancy with emotion or declarations of love. She began to call him "Dr. Loyal" while waiting for him to tell her to call him "Daddy" or "Dad." She had a long wait: it was only after her own children started calling Dr. Davis "Bopa" that Nancy dropped "Dr. Loyal" and began to call him "Bopa" too. In her biography, Mrs. Reagan refers to her stepfather as "strict but fair," and admits she found it difficult to share her mother with someone else.[13]

Over time, Nancy came to love and respect Dr. Davis, and was delighted when he finally adopted her—something he had been reluctant to do as long as her birth father was still alive. Nancy was so eager to be adopted by her stepfather that she approached a local judge living next door to the family and asked him what she had to do to adopt Dr. Davis. The judge informed Nancy's stepfather of her wishes. Dr. Davis told her that there was nothing he wanted more than to be her real father, but that if it was what she wanted, she would have to make it happen. Thus, when Nancy was only fourteen, she took the extraordinary step of bringing adoption papers with her on a visit to her father and asking him to give up his parental rights. She returned to Chicago with the adoption papers signed.[14]

Edith's marriage to Loyal Davis did not cause her to give up her fascination with the stage and her friendship with many prominent actors of the day. The Davis family moved at the top of the Chicago social world but was also very well known in the city's theatrical circles. At the time, Chicago was a center of entertainment in the United States. Among the national radio programs produced there was *Betty and Bob,* an NBC radio production in which Edith worked. Chicago was also a stop for national touring theater productions and originated productions as well. Because of her mother's connections, Nancy got to know many famous actors. Alla Nazimova, the stage and silent movie star ("Zim" to Nancy), was her godmother. Nazimova was the first Stanislavsky-trained actress to play a lead role on Broadway, and her Hollywood séances impressed even Rudolph Valentino. Comediennes Colleen Moore ("Aunt Colleen") and ZaSu Pitts were other famous performers who became close family friends.[15]

There was also "Uncle" Walter Huston, who regaled the household with stories of other Hollywood stars, such as Katharine Hepburn and Spencer Tracy (Nancy called him "Spence"). The Davis family often spent summer weekends with Uncle Walter at Lake Arrowhead. While at the lake, Nancy met established actors and many Hollywood principals, including agent Myron Selznick and actor Reginald Denny, and up-and-coming stars such as Jimmy Stewart (on whom she had a bit of a crush).[16] To Nancy, these actors became more than faces on the screen or pictures in a movie magazine. They were talented, entertaining, and real people who fueled her interest in the theater. Through her mother and Uncle Walter, Nancy also met producers and writers, in the process becoming interested in the many aspects of theatrical performance. One summer day she sat by the Hustons' pool while Josh Logan, a young Hollywood producer, read a script to Walter Huston. Nancy listened to the two men discuss the casting of the movie. When they were done, Uncle Walter asked for her opinion of the script.[17]

Nancy attended the prestigious Girls Latin School in Chicago. There she was involved in many activities: field hockey, student government, and student theater. Nancy got her first taste of real acting in her senior year, when she won the lead in her class production of (ironically) *First Lady* by George S. Kaufman. Nancy dominated the production, learning the lines of everyone in the play, feeding her fellow players reminders when they forgot their lines, and even tailoring some of her own lines to fit what they remembered.[18]

After graduation, Nancy entered Smith College, one of the nation's best-known women's colleges. She was, however, not much of a scholar, and her weakness in math and science ruled out most of the traditional majors. Therefore, Nancy became one of the few students to major in drama. She appeared in many of the school's theater productions, getting rave reviews for the student-written and

-produced *Ladies on the Loose*. She also did summer stock productions during her vacations.[19]

At Smith, Nancy was taught by Hallie Flanagan Davis, at the time one of the most famous and controversial women in American theater. Davis believed that theater was for everyone—the masses as well as the elite. During her four years with the National Theater program, she created a new vision of the theater and left a legacy of active regional theaters across the United States. She also felt that the theater should have a politically active social conscience. Nancy did not agree with this approach. She wanted to be taught about acting, not social issues. Despite their differences, Nancy won a role in *Susan and God*, the first major production of the Davis tenure at Smith.[20]

During this period, Nancy had her first serious romance, with Frank Birney, a Princeton man. The two had a great deal in common. Like Nancy, Frank was from the Chicago area and had parents who were divorced. He also aspired to a career in theater, but as a writer rather than a performer. For a time, the young lovers were inseparable. Unfortunately, the relationship ended tragically on 13 December 1941, when Birney was found crushed to death in a train yard. Though the circumstances surrounding his death were never determined with certainty, it was reported that he had missed his train to New York while on his way to see his sister, and was walking down the tracks when he was struck by a train going in the opposite direction. There was speculation that Birney might have committed suicide because he was worried about his grades and possible dismissal from Princeton.[21]

Nancy was distraught when she received the news. She took to her room for several days and then left the campus for Chicago, where she spent most of her Christmas holidays consoling Frank's mother. Perhaps because of her own deep feelings of loss, Nancy embellished the story of Frank's death. Over the years, she told several friends and even her own daughter that she and Frank were engaged and that he was on his way to pick her up for a trip to New York when the accident occurred. According to Nancy's housemates, however, she had had no plans for that weekend; and Birney's friends have said that if the two were engaged, it had not been made public.[22]

Soon after the tragedy, Nancy graduated from Smith. Without a career and having lost the man she loved, she returned to Chicago to stay with her mother while her stepfather served with the U.S. Army. To keep busy and help support the family, she worked at Marshall Fields department store and as a nurse's aide. However, Nancy had not given up her acting aspirations. She continued to perform in summer stock whenever possible, and with the help of ZaSu Pitts, landed her first professional role in a touring company of *Ramshackle Inn*.[23] By the time the tour ended in New York, Dr. Davis had returned home from Europe. As a result, Nancy decided to remain in the city. She lived on East 51st Street, close to Walter Huston and Spencer Tracy.

Nancy soon landed a small role in the Broadway production of *Lute's Song,* starring Yul Brynner and Mary Martin. She also did some work in the new medium of television, appearing in another production of *Ramshackle Inn* and a play called *Broken Dishes*. In 1949, Spencer Tracy introduced Nancy to a Hollywood casting director, Benny Thau, who arranged a test for the fledgling actress. As a result of her screen test, Nancy was signed to a beginner's contract of $250 per week with MGM.[24]

At the time, Nancy did not realize how important her family connections were to her screen test. Her mother called Spencer Tracy and asked him to arrange for the well-known director George Cukor to oversee the test. Benny Thau used his influence to have the "right" script for her test and to have George Fosley, one of the best Hollywood photographers, take the required still shots.[25] After the successful completion of her screen test, Nancy became part of the Hollywood community. Her future seemed set.

Nancy Davis never became a major Hollywood star, but her career did have its high points. In 1949, she appeared with Glenn Ford and Janet Leigh in *The Doctor and the Girl* and in a lavish production of *East Side, West Side*. In total, Nancy appeared in eleven movies, including *Night into Morning* (1951) and *Donovan's Brain* (1953)—almost always in a supporting role. She did manage to garner some favorable reviews for her performances: A. H. Weiler of the *New York Times* described her as "beautiful and convincing," and Lloyd Shearer of the *New York Herald Tribune* commended her for "good solid acting."[26] Nancy was also popular with the public, and in a 1950 *Photoplay* "Choose Your Stars" contest, readers chose Nancy fifth of ten up-and-coming players likely to achieve stardom, behind such actresses as Mercedes McCambridge and Piper Laurie.[27] Despite her good reviews, they were for smaller supporting parts, and it was soon clear that Nancy was not destined for stardom. Her studio reputation was as a well-groomed actress who was easy to work with, but not an Elizabeth Taylor, Ann Sothern, Jane Russell, Marilyn Monroe, or Lana Turner, the leading "sexy" starlets of the day. Unfortunately, Nancy was not even considered in the same league as a Jane Powell, Debbie Reynolds, or June Allyson, the Hollywood girls next door. Hollywood columnist Louella Parsons wrote: "Nancy looks very unlike the usual conception of an actress. She might be the daughter of any town's leading citizen or the competent secretary of a big official, but you would never label her an actress."[28] This analysis of her persona wasn't lost on Nancy, who would write in her biography, "Actors tend to play the roles that they are suited for, and unlike many young actresses, I wasn't the big-bosomed sweater type girl. As a result, I was usually asked to play a young mother or a pregnant woman."[29] Nancy did have some assets as an actress. Besides her professional conduct, she was also well known for her large, expressive eyes, which she could use to communicate a variety of emotions.[30]

Another reason why Nancy's career never blossomed may have been that acting was not her highest priority. On the biographical information form that she filled out for MGM, Nancy wrote that her greatest ambition was to have a successful marriage. In 1975 Nancy responded to a Smith College alumni information form in part by writing, "Because I hadn't found the man I wanted to marry, I couldn't just sit around doing nothing so I became an actress."[31]

Nancy met her future husband through an unusual set of circumstances. As she herself recalled, she was reading a Hollywood newspaper in late 1949 when she noticed her name on a list of alleged Communist sympathizers. Given the fact that the "Red Scare"—the fear that Communists had infiltrated American institutions—was particularly strong in Hollywood at that time, she became quite alarmed. Unsure about how to deal with the problem, she contacted Mervyn LeRoy, her director in *East Side, West Side*. In turn, LeRoy contacted Ronald Reagan, the president of the Screen Actors Guild

(SAG).[32] Reagan discovered that the problem had arisen from the fact that there was another actress with the same name, and met with Nancy (over dinner, at her request) to explain the mix-up. He later told her that he had convinced the other Nancy Davis to change her professional name. This story of how Nancy met Ronald Reagan doesn't quite ring true, mainly because Nancy had enough influential Hollywood friends to ensure that she would not be confused with some other Nancy Davis. It seems likely (particularly given her insistence that they meet over dinner) that Nancy was more interested in being introduced to Ronald Reagan than in resolving any confusion over names.[33]

In 1950, perhaps in an effort to remain close to Ronald Reagan, Nancy was appointed (at her request) to the Screen Actors Guild to serve out the term of a member who had resigned. That November, she ran for her own seat on the board, but lost. The day after the results were made public, Nancy was again appointed to the board, with the help of SAG president Ronald Reagan. Even though she had never shown much interest in industry-related functions, she ran again in 1951, this time winning a three-year term. Reagan's involvement in SAG activities had been a major source of friction in his first marriage, to actress Jane Wyman, who felt that her husband spent too much time on SAG activities and not nearly enough time at home. By supporting Reagan's interest in SAG, Nancy may have been trying to avoid an obvious point of conflict.[34]

Nancy Reagan has often said that her life began when she met Ronald Reagan, but her future husband was far from ready for remarriage. Reagan's first marriage had just ended, and he was trying to cope with being a divorced father to his daughter, Maureen, and adopted son, Michael. In fact, Hollywood stories suggested that he was still so much in love with his former wife that he had rented their honeymoon apartment and continued to drive the Cadillac convertible she had given him.[35] While recovering from the trauma of his divorce, Reagan dated many young Hollywood starlets and soon gained a reputation as a lothario. A serious relationship with Nancy was clearly not on his immediate agenda.

Ronald Reagan's aloofness was also a factor in his reluctance to commit to a new relationship. Perhaps as a result of being abandoned by his alcoholic father, Ronald Reagan had great difficulty forming close relationships throughout his adult life.[36] He had many acquaintances, but few real friends. It would take time for Nancy to break through the shell that he had built around his feelings and convince him that he could trust her. In her memoirs, Mrs. Reagan explains her husband's detachment in terms of his past: "It's hard to make close friends or to put down roots when you're always moving, and I think this—plus the fact that everyone knew his father was an alcoholic—explains why Ronnie became a loner. Although he loves people, he often seems remote, and he doesn't let anyone get too close. There's a wall around him. He lets me come closer than anyone else, but there are times when even I feel that barrier."[37]

Jane Wyman and Nancy Davis shared several characteristics. They were about the same size and weight; they had the same color eyes as Reagan's mother, Nellie; and they were both actresses when he met them. Jane and Nancy were both the daughters of absentee fathers whose names they never spoke. Both loved the color red, and neither was much of a cook. Finally, both women virtually had to shanghai Reagan into marrying them.[38]

Ronald Reagan and Nancy Davis dated sporadically over the next two years, usually accompanying each other to the openings of their movies. Not yet ready to settle down, Reagan played the field by dating sixteen different actresses during that time, including Doris Day, Rhonda Fleming, Piper Laurie, Patricia Neal, and Ann Sothern. Doris Lilly, the future author of *How to Meet a Millionaire,* claimed that Reagan proposed to her but that she turned him down because he was only looking for someone "who was willing to make the big moves, push, be there, encourage him, never leave him alone for a moment. . . . I couldn't do it."[39] Nancy also dated others, none seriously.[40]

In the meantime, Nancy continued her movie career, starring with James Whitmore in *The Next Voice You Hear,* a parable about God saving the world. The Hollywood buzz was that the movie had the potential to be a huge success, and might even be a "breakout" movie for Nancy. Unfortunately, critics panned the film, and the public ignored it. In the movie, Nancy played Mrs. Joe Smith, James Whitmore's pregnant wife, an extremely sympathetic and moving character in a bad movie. Bosley Crowther of the *New York Times* said that Nancy was "delightful" as the "gentle, plain, and understanding wife."[41] After the film's demise, she found herself typecast as a pregnant wife in a series of at best average films. If her Hollywood career continued, it would be difficult for her to move beyond supporting roles. Frustrated with being typecast, Nancy Reagan asked MGM to cancel her contract, saying, "I'm tired of playing pregnant housewives."[42] Nancy was also thirty-one and would soon be unable to play such roles.

Meanwhile, Ronald Reagan's movie career had also stalled. His last successful picture had been almost ten years earlier. Having come from a broken home as a child, he was deeply affected by his divorce, and his work as head of the Screen Actors Guild was becoming increasingly difficult because of the divisive Communist issue. After more than two years of dating, Reagan and Nancy were finally ready to make their relationship permanent, and on 4 March 1952 Nancy Davis became Mrs. Ronald Reagan. The Reagans' first child, Patricia Anne (Patti), was born on 22 October 1952; their son, Ronald, Jr., followed some years later, on 20 May 1958.

Given the time between her marriage and Patti's birth, it is clear that Nancy was pregnant when she married Ronald Reagan.[43] What is less clear is whether she used the pregnancy to prod Reagan to the altar. Given his reluctance to form lasting attachments, it is a possibility. But their relationship did seem to be moving in the direction of marriage. Reagan had invited Nancy to his ranch and introduced her to his children. Nancy says that it was at this point that she realized that Ronald Reagan was serious about their relationship.[44] However, the only two people who knew for sure never discussed the issue publicly.

Ronald and Nancy Reagan had several things in common. They were both children of divorce, although this fact seems to have affected Ronald Reagan more deeply than his wife. Both had acting careers that had slowed down. He got along famously with her mother. He and his mother-in-law both loved to tell bawdy stories, and he would sometimes call Edith on the phone just to tell her the latest. Reagan came to admire Loyal Davis, whose conservative opinions were partially responsible for his evolution from Democrat to Republican. With an alcoholic father, Ronald Reagan lived a difficult life growing up. He never had his wife's film connections and never really felt part of the Hollywood establishment. He was amazed by his wife's familiarity with the Hollywood elite—that she had known Walter Huston and Spencer Tracy since her childhood, and that she had actually dated Clark Gable.[45]

Their disparate backgrounds increased their attraction to each other. Nancy's more sheltered upbringing, her elite private schooling, her family's wealth, what some have referred to as her "champagne laugh," and her relentless attention and commitment to him appealed to Ronald Reagan. Nancy, for her part, was fascinated by the very roughness of Reagan's upbringing, his nomadic early life, his having to work his way through Eureka College by washing dishes, the variety of jobs he had held, and his intense pride at having made it on his own. Naturally shy, she was also drawn to his outgoing and gregarious personality. Ronald Reagan loved to talk, and Nancy loved to listen. She was a compulsive worrier, he was an eternal optimist—she often describes him as the most optimistic man she ever met.[46] The differences in their life experiences and personalities made for mutual attraction; each provided what the other was missing. They made each other whole. The Reagans were deeply committed to and protective of each other and their marriage. The stability of their relationship also resulted from their parents' failed marriages, Nancy's mother's remarriage, and Ronald Reagan's unpleasant divorce from Jane Wyman.

Neither of the Reagans was ever a major Hollywood star. Ronald Reagan had once been on the edge of becoming a leading man, but had never quite made it to the inner circle. He had, however, come close enough to stardom to receive and value the star treatment. Nancy never broke out of the supporting actor category. For Nancy, like her mother, giving up her acting career to become her husband's best supporting player was an easy decision. For Ronald Reagan, who didn't understand why he was not a major film star and who now had a larger family to feed, his decline as an actor was a significant blow.

Although Ronald Reagan had made some successful movies, including *Knute Rockne—All American* and *Kings Row,* his Hollywood career was virtually finished by 1952. He was finding it extremely difficult to get what he considered appropriate parts. Money was so tight that Mrs. Reagan, who had sworn that she would not be a working wife and mother, went back to work for four months, making the film *Donovan's Brain* to help support the family.[47]

This was undoubtedly Ronald Reagan's low point. The failure of his first marriage had left him deeply shaken. Now it seemed that his career was also over. The only work he could get was on the Las Vegas circuit, but even there his marketability was marginal because of his inability to either sing or dance. His only alternative was to emcee stage shows. Nancy's role was to see him through and to assure him that better days were coming. She is one of the very few people who have seen Ronald Reagan without his perpetual optimism. Thus, she understood the need to keep his spirits up, a role she would assume during his political career.[48]

Fortunately, Ronald Reagan's stint in Las Vegas was brief, and he was soon offered a job as the official spokesman for General Electric. The position involved hosting a weekly television series, *General Electric Theater,* and traveling around the country giving speeches at the company's factories and conventions. For Reagan, this was an ideal job. He got to act a bit (in some *General Electric Theater* dramas), and he had a steady income and was given a number of perks, such as a new, all-electric home. Crossing the United States, he made many contacts that would be important for his future political career. During this period, Reagan's political conservatism—born out of his experiences as SAG president and complemented by his association with Dr. Davis—matured. As his speeches for General Electric became more conservative, he began to realize that his own politics had changed. He now had more in common with the Republican Party than with the Democrats. Both Reagans voted for President Eisenhower in 1956, and Ronald Reagan led a group of Democrats for Richard Nixon in 1960. However, it was not until 1962 that Reagan officially changed his voting registration to Republican.[49]

Home for the Reagans was a small ranch house in Pacific Palisades. When Patti was born, Ron gave Nancy a brooch inscribed with the words "Tuesday's Child." An accompanying card read, "so you won't have to be too far from our Tuesday's child ever. And because I intend to be as close to both of you as Eggs are to Easter."[50] The future president found himself unable to keep his promise, as his work for General Electric kept him on the road for long periods of time. While Mrs. Reagan assisted her husband by traveling with him when she could and appearing in some *General Electric Theater* dramas, she was often left at home by herself to raise their two small children.

Life was lonely for Nancy during the first several years of her marriage. She had few close friends in Pacific Palisades and was isolated from most of her Hollywood friends and contacts, who had not yet made the move to suburbia. Most of her neighbors were the wives of doctors and lawyers with whom she had little in common besides their children. Fortunately, the Reagans' social life substantially improved in 1954, when Robert Taylor and his wife, Ursula, moved to a house within walking distance of the Reagans. Bob and Ron had long been Hollywood friends, and soon their wives also became close. The two women would sometimes get away for lunch or an afternoon fashion show. For weekend entertainment, the two couples would drive over the border to Tijuana, Mexico, to watch a bullfight.[51]

In 1956, General Electric built the Reagans a new home located in Riviera, a more exclusive section of Pacific Palisades. Because Mrs. Reagan supervised most of the construction they called their new home the "Nancy House." As soon as the house was finished, Mrs. Reagan began decorating, using bright colors muted by soft pastels, soft grays, and pale greens. The kitchen featured red lacquered Chinese cupboards, and the living room, with its huge fireplace and floor-to-ceiling windows looking out on the swimming pool, contained two yellow couches, a black cocktail table, and red rugs.[52]

Life in Pacific Palisades in the 1950s was typically suburban. Mothers took turns driving their children to school and then spent a good portion of the day lounging around each other's pools, discussing the problems of raising children. Late in the afternoon, the children arrived home from school and it was soon time to start dinner. Mrs. Reagan did her best to join in, carpooling children back and forth to school, doing her weekly grocery shopping at the Brentwood market, and occasionally driving to Colvy's store in Pacific Palisades to pick up items for her husband. She read articles in *Life* and *Look* magazines on current events and best-selling novels for entertainment, and she also kept abreast of Hollywood and the television industry.[53] When her husband was home, the family went to church together, but when he was on the road, Mrs. Reagan and the children rarely attended.[54]

Even then, Mrs. Reagan was a perfectionist. Her house was impeccably clean, the children were nicely groomed, and meals were always on time. She tried to pass on to her children the discipline she had been taught by her stepfather. Her children, however, especially Patti, were high-spirited, constantly testing their limits and not eager to take their mother's discipline. Mrs. Reagan's frustration was heightened by a steady regimen of diet pills. She had put on some extra pounds during her pregnancy with Ron, Jr., and turned to diet pills when she had trouble losing the weight. Although the pills helped her shed a few pounds, they also increased her natural anxiousness. Eventually her doctor gave Mrs. Reagan another pill to calm her nerves and still another to help her sleep.[55] Years later, the first lady acknowledged that this was one of the most difficult (though simultaneously rewarding) periods of her life.[56] Her problems would later be reflected in her many conflicts with her increasingly rebellious children.

Although Mrs. Reagan did her best to fit the model of a 1950s wife, she was never really happy at home raising children. She had not intended to give up her movie career to become yet another suburban housewife, but to take on a new job—tending to her husband's needs. When he wasn't home, Mrs. Reagan felt at loose ends.

Reagan's job not only heightened his national visibility, it also provided an opportunity for him to hone his speaking skills. During the ten weeks each year that the television show was not in production, he crisscrossed America, making personal appearances at General Electric plants. In his ten years with General Electric, Reagan visited all of the company's thirty-five factories and met most of its 25,000 employees. In the process, Reagan would sometimes make as many as fourteen speeches per day.[57]

It was during this period that Ronald Reagan's politics became more conservative. His father-in-law was a well-known conservative doctor, who was outspoken and convincing in his beliefs. His work for General Electric had Reagan moving in high corporate circles for the first time. As a result, he developed a much greater respect for corporate America's role in creating economic growth. He came to believe that government was becoming a danger to the very individual freedoms it was created to protect. He also thought that government intervention in the economy, while it protected workers, ended up limiting economic growth. Reagan soon became a popular speaker. As the politics and tone of his speeches became more conservative, he came into conflict with General Electric. In one of his standard speeches, Reagan attacked the Tennessee Valley Authority (TVA), a hallmark of President Franklin Roosevelt's New Deal. But the TVA was a very large customer of General Electric, generating $50 million in contracts. General Electric executives were not happy having one of their largest clients disparaged in public by their own spokesman.[58]

In 1962, Ronald Reagan lost his position with General Electric, primarily because he had become increasingly vocal in expressing his newfound political conservatism. Without a full-time job, he had to rely on his speechmaking for income. In 1964, with his brother Neil's help, he was hired to host the television program *Death Valley Days*. However, it was now politics, not acting, that was Ronald Reagan's real interest.

In 1960, Reagan gave speeches as a Democrat supporting Republican Richard M. Nixon for president, and in 1962 he officially changed his party registration to Republican. In 1964, Ronald Reagan became the cochairman of the California Republicans for Barry Goldwater and stumped the state, giving speeches and raising money for the Goldwater presidential campaign. On 27 October 1964, Ronald Reagan made his national political debut with a passionate, televised speech for Goldwater, entitled "A Time for Choosing." The concluding paragraph was vintage Reagan: "You and I have a rendezvous with destiny. We can preserve for our children this, the best hope of man on earth, or we can sentence them to take the first step into a thousand years of darkness. If we fail, at least let our children and our children's children say of us we justified our brief moment here. We did all that could be done."[59] The speech was very well received, adding significantly to the coffers of the Goldwater campaign. It also got prominent California Republicans thinking about Reagan as a potential candidate for governor. One national magazine called the speech "the one bright spot in a dismal campaign."[60]

Barry Goldwater's crushing defeat at the hands of President Lyndon Johnson convinced Reagan to get off the sidelines and into the political game. George Murphy's 1964 success in beating Pierre Salinger for one of California's U.S. Senate seats proved that being a former actor was not necessarily an impediment to political success—at least in California. While Reagan considered entering politics, Henry

Salvatori, finance chairman of the Goldwater presidential campaign, and Holmes Tuttle, a multimillionaire Republican fund-raiser, approached him about running for the governorship. To encourage Reagan to run, Tuttle, Salvatori, and forty-one California businessmen formed an organization called "The Friends of Ronald Reagan" and purchased the public relations skills of the Spencer-Roberts firm, which had managed Nelson Rockefeller's 1964 presidential primary campaign. With their backing, Ronald Reagan agreed to become a candidate, and he easily won the Republican nomination.[61]

Her husband's growing enthusiasm for politics came as a surprise to Nancy Reagan, although she realized later that it should not have. As she writes in her memoirs, "When I married Ronnie, I thought I married an actor. But looking back now, I really should have known that acting wasn't fulfilling enough for him. He had already served five terms as president of the Screen Actors Guild and two more as president of the Motion Picture Industry Council. And he had always been active in supporting candidates for public office. All that should have been a signal to me, but somehow I missed it. . . . Looking back now, I am amazed at my own naïveté. But I honestly never expected that Ronald Reagan would go into politics."[62] Stuart Spencer, one of Reagan's closest and most trusted political advisors, later remarked that he had sensed early on in Reagan a subtle desire to go into politics, but not so Nancy, who valued her privacy way too much for the public arena.[63]

When Reagan announced his campaign for governor, there was no longer any doubt that he was serious about a political career. At first, Nancy thought that being a politician's wife would be similar to being an actor's wife, but she soon found out that the political life was much more rigorous and less private. She was characteristically supportive of her husband's efforts in his first campaign, but she played only a very small public role.

Mrs. Reagan especially disliked giving campaign speeches. Surprisingly, she found that her years as an actor had not prepared her for campaigning: she recalled that "this wife wanted no part of campaigning. I was shy in those days and terrified that I'd have to give a speech. I have often been asked why I felt that way, given all the years I had spent in theater and film. But to me the difference is enormous. When I was acting, I wasn't being myself—I was playing a role that had been created for me. But giving a speech is completely different. You can't hide behind a made-up character, and I was far too private a person to enjoy playing myself."[64] However, she could not avoid at least some participation in the campaign. As an alternative to written speeches, Mrs. Reagan adopted a question-and-answer format for her public appearances. With practice, she became fairly comfortable with this approach and used it regularly in future campaigns.[65]

During the campaign, Mrs. Reagan began to influence her husband's schedule. She knew him better than any of his staff and felt that she could help him best by monitoring the use of his time. Mrs. Reagan realized that if her husband was overtired or overstressed, he was prone to mistakes. Therefore, she often insisted that his staff cut back on his schedule. This practice of her overruling Ronald Reagan's staff continued throughout his political career. To some members of the press, who were not used to candidates' wives being so involved in their husbands' campaigns, she seemed like a tigress protecting her cub.[66]

Fortunately for candidate Reagan, Pat Brown, the two-term governor of California, did not consider him a serious threat. Unopposed in the 1966 Democratic primary, Brown focused his attention on Reagan's opponent in the Republican primary, giving Reagan a free ride until the general election. Ronald Reagan, however, confident that he would win the Republican nomination, focused his attention and considerable rhetorical skills on Governor Brown. The governor was fairly popular, but he was seeking a third term and had overstayed his welcome. Candidate Reagan skillfully exploited this weakness. As the general election grew closer and the possibility of a Reagan victory became more realistic, the tone of the governor's campaign became harsher. Brown began attacking Reagan as a right-wing zealot. But because of Reagan's genial demeanor, the attack had little success (a lesson future Reagan opponents would also learn). When the votes were counted, Ronald Reagan had scored a major political upset, handily defeating Governor Brown, 58 percent to 42 percent.[67]

The next eight years as the wife of California's governor in many ways foreshadowed Mrs. Reagan's tenure as first lady. First, Mrs. Reagan was known to be very protective of her husband. As a consequence, she was sometimes criticized for becoming too involved in his affairs. Second, she also had a tendency to stir up controversy (even when that was not her intent) and as a result often had a stormy relationship with the press. Mrs. Reagan also developed a reputation for style and elegance, and she was a popular fixture in the style sections of newspapers, if not on the editorial pages. Finally, she became interested in various social causes.

As first lady of California, Mrs. Reagan often appeared uninterested and uninvolved in many of her husband's policies as governor. To many Californians, Mrs. Reagan seemed to have no real policy concerns. By contrast, she was obsessed with her husband's well-being and public image, and the governor's staff considered her to be overprotective. She never hesitated to call them when she thought he was being overworked and to suggest that an item or two be dropped from his schedule. She was also not shy about letting her husband know when she thought that a staff member did not have his best interests at heart. One of her favorite targets was Lynn Nofziger, the governor's director of communications. Mrs. Reagan believed that Nofziger's rumpled suits presented the wrong image and that he had a tendency to talk down to the governor.[68]

Mrs. Reagan's constant phone calls to the governor's office (even during cabinet meetings) soon led some staff members to refer to her as Governor Nancy.[69] Some on the governor's staff believed that he was "henpecked" and found Mrs. Reagan demanding, impatient, and cold. Ronald Reagan, however, knew that his wife was only concerned with his well-being, and rarely resisted her involvement.[70]

Both Reagans realized the needs they filled in each other. Nancy Reagan needed to feel needed, while Ronald Reagan required his wife's constant attention. Far from resenting her involvement, the governor came to recognize and value his wife as a shrewd judge of character, and often turned to her for advice. From the beginning of Reagan's tenure as governor, Nancy played an important role in staff decisions. Ronald Reagan's instincts sometimes failed him in judging people, particularly those close to him. Nancy had an almost sixth sense about who would serve her husband well and began to promote them for higher positions within the administration.

Thus the idea of "Governor Nancy" began to take shape—the notion that Mrs. Reagan was the power behind the throne. Mrs. Reagan certainly had her hand in personnel matters, and she may also have occasionally influenced the governor on policy, such as his opposition to the Equal Rights Amendment. However, the idea that Mrs. Reagan was the one who was really running the state of California is ludicrous. She was not that interested in public policy. Her main concern was in protecting her husband. She was much more likely to be upset with a negative newspaper story about her husband than a piece of legislation he sponsored being defeated in the state legislature.[71]

Mrs. Reagan's relationship with the press while first lady of California resembled her tenure as first lady of the United States. After an early honeymoon period, she began to generate controversy and had difficulty in managing the press. Some of Mrs. Reagan's press coverage was very favorable, particularly concerning her appearance. One writer described California's new first lady in glowing terms: "Nancy Reagan looks like a Republican version of Jacqueline Kennedy. She has the same spare figure, the immaculate chic."[72]

Mrs. Reagan's biggest controversy during her husband's tenure as governor involved the governor's official residence in Sacramento. Essentially, she loathed her new home. The governor's mansion had almost no grounds, and its location next to an American Legion hall, two gas stations, and a motel was not ideal. Mrs. Reagan made public her feelings that the mansion was an inappropriate residence for the governor of such an important state. She also thought that it was a fire hazard and an unsafe place to raise their son. She once tried to open a window to show Ron, Jr., how to get out in case of a fire, but could not get the window open. During the winter it was often so cold that she had to wrap herself in blankets just to keep warm. Its downtown location made entertaining guests difficult: conversations would have to be halted until the noise from passing vehicles died away.[73] Nancy was not the only first lady of California to object to the governor's residence. Her predecessor, Mrs. Brown, had described the mansion as "Victorian ugly" and "a firetrap."[74] Built in 1877, the building was so run-down that Mrs. Brown had tried to have it condemned.

Publicly, Governor Reagan expressed many of the same opinions about the governor's mansion as his wife. However, those closest to the governor thought that he was only doing so to defend his wife. Among members of his staff Reagan was known for a remarkable ability to ignore his environment when concentrating on issues, and they felt that this trait made it unlikely that he was actually bothered by the physical deterioration of the governor's mansion.[75] However, since Nancy was unhappy, they would leave. After staying in the mansion only four months, the Reagans moved into a twelve-room Tudor-style house in a quiet suburb of Sacramento. Their new home was purchased by the Reagans' rich friends and leased to the governor and his wife.[76] Mrs. Reagan argued that their new residence was much more appropriate, but the public and the press were critical of the Reagans. Some suggested that they were putting on airs—that they thought they were too good for the residence that had served other governors and their families. The press even started referring to Mrs. Reagan as "Queen Nancy."[77]

Mrs. Reagan's relationship with the press remained rocky for the remainder of Governor Reagan's term. Some California political reporters commented negatively on what came to be called the "stare"—a glassy-eyed gaze of rapt attention with head slightly tilted that the governor's wife fixed upon her husband whenever he was speaking. To many feminists, the stare was especially upsetting. To them, it suggested that Mrs. Reagan did not have a thought in her mind, and represented her complete subordination to her husband.

What many critics did not realize was that "the stare" began long before Ronald Reagan's election as governor. It began back in the days when Reagan was head of the Screen Actors Guild. Whenever her husband spoke in public, he had Nancy's full attention. Her expression was neither recently created nor a pretense.

Her expression may also be related to a certain quality of her eyes, which are large and expressive. They are also unusually widely spaced. As noted by one author, "spaced out eyes can not only be disguised, in profile or three-quarter shots (which Claudette Colbert used to insist upon), but exploited. They give that intensity of gaze without specific suggestiveness that the movie stills encouraged, a kind of blank urgency capable of being taken in a number of ways."[78] This perfectly describes the look that Mrs. Reagan cast upon her husband when he was speaking.

Nancy was well aware that her eyes were her best feature. In her memoir, *Nancy,* she describes the preparation for her first day of shooting on a Hollywood set:

As I was being made up the first day, Bill [Tuttle] came in to introduce himself and said, "Well, I guess that's all right, but we'll have to do something about her eyes—They're too big for pictures." He was joking, but I was so nervous I thought he was serious, so I went around the rest of the day with my eyes half closed. Finally, George Folsey took me aside and asked me if I was tired, what was the matter? I told him what Bill Tuttle had said, and I thought he would never stop laughing. Finally, wiping the tears from his eyes, he said, "Nancy, don't you know your eyes can never be too big for pictures."[79]

Mrs. Reagan's movie characters were often tailored to take full advantage of her eyes. The sympathetic child psychiatrist in *Shadow on the Wall*, the understanding daughter of a Park Avenue neurosurgeon in *The Doctor and the Girl*, and the pregnant wife in *The Next Voice You Hear* were all roles that called for numerous close-ups of Mrs. Reagan's large eyes. Once she learned how to make use of her best physical attribute, Mrs. Reagan would not forget.

Michael Deaver has suggested another reason for the stare, arguing that Nancy's look might appear to be vacant just because her thoughts were turned inward. Although Mrs. Reagan had heard most of her husband's stump speeches many times, he often made subtle changes in them. He would alter a phrase or a story to suit a particular audience. One reason Mrs. Reagan was listening so intently might be to pick up on the changes and let her husband know which he should keep.[80]

Ironically, some of the harshest criticism of Mrs. Reagan resulted from one of her few efforts to cultivate the press. With the idea of improving her public image, she agreed to an in-depth interview conducted by novelist and essayist Joan Didion. Much to her dismay, the interview resulted in a scathing profile entitled "Pretty Nancy," published in the 1 June 1968 issue of the *Saturday Evening Post*. In the article, Didion described Nancy as seeming to live in a perfect daydream world, full of phoniness and playacting, and characterized her as insincere and overly dramatic.[81] Nancy was extremely upset with the profile and as a result grew even more wary of the press.[82]

Not all of Mrs. Reagan's press coverage was negative. While she was generally panned on the editorial pages, she often received accolades on the society pages. As first lady of California, Mrs. Reagan spent much of her time shopping in the most prestigious Beverly Hills shops, lunching with millionaire friends such as Betsy Bloomingdale, and attending society and cultural events around the state. Before long, Mrs. Reagan had cultivated an image of style and elegance and was drawing comparisons to former first lady Jacqueline Kennedy. In 1967, Warren Steibel, the producer for William Buckley's *Firing Line,* filmed an hour-long documentary entitled *Nancy: First Lady of California* for broadcast on NBC television. Steibel explained his choice of Mrs. Reagan by saying, "The interest in her is tremendous. She seems to fascinate people."[83] The following year, she was named to the list of best-dressed women in the United States and had a rose named after her.[84]

As is expected of governors' wives, Mrs. Reagan also championed a number of important causes. Both she and Governor Reagan were interested in the plight of returning Vietnam veterans and of those servicemen still listed as missing in action. Mrs. Reagan often visited veterans' hospitals, meeting injured soldiers. At their request, she placed phone calls to their wives and/or mothers, letting them know they were on the road to recovery. She also became involved with the Foster Grandparents organization—a program started by Sargent Shriver that puts children with special needs in close contact with older adults.

The Foster Grandparents program first touched Mrs. Reagan on a visit to Pacific State Hospital in 1967. She was so moved by the interaction between the children and the adults that she became involved in the organization. Mrs. Reagan regularly visited Foster Grandparents programs, taped public service announcements to attract the interest of the business community, and even encouraged the Australian government to set up a similar program.[85] What Mrs. Reagan liked most about this group was that both the children and the adults benefited. Older adults who might otherwise feel lonely, without purpose, and unloved were matched with children who needed more love and attention than they received in an institutionalized setting. Through their association, both helped fulfill each other's needs.[86]

Because of California's size and electoral importance, that state's governors are often viewed as prospective presidential candidates.

Ronald Reagan was no exception. He had no sooner won the governor's office than he was fielding questions from the press about his presidential ambitions. His entrance in the 1976 Republican presidential primaries was not the first time he had thought about a future in the White House. In 1968, while he was governor, Reagan went to the Republican convention as the favorite son candidate of California. He was even then aiming for the White House. He had, however, waited too long before announcing his candidacy, and had lost any chance of gaining his party's nomination. Nancy learned of her husband's 1968 presidential decision over the radio. It was the first (and last) time that her husband had made a decision without consulting her. At least on paper, Ronald Reagan's candidacy in 1968 was not a bad plan; he had little to lose and potentially could gain a great deal. However, the Nixon campaign undercut Reagan's chances by shrewdly wooing Barry Goldwater and Southern conservatives such as Strom Thurmond and John Tower, thus isolating Reagan from his political base.[87] After Nixon's victory in the general election, Reagan and his advisors realized their lost opportunity, concluding that he should have pursued the Republican nomination earlier and with more vigor.

In early 1973, Ronald Reagan briefly considered a run for the U.S. Senate. While the governor and his advisors were sure that he would win, he ultimately decided not to run. His wife's lack of enthusiasm was one factor influencing his decision. When she was approached with the idea, Mrs. Reagan replied that the life of a senator's wife did not appeal to her.[88] Perhaps both Reagans had their eyes on a higher office.

In 1974, Governor Reagan met with a group of close advisors to discuss his presidential prospects. The biggest impediment to his candidacy in 1976 was the incumbent Republican president, Gerald R. Ford. Reagan and his advisors realized that challenging an incumbent Republican president (even one who had not been elected) would be difficult. However, when President Ford chose the liberal Nelson Rockefeller as his vice-presidential running mate, Reagan concluded that the conservative wing was losing control of the Republican Party and began to think seriously about running against Ford.[89] After finishing his second term as governor in 1974, he spent the next two years traveling around the country as the spokesman for the conservative wing of the Republican Party. In the process, he won converts to his cause and picked up many political IOUs.

By 1976, Ronald Reagan was well positioned to make a serious run at the Republican nomination for the presidency. But before he launched his campaign, he had to convince his most important "advisor"—Mrs. Reagan. Nancy was reluctant to give her approval. She did not want her husband to make the attempt if it would harm either his health or his future chances. She also had mixed feelings about her husband's continuing in politics. Her experience in Sacramento had not been entirely positive, and part of her longed to return to Los Angeles and a more private life. After deliberating long and hard, Mrs. Reagan finally agreed to the 1976 campaign, primarily because it was what her husband wanted.[90]

In public, Mrs. Reagan again played a very quiet role in the campaign. She made her usual question-and-answer campaign appearances, traveled with her husband, and attended his speeches. She tried to draw a distinction between herself and first lady Betty Ford, who Mrs. Reagan thought was too liberal (as a result of Mrs. Ford's seeming to condone premarital cohabitation in a *Sixty Minutes* television interview) and too interested in pushing her own agenda (Mrs. Ford's support for the Equal Rights Amendment being the most obvious example).[91]

Behind the scenes, however, Mrs. Reagan was an important campaign advisor. Even as she was unsure she even wanted her husband to continue in politics, she was determined to do her best to help him get what he wanted. She monitored her husband's campaign schedule and began to assume a more active role in overseeing personnel. Mrs. Reagan was a strong supporter of John Sears (who had taken the time to cultivate her) for campaign director. She opposed Lynn Nofziger, a longtime Reagan supporter and aide, who as head of Citizens for Reagan had raised millions of dollars for the campaign. Nancy blamed Nofziger for a scandal involving homosexuals on the governor's staff that had tainted her husband's administration.[92] As a result, Sears gained control of the campaign and Nofziger was limited to coordinating the campaign in California. When the campaign was over, Mrs. Reagan would make sure that Lynn Nofziger never again assumed a prominent role in any future Reagan administration.[93]

Although the 1976 campaign was not successful (in her biography, Mrs. Reagan refers to it as the "glorious defeat"), it resulted in the Reagan team being better prepared for 1980. When the 1976 campaign was over, $1 million remained in the campaign coffers. The money was used to start a Political Action Committee (PAC) called Citizens for the Republic, whose goal was Reagan's election in 1980. The PAC developed a mailing list of 100,000 people, which was used to push the available campaign funds up to $4.5 million by the end of 1978.[94]

During the 1980 campaign, Mrs. Reagan's involvement in managing personnel became even more apparent. When John Sears and longtime Reagan aide Michael Deaver argued over their relative positions in the campaign, in order to try and reconcile their differences, she arranged a meeting between Sears, Deaver, and her husband at the Reagans' Palisades home. Unfortunately, the meeting was unsuccessful, and Michael Deaver left the campaign, which put Sears firmly in charge. When the Reagan campaign lost the Iowa caucus to George Bush and fell behind in the New Hampshire polls, Nancy organized another meeting in which the decision was made to dump Sears and his associates.[95] Before the New Hampshire votes were even counted, Mrs. Reagan called Sears in and gave him a copy of the press release announcing his removal from the campaign. As soon as Sears was gone, Deaver was back in the campaign, and Mrs. Reagan was happy, as she would now be working with an old friend and ally.[96]

Ronald Reagan won the Republican nomination, but his team made some mistakes in the early days of the general election campaign. Nancy thereupon insisted that a more centralized campaign command structure was needed. Stuart Spencer, who had guided the Reagan gubernatorial campaigns, was approached about directing the presidential campaign. The first question he asked was whether Mrs. Reagan wanted him. Assured that she did, he signed on and helped lead the campaign to a successful conclusion.[97] Mrs. Reagan played such a prominent part in the campaign that some political insiders wondered whether she would assume an equally active role as first lady.

To those outside the 1980 campaign, however, Mrs. Reagan's role seemed routine. She conducted the same question-and-answer sessions she had always given. Occasionally, when the need was especially great, she would give a speech, but she was clearly most content to be by her husband's side at rallies, dinners, and receptions—always well groomed and usually smiling graciously.

As in 1976, Mrs. Reagan tried to draw a clear distinction between herself and first lady Rosalynn Carter. When the press asked whether she intended to have as substantive a role in policy decisions as Mrs. Carter, Mrs. Reagan replied that she did not think it was proper for first ladies to sit in on cabinet meetings. She went on to say that while her husband sometimes discussed issues with her, she served merely as his sounding board and rarely made any suggestions.[98] In fact, her role in the presidential campaign indicated more involvement in the soon-to-be-president's affairs than she was willing to publicly admit.

During the campaign, some of the younger female members of the press corps criticized Mrs. Reagan. Much of the criticism had more to do with style than substance: the continued focus on the stare which had now been renamed the "gaze," the way she sat, the way she presented herself (which some saw as artificial and pretentious), and the deference she paid to her husband. Sally Quinn of the *Washington Post* criticized the way Mrs. Reagan sat—"She never seems to get an itch, her lips never stick to her teeth, she hardly blinks"—and Julie Baumgold of *New York* magazine named Nancy "Ronald Reagan's Total Woman."[99]

She was also criticized for her unwillingness to address issues of significance—particularly women's issues. Mrs. Reagan's reticence contrasted with the activism of the two previous first ladies, both of whom were more than willing to take on prominent topics. As a result, she was portrayed as lacking substance. The irony, of course, is that Mrs. Reagan was proving to be a very powerful political wife—though her power was not grounded in causes, constituencies, or office, but rather in her unwavering commitment to her husband.

Fortunately for the Reagan campaign, presidential elections are determined on the perceived merits of the candidates and not on criticisms of their wives. In November 1980, Ronald Reagan won a decisive victory over President Jimmy Carter, becoming the newly elected president of the United States and Mrs. Reagan the new first lady. She would go on to be the first first lady since Mamie Eisenhower to serve for eight full years.

By the end of the 1980 election, the characteristics Mrs. Reagan would display as first lady were fully developed. Most important would be her interest in creating an environment in which her husband could flourish. Mrs. Reagan had said on numerous occasions that Ronald Reagan was her career, and there was no reason to think that once in the White House she would consider a career change. To assure her husband's political success, she would continue to manage his time and his schedule, protect him from aides who she felt were not serving his best interests, and when necessary interject herself into the management of his campaigns. Although it was not widely recognized at the time, there were numerous indicators that Mrs. Reagan would become one of the most influential members of the new administration.

Her years as first lady of California also suggested that the country would be in for some interesting times. Based on her past, Mrs. Reagan's relations with the national press would likely be stormy. She had been associated with either the theater or Hollywood for a major portion of her life and was used to receiving special treatment from the press. It was not unusual for Hollywood actors to receive special perks, and she gave every indication that she expected the same as first lady. Mrs. Reagan would also bring the same sense of style and glamour to the White House that she had been recognized for as first lady of California—for which she would receive the same mixture of praise and criticism.

CHAPTER 2

LEARNING THE ROLE OF FIRST LADY

Although Nancy Reagan has often said that she pays little attention to her image, many who know her disagree. According to Michael Deaver, there are "few public relations professionals with a better public-relations antenna than her."[1] That acumen would prove very important to the first lady during Ronald Reagan's first term as president. During these years, Mrs. Reagan succeeding in modifying her initially negative public image into a more positive one that better served the president's agenda and that fit her role as the president's chief supporter. Her skill at public relations would help her manage the change.

As the Reagan administration planned to take office, Mrs. Reagan prepared to take on the most important assignment of her life. In American politics, there are no more major roles than president and first lady. Nancy at last had the opportunity to be a star—something that had been denied her in Hollywood. She would soon discover, however, that she would have to temper her desires in the interests of her husband's presidency and resume the supporting role she played so well. Mrs. Reagan understood that her part as first lady provided a unique opportunity to merge her talent for shaping her image with the requirements of her new position.

After her husband's election, Mrs. Reagan exercised a star's prerogative and suggested that the Carters leave the White House early, to facilitate the transition for the new presidential couple. Reportedly, she wanted to redo the White House before the inauguration, and even planned on knocking down a wall in the Lincoln bedroom.[2] In an interview, the new first lady implied that the Carter years had not been kind to the White House, which now, she said, needed a thorough revitalization.[3] In addition, several of Mrs. Reagan's friends publicly expressed their opinion that "class and dignity" would be returning to the White House with the new administration.[4] This was one of several slights originating from the Reagan camp that President and Mrs. Carter found tactless and that contributed to the awkwardness of the transition. The Carters felt that they had been good stewards of the White House, substantially adding to the art collection, for example. They had also invited internationally known musical stars to perform at the White House. But to them it seemed that the Reagans were implying that the Carters constantly wore blue jeans and drank beer out of bottles. The Carters were hurt and angered. It was difficult enough losing an election that they felt they deserved to win, but being held up to ridicule in the national press by their opponents was rubbing salt in their wounds.[5]

Mrs. Reagan had long thought that Jackie Kennedy was the most elegant and stylish of first ladies. She was determined that the administration would be a Republican Camelot and that she would play the role of Mrs. Kennedy. The new first lady hired Letitia Baldrige, Mrs. Kennedy's former chief of staff and social secretary as well as a longtime Washington insider, to help with the transition.[6] Baldrige introduced the Reagans to the Washington social scene and oversaw the selection of Mrs. Reagan's staff.

Mrs. Reagan's Office of the First Lady was the first to benefit from public law 95–570, passed in 1978, which declared that "assistance and services are authorized to be provided to the spouse of the President in connection with the assistance provided by the spouse to the President in the discharge of the President's duties and responsibilities."[7] As a result, the Office of the First Lady had a budget of $650,000 and a staff that would grow to eighteen people (compared to twenty-six for Betty Ford and twenty-one for Rosalynn Carter), with a number of calligraphers and social office personnel who worked under her chief of staff.[8] Mrs. Reagan's staff was primarily made up of professional women with backgrounds in business and/ or politics, who took their work seriously. Among the key staff members were Lee Annenberg, Sheila Tate, Nancy Reynolds, Muffie Brandon, and Elaine Crispen. Lee Annenberg, an old friend of Mrs. Reagan, also served as the White House chief of protocol during the early years of the administration.[9]

Robin Orr was Mrs. Reagan's initial choice as press secretary, but she lasted only a month into the new administration. Orr, who had been a society columnist for the *Oakland Tribune,* had no experience working in public relations or with the Washington community. After a very rocky start, Orr was replaced with Sheila Tate, who came to the White House from a highly regarded Washington, D.C., public relations firm. The newly appointed press secretary soon realized that former President Carter had been correct when he told her that she "had the toughest job in the White House."[10] It was she who bore the brunt of the relentless press scrutiny of Mrs. Reagan's refurbishment of the White House, the purchase of new china, and the first lady's new wardrobe. Tate handled press questions with honesty and humor, but occasionally could lapse into sarcasm. After hearing that an animal rights group questioned the first lady's wearing of fur, Tate's reply was that "it was just a dead animal." She later noted, "if I were first lady, I would probably take on some kind of nice animal issue, so I could be photographed with puppies for the next four years."[11] When the press questioned her about her personal feelings toward Mrs. Reagan, Ms. Tate earnestly responded, "I like her, I really do. I'm a different person, but that does not mean I don't appreciate Nancy Reagan for the person she is."[12]

Sheila Tate and Larry Speakes, who succeeded James Brady as the president's press secretary, worked for the same public relations company before going to work in the White House. Because of their past association, Speakes invited Tate to sit in on West Wing meetings. According to Tate, the practice greatly improved the coordination of East Wing and West Wing activities and schedules and contributed to the generally positive relations between the two staffs.[13]

Muffie Brandon (wife of Harry Brandon, chief diplomatic correspondent for the *London Times*) was Mrs. Reagan's social secretary. Responsible for every social function relating to either the White House or Mrs. Reagan, Brandon was one of Mrs. Reagan's staunchest defenders. She was openly critical of what she saw as a new breed of reporters covering the White House: "The president and Mrs. Reagan live in the manner of their generation, which is not exactly the manner in which the young reporters in their 20s and early 30s live. Some of the young reporters are unfamiliar with this manner, the politeness, the charm, and the attitude toward life."[14] She was also appalled at the casual style of dress that had become common among White House visitors and employees: "I'll tell you in the corridors of the White House, the difference in the way women are dressed and the way they were dressed in previous administrations. We don't have to be super chic. But I remember a girl greeting me not too many years ago in clogs at the diplomatic reception door. I never got over it. We do not wear pants. We do not wear clogs. We represent our country."[15]

Nancy Reynolds, another of Mrs. Reagan's longtime friends, served as her personal assistant. Reynolds had an extensive background in television. She became a converted Reaganite in 1966, serving with Governor Reagan's administration in California. Reynolds helped Mrs. Reagan with her mail and served as informal press secretary and traveling companion. Her personal friendship with Mrs. Reagan permitted her to do much more. When the Reagans came to Washington, D.C., after the election, Reynolds, who was then Vice-President for National Affairs for the Bendix Corporation and a D.C. resident, helped her friend meet the capital's movers and shakers. Reynolds also served as a liaison for Mrs. Reagan, meeting several times with the outgoing East and West Wing staffs about their operation.[16] In late 1981, President Reagan named Reynolds the U.S. representative to the Commission on the Status of Women of the United Nations Economic and Social Council.[17]

When Reynolds left the first lady's staff in 1982 to take up her U.N. post, Gahl Hodges replaced her, and Linda Faulkner replaced Hodges in 1985. Faulkner's response when asked about working in the Reagan White House was typical of many East Wing employees: "I admired the Reagans tremendously. I remember thinking, 'If I had my choice of presidents, this would be the one I'd choose.'"[18]

Elaine Crispen, Mrs. Reagan's personal secretary and assistant during the 1980 presidential campaign, accompanied the first lady to Washington, eventually serving as the first lady's press secretary (after Sheila Tate left to pursue a corporate career). In 1988, as she prepared to leave the White House, Crispen said that what she would remember most about working in the White House were the children: "When I close my eyes, all I can see is her with kids—on Bali or in Thailand. I just see all of these little faces all over the world."[19] She also mentioned that her one regret was that "she never had the time to return all the calls, answer all the questions, and satisfy all the requests."[20]

Mrs. Reagan thought that the East Wing should follow the administration's lead in controlling the size and cost of government. She closely monitored the size of her staff and their expenditures. It was a common East Wing joke that even "if a staff member were offered a complimentary, upgraded hotel room that would have meant no additional expense, he was to refuse it."[21] Mrs. Reagan readily admits to being a perfectionist (a trait she undoubtedly learned from her stepfather), and expected the same from her staff. The number of staff members who passed through the East Wing leaves little doubt that Mrs. Reagan was a demanding boss. While she was first lady, Mrs. Reagan would go through three speechwriters, three social secretaries, three project directors, three press secretaries, and five chiefs of staff.[22]

Some staff members thrived under the first lady's perfectionism. Elaine Crispen suggests that while the schedule was difficult, the East Wing staff appreciated Mrs. Reagan's commitment: "You put in incredibly long hours. You put your own life on hold, just like the President and first lady. You know they don't have time for personal things anymore. I wouldn't have wanted to make those sacrifices and done it for someone who didn't give a damn. But she did give a damn, she did care. She cared very much about her husband. I can't fault her for that. She cared about her family, her parents. She cared about her country and a mark she would leave."[23]

James Rosebush, Mrs. Reagan's third chief of staff (1982–1986) thought that it was not so much that the first lady was demanding, but that she worked so hard herself that staff members had to demand a lot from themselves to keep up with her. He often needed to get up quite early to prepare for his 7:00 a.m. meeting with Mrs. Reagan, because he knew that she would have already read the daily papers and her briefing papers and that she would set the agenda if he was not prepared.[24] Sheila Tate also thought that Mrs. Reagan was not particularly demanding. Her clarity about what she wanted made her easy to work for. Tate thought it would be much harder to work for someone whose goals were less clear. Like Rosebush, Tate thought that preparation was the key. If you needed Mrs. Reagan to travel and speak to a meeting of an important group, you needed to be ready when she asked you why. As long as you provided her with a good reason, Tate felt, Mrs. Reagan would agree to do what you asked.[25]

With these expectations went loyalty. When her maid, Anita Castelo, was arrested and charged with attempting to purchase and smuggle small arms ammunition back to Paraguay, the first lady not only offered a character affidavit, but also welcomed Castelo back to the White House after she was found innocent. Speaking for the first lady, Elaine Crispen said that she was "very happy that the charges were dropped and that Anita was found innocent and that she was looking forward to her return."[26]

During the Reagan years there were many fewer problems between the West and East wings of the White House than in previous administrations. One former White House staff member during the Carter years characterized the relations between the two staffs as "Hate. Hate. Kill. Kill."[27] James Rosebush attributed the good relationship between the East and West wings in part to Mrs. Reagan's interest in politics and her husband's schedule and to members of the president's staff who had a genuine interest in the first lady's success (particularly Michael Deaver).[28]

Inevitably, though, there was occasional tension between the president's and first lady's staffs. Some East Wing women were made to feel like second-class citizens when they were reportedly excluded from a staff Christmas party to which female staffers from the West Wing were invited; they were also denied tennis court privileges unless invited to play by someone who worked in the West Wing.[29] However, Sheila Tate insists that there was no systematic discrimination against East Wing female employees. She suggests that if there had been and a staff member had mentioned it to Mrs. Reagan, she would have stopped it immediately. Tate does recall one occasion when an advance man tried to economize at the end of a fiscal year. He assigned East Wing female staffers to shared single rooms, while West

Wing staffers doubled up in two-bedroom suites. Once Tate complained, the decision was reversed and it never happened again.[30]

The natural political and institutional differences in status between the president and the first lady explained the perceived unequal treatment experienced by East Wing staff. However, some members of the first lady's staff felt that Mrs. Reagan's reliance on the president's staff (particularly Michael Deaver) to solve her problems devalued their importance throughout the administration. Some East Wing members also suspected that Mrs. Reagan was more comfortable working with men than with women.[31]

Her staff was in agreement, however, that Mrs. Reagan, like other first ladies, needed a cause to promote. Many in the East Wing assumed that she would continue her work with the Foster Grandparents program. The first lady was very enthusiastic about the program: "It gives grandparents a whole new life, a purpose, a reason for getting up in the morning. They don't think about themselves any longer. That child becomes their child. I am talking about severely retarded children. With such pride and love, a grandparent will say, 'I want you to meet my grandson.'"[32] During Mrs. Reagan's first nine months, she visited local Foster Grandparents programs numerous times. Tom Pauken, director of Action (the federal agency that administered the program), felt that the first lady's involvement was very important: "It allows the American public to know more about this wonderful program, it encourages those Foster Grandparents who work with severely handicapped and troubled youth to continue their outstanding work, and lets everyone know how much older Americans can contribute to help those young people with significant needs."[33] Despite Mrs. Reagan's commitment to the Foster Grandparent program, however, there were only two such programs in the Washington, D.C., area, and she couldn't just keep visiting the same two programs over and over again. Nevertheless, Mrs. Reagan's involvement in the Foster Grandparents program continued well into the president's first term. In 1983, there was a suggestion within the White House to establish a Foster Grandparents Foundation at least partially to provide greater visibility for the program.[34]

The initial public response to Ronald Reagan's election was very favorable. While all presidents enjoy a honeymoon period, the Reagans experienced a virtual love fest. Many leading news magazines, such as *Time, Newsweek,* and *U.S. News and World Report,* as well as personality magazines, such as *People,* reported the Reagans' plans for bringing style back to the White House. Nancy Reagan in particular was the object of endless fascination. No detail was too small to be examined. One learned the types of gowns she preferred (by designers Galanos, Adolfo, and Bill Blass), the style of her hair (lightly frosted by Monsieur Marc), and the name of her decorator (Los Angeles interior decorator Ted Graber). Her closest friends, including Betsy Bloomingdale, Bonita Granville Wrather, Martha Lyles, Jean Smith, Jane Dart, Virginia Tuttle, Marion Jorgenson, and Betty Wilson—often described as world-class partygoers and -givers, and as movers in California society—attracted national press attention. There was a sense of a return to style and elegance that Washington society had not seen since the Kennedy years. To many Americans, the Reagans represented a welcome relief from the perceived austerity of the Carter administration.[35]

Beginning with the inauguration, the Reagans changed the social tone of Washington. Jimmy Carter's inauguration had a common-man, folksy, down-home theme. In contrast, the Reagan inauguration was one of grace and luxury (detractors said opulence). When Ronald Reagan became governor of California, the Reagans staged the most expensive inauguration in Sacramento's history. They did the same for Washington, D.C. The Republican National Committee pumped more than $5 million into the Reagan inauguration celebration. During the Carter inauguration, there were twenty-five events open to the general public at no charge. Such free events were nonexistent during the Reagan inaugural. There also were no longer inexpensive $20 seats for the Inaugural Ball. Tickets for the Reagan Inaugural Ball ranged from $100 for standing room only to $2,000 to $3,000 for a seat. The total cost of the inauguration exceeded $16 million.[36]

The Reagans worked hard to cultivate the Washington community. After the November election, the Reagans hosted a party to which some of the most influential people in the capital were invited. The list of invitees included Joseph Hirshborn, the noted philanthropist; Mstislav Rostropovich, conductor of the National Symphony Orchestra; Edward Bennett Williams, attorney and

Baltimore Orioles owner; Austin Kiplinger, financial newsletter publisher; the governors of Maryland and Virginia; Marion Barry, Washington, D.C., mayor; Melvin Paine, chairman of the board of *National Geographic;* and John T. Walker, bishop of Washington's Episcopal diocese.[37]

The Reagans were a hit in official Washington. Social affairs now required the men to wear black ties and the women to appear in designer gowns costing thousands of dollars. Formal dances with private orchestras or bands became commonplace. The wine and cheese of the Carter administration gave way to salmon, escargots stuffed with mushrooms, and calamari in garlic butter. Reaganites dominated the city. The best Washington hotels filled up with the rich and the well known. The affluent no longer had to be ashamed of their wealth.

At the center of it all was Nancy Reagan, who quickly became known for organizing elaborate and splendid social functions, and for dressing the part of the glamorous first lady (her "borrowing" gowns from top designers helped her cope with the expense). Hollywood guests were in, and so were the movies. The Reagans added a new social event to the White House: movie screenings. Hollywood stars and entertainers attended the more than four dozen state dinners held during the Reagan years. The guest list for the state dinner held in early November 1984 included Charlton Heston, Jim Nabors, Jimmy Dean, Stephanie Powers, Twyla Tharp, Henry Winkler, and Stephanie Zimbalist. Additional star power was provided by Nancy Hogshead, 1984 Olympic gold medalist; James Lovell, former astronaut; Kathryn Sullivan, astronaut; and Floyd Patterson, former boxer. The Twyla Tharp dance company performed to a recording of Frank Sinatra singing "My Way."[38]

Mrs. Reagan determined that at her formal events only the most elegant manners would suffice. She insisted that the most prominent guest enter the room first, regardless of gender. She also ended the practice of female social aides asking lonely-looking male guests to dance, which after all was unladylike.[39] They could talk to a male wallflower, but could dance only if he invited her to do so. Mrs. Reagan took a personal interest in organizing the state dinners. She chose the flower arrangements and pretasted the entire meal, often recommending changes in sauces and vegetable. Desserts usually involved raspberries, either simply presented in a tart or sometimes served by themselves. Jane O'Reilly notes "that for certain circles, Nancy Reagan had transformed a sprinkling of fresh raspberries in a tart shell into something approaching a national food."[40] Although keeping up with the first lady was a difficult task for many Washington wives, such affairs were routine for Nancy's out-of-town guests, who had both money and time.

The fancy dinner parties and balls were only one way in which the Reagan influence was felt at the White House. Mrs. Reagan thought that the official presidential residence was drab, dreary, and somewhat uninviting—not at all the kind of place fit for entertaining the heads of other countries. Like her predecessors Jacqueline Kennedy and Pat Nixon, the first lady set out to refurbish her new home. Her first step was returning the standard $50,000 decorating funds allotment to the government and then raising the amount she felt she needed through private donations. Over $822,000 was contributed, with most of the donations coming from wealthy Reagan friends.[41] The Annenbergs contributed $70,000 (more than the entire government allotment alone), the Jorgensons $50,000, the Bloomingdales $20,000, and the Darts and Tuttles $10,000 apiece.[42]

However, elegance can cross the line to elitism, and the national press began referring to the first lady as "Queen Nancy." The new administration's conspicuous consumption also elicited a strong critical response from many Americans, beginning as early as the inauguration. The $16 million price tag for the three-day festivities came at a time when national unemployment had risen to 7.4 percent.[43] Even though the first lady had no control over the pricing of tickets, the planning of events, or the budgeting costs (which were set by the Inaugural Committee), many of the complaints were directed at her. The criticism mounted even higher with the White House refurbishment and the purchase of new china.

The first lady was soon subjected to a barrage of negative comments. The press, which just weeks earlier had been so enthusiastic about the Reagans, began running stories detailing Mrs. Reagan's extravagance. Nighttime talk show host Johnny Carson joked about her new favorite junk food—caviar.[44] Critics pointed out that with much of the donated money being tax deductible for those in the 50 percent tax bracket, money was indirectly being spent from the public treasury.[45] When the White House would not make public the names of donors, some raised the possibility that the secret donors were buying influence with the new administration.

The White House announcement of the purchase of a new set of formal china for $209,508 was particularly controversial. The 4,732-piece ivory china set was designed to replace the existing White House china that had been bought fourteen years earlier during the Johnson administration, and was chipped and cracked from age and use. For only the second time in history, the cost of the new china was paid for by private funds (by the tax-exempt Knapp Foundation).[46] Unfortunately, the revelation of the purchase came on the same day the Department of Agriculture announced cutbacks in the school lunch program. The press release also stated that for the first time, ketchup would be considered a vegetable. Not surprisingly, controversy followed. Newspaper columns were soon joking about the first lady's "china policy."

Ironically, Mrs. Reagan herself helped create some of the controversy by inadvertently leaking the story about the new china. The first lady had just finished writing the last chapter of her autobiography, *Nancy,* which was serialized in a women's magazine. In that chapter she mentioned ordering the china. When Associated Press reporter Maureen Santini read it, she realized she had stumbled across some major news. Mrs. Reagan had accidentally thwarted her staff's plans to release the information only after the china had gone into production, with photographs of the prototype. Instead, the press stampede was on.[47]

Both the first lady and Sheila Tate were frustrated by the press's fixation on the cost of the china while ignoring the fact that it was being donated to the White House. Attempting to put the china purchase in perspective, Tate conducted historical research on White House china. She found that Eleanor Roosevelt bought new china during the depths of the Depression. Her china purchase was paid for by the Department of the Interior and in current dollars cost as much as the Reagan china.[48] Unfortunately for the first lady's press secretary, she found that the press was not much interested in historical comparisons that might ruin an otherwise good story.

The president's and first lady's staffs brainstormed about how to best defuse the controversy, as it was beginning to affect the president's agenda. An especially touchy question was how to display the new china once it arrived at the White House. Ronald Reagan's deputy press secretary, Peter Roussel, suggested that to inaugurate the purchase, Mrs. Reagan should invite one "mainstream" couple from each of the fifty states to a White House dinner using the new china.[49] This suggestion turned out to be a nonstarter. Sheila Tate suggested instead that the new china be displayed in the "China" room for the press, with a representative of the Knapp Foundation, officials from Lenox (makers of the china), Margaret Klapthor of the Smithsonian Institution, and Barbara Bush in attendance. Tate stressed that all pictures should be group pictures and that Mrs. Reagan not handle any of the china or make any remarks at the ceremony.[50]

The final decision was to present the china in conjunction with a state dinner for President Hosni Mubarak of Egypt. Before these dinners, the White House usually conducts a press walk-through in the afternoon, mostly for photographers, who might want pictures of the table settings. The first lady never attends these sessions; no one but the chief usher is there. Under normal circumstances, only photographers, not writers, would attend. In this case, because of the tremendous interest in the china, the attendance was huge.[51] Mrs. Reagan was not there, but her staff provided the press with a chart comparing the cost of the Reagan china to the five most recent china purchases. Only the Roosevelt china (when adjusted for inflation) was cheaper than the Reagan china, costing $43.04 per piece compared with $47.92 per piece for the Reagan china.[52] At the unveiling, the first lady's press secretary again stressed that the Reagan china was purchased with private funds.

Mrs. Reagan's expensive taste in clothes also drew heavy criticism. Beginning with the inauguration, Mrs. Reagan was determined to dress the part of the first lady. She wore a gown costing $10,000, a $10,000 Maximillian mink coat (a gift from her husband), a fur-lined raincoat worth $1,000, and other gowns and day suits with a cumulative minimum estimated worth of $25,000.[53] First ladies of course do not have an unlimited supply of funds to keep them in fashionable attire. Mrs. Reagan therefore resumed a practice that she had used for years. Like many other socialites, she was regularly offered and had accepted free gowns. Designers encouraged this practice because it was good advertising for the American fashion industry.

Some of Mrs. Reagan's favorite designers, such as Galanos, Blass, and Adolfo, donated their gowns and daywear for her use. How many such outfits Mrs. Reagan accepted was never disclosed. At least one designer, Jean Louis, is known to have sent her $22,000 worth of clothes.[54] Mrs. Reagan kept some of the gowns and donated others to costume collections. By taking a tax deduction for her donations, she not only received a gift, but also saved money on her taxes.

The first lady's taste in fine clothes was undoubtedly cultivated during her days on the stage and screen. An upcoming actress was expected to dress the part, both on and off the set. In discussing Mrs. Reagan's clothes problem, Michael Deaver writes that she "also had grown up around the stage and in Hollywood, two venues where a little elegance in dress is part of the air that everyone breathes."[55] The first lady was used to not only dressing the part, but also having well-known fashion designers supply the costumes.

Early in the Reagan first term, Richard Allen, the president's national security advisor, was forced to resign after accepting a $1,000 gratuity for arranging an interview with Mrs. Reagan. The first lady subsequently sought the opinion of the president's staff as to whether she could continue her method of acquiring designer clothes. By accepting the gowns as gifts, Mrs. Reagan may have violated the 1977 Ethics in Government Act. Under the provisions of the act, the Reagans were required to report on public disclosure forms not only all gifts valued at over $35, but also financial liabilities exceeding $10,000.[56] Mrs. Reagan had not listed her gowns. The possible violations were serious enough that White House lawyers raised concerns within the administration that Mrs. Reagan's practice could generate an Internal Revenue Service investigation.

The first lady's critics argued that the issue was broader than whether she had violated the Ethics in Government Act. By wearing donated designer clothes, she may have been supporting the American fashion industry, but she was also helping specific designers make huge profits. In the midst of a recession, Jean Louis saw his profits increase by one-third. Noted fashion designer Geoffrey Beene suggested that the whole scheme had "the overtones of a commercial."[57] Sidney Cohen, a Democrat and former commissioner of the Internal Revenue Service, was even harsher in his criticism, saying,

"Those people don't understand that maybe you shouldn't do something like this. It is more a question of taste than anything else. It smacks of favoritism and gives the appearance of privilege to a certain group. You can bet your life that the designer who provides the gowns will be invited to the White House regularly, be put on some advisory group and maybe be part of a delegation to the Vatican."[58] In September 1981, Fred F. Fielding, counsel to the president, specifically noted in a memo to Michael Deaver that because the first lady was not an officer of the United States, she was not prohibited from accepting gifts as long as there were no conditions attached and the Reagans reported the gifts as income as required by federal law.[59] However, Fielding also questioned the wisdom of accepting gifts of clothes and jewelry because it might convey the impression that President and Mrs. Reagan "were 'indifferent' and 'insensitive' to the poor, and so forth."[60] In her autobiography, the first lady defends her decision to "borrow" clothes, stating:

> Then there are state dinners, which take place almost every month. During our eight years in Washington, Ronnie and I hosted almost eighty of them. Even if you wear outfits more than once, as I did, that adds up to a lot of formal dresses. . . . Because I needed more clothes—far more than I could afford to buy—I borrowed outfits for specific occasions from some of my favorite designers and old friends. And here I made a big mistake. No, not by borrowing, but by announcing from the start that I was going to do this, and I would return them. But I honestly never expected that this would be seen as a problem. Borrowing designer clothes is such a widespread and accepted practice in the American fashion industry that it never occurred to me that I would be criticized for it.[61]

The first lady claimed that because the clothes were either borrowed and returned or donated to fashion museums, they were not gifts, and therefore not subject to the Ethics in Government Act. Mrs. Reagan's creative interpretation kept the question of a possible violation from being resolved, but the damage to her image was significant. Continuing her streak of bad timing, the story about the designer gowns appeared in the news the same week as stories about the poor standing in long lines to get handouts of free cheese. The first lady's lifestyle was becoming a political liability to the president, who was forced to defend his wife by saying that she had been given a "bum rap."[62] Despite the president's support, a 25 November 1981 poll by the *Washington Post*/ABC News showed that 23 percent of the American people said that their impression of Mrs. Reagan was unfavorable, and that a substantially higher percentage of Americans disapproved of Nancy Reagan than they did of Rosalynn Carter and Pat Nixon early in their husbands' administrations.[63]

The press was soon filled with stories about "Queen Nancy." A postcard picturing Mrs. Reagan wearing a jewel-encrusted crown, a dress of the finest brocade, and a cape of snowy ermine became the hottest-selling Washington souvenir. The first lady's staff was constantly beset with questions about her attire. Where did she obtain a particular garment, was it a gift, and had it been declared under the Ethics in Government Act? In response, Mrs. Reagan noted that wearing gowns donated by prominent fashion designers was a common European practice, and asserted that her doing so was good advertising for the American fashion industry.[64] Finally, attempting to quell the criticism, she announced that she would donate all of the gowns to American fashion museums.

> I have long felt that American fashion is the best in the world, and because there are so many talented young American designers, it occurred to me that I might find a way to encourage them. To provide these promising young students with an opportunity to study the workmanship of established American designers, I am happy to announce that a representative group of clothing worn by me since becoming First Lady will be distributed regularly to the costume collections of a number of U.S. museums.[65]

In reality, after very publicly donating a couple of gowns, Mrs. Reagan quietly returned to her previous habits.

Meanwhile, the first lady's critics had broadened to include not only the administration's opponents, but also its friends. The conservative *Wall Street Journal* argued that Mrs. Reagan was the reason for women leaving the Republican Party. William Schneider, a Republican political analyst, argued that she had compromised the new presidency by demonstrating that the administration had a "bias toward the rich."[66]

A *Newsweek* poll published on 21 December 1981 provided additional evidence that the general public was equally unhappy with the first lady. The poll showed that Mrs. Reagan had about the same public approval rating as Mrs. Carter had at the low point of the Carter presidency (26 percent for Mrs. Reagan versus Mrs. Carter's 19 percent). Of those polled, 62 percent thought that Mrs. Reagan put too much emphasis on style and elegance, given that the country was in a recession at the time. In addition, 61 percent said that Mrs. Reagan was less sympathetic to the problems of the poor and disadvantaged than other first ladies. An early December poll from *Washington Post*/ABC News brought equally bad news. The first lady had a 23 percent disapproval rating, it found, with the sharpest criticism of Mrs. Reagan coming from the poor, African Americans, and of course Democrats.[67]

The White House claimed that the public was not nearly as concerned about these issues as the press. A Gallup poll published on 24 December 1981 provided support for their position. In the poll, which ranked America's ten most admired women, Mrs. Reagan was first (up from eighth the year before).[68] Obviously, the public had mixed feelings about the first lady's interpretation of her role.

Mrs. Reagan did have her supporters. Those familiar with the fashion world pointed out that the general public's perception of the industry was inaccurate. Most people who heard the term "fashion" tended to think of only three or four top designers, not realizing the major economic scope and impact of the clothing business. In the early 1980s, fashion was actually the third largest industry in the United States, employing more people and paying more taxes in New York than any other business. Every year, more than 900 manufacturers contributed $16 billion to the New York City economy and employed over 6,000 people.[69] Others noted that with the American fashion industry in a downturn, Mrs. Reagan's fondness for American designers might help the industry in the international market.[70]

Given Mrs. Reagan's reputation for having a sensitive public-relations antenna, it is curious that her tenure as first lady started so poorly. Certainly she badly misread both the mood of the country and the nature of the Washington press. She clearly did not realize the extent of Americans' suffering or understand that her life was now an open book. Mrs. Reagan's role model as first lady was Jackie Kennedy, but the times called more for an Eleanor Roosevelt.

While on the 1980 campaign trail, Mrs. Reagan indicated that she intended to keep some aspects of her Washington life private.[71] That may have been possible with the Hollywood or Sacramento press, but it certainly wouldn't happen with the Washington press. As Lewis Gould noted of the press during the Carter administration, "The twin forces of celebrity journalism and eroding professional skills among reporters started the long decline into relentless triviality that now marks much of the nation's public discourse in the press."[72] Not much had changed by 1980.

On 30 March 1981, just slightly over two months into the administration, Mrs. Reagan also had to deal with an attempt on her husband's life. For all the jokes President Reagan made after he was shot ("I'd rather be in Philadelphia," etc.), the president's situation was much more critical and his recovery more arduous than the public was led to believe. Although Ronald Reagan was in very good physical condition, he was hardly a young man. He had been shot in the chest with a twenty-two-caliber handgun and had lost a significant amount of blood; doctors estimate that if he had arrived at the hospital five minutes later, he might have died. Although no one realized it at the time, John Hinckley, the shooter, had used deadly devastator bullets, which are designed to explode on impact. One of the bullets was lodged near the president's spine. The bullet was removed safely during surgery, but it later exploded while being analyzed in an FBI lab, destroying a microscope and spraying the room with metal fragments.[73]

The president developed a postoperative infection and fever. He was often in a great deal of pain, and his full recovery was far from assured. In her autobiography, Mrs. Reagan writes compellingly of her anxiety during this time:

> It was a nightmare—the panic and confusion, the waiting, the not knowing. But something takes over at these times and somehow I held myself together. They're doing what they can, I told myself. Stay out of their way. Let the doctors do their work. My father, a doctor, had told me that so many times—it was like an echo in my head. Around me, the hospital was bedlam. I still

wake up at night remembering that scene—confusion, voices, sirens, reporters, doctors, nurses, technicians, the president's men, the Secret Service with their walkie-talkies. People running through the corridors, doctors barking out orders and the police shouting again and again, "Get those people out of here!"[74]

Mrs. Reagan had always been deeply concerned about her husband's health and well-being; she was now confronted by her worst nightmare made even worse by her helplessness. She had previously "nursed" Ronald Reagan through the difficult period resulting from his divorce and the collapse of his movie career. She had always worked tirelessly to protect him from those she thought did not have his best interests at heart. Now she was faced with a situation that she could not control.

When the Secret Service notified her that there had been a shooting, Mrs. Reagan rushed to George Washington University Hospital, where Michael Deaver met her. He attempted to calm her down, but he also prevented her from seeing President Reagan while the doctors determined the extent of his injuries. Finally, the first lady demanded to see her husband. She was escorted to a room filled with medical staff where the president was laying on a gurney, smiling at her from under his oxygen mask. After giving permission to operate, she waited outside the operating room while doctors worked to save the president.[75] With her husband's life at stake, the wait was excruciating.

She had to face the possibility that the president might not recover—a scenario made more real by the difficulties she had encountered in attempting to see her husband and in receiving accurate information immediately after the shooting. As the daughter of a world-renowned surgeon, Mrs. Reagan knew enough medicine to understand the degree of trauma her husband had experienced and to realize that he might not survive. Although the possible death of a loved one would be painful for anyone, it would be especially devastating for a woman who had devoted so much of her life exclusively to her husband.

While the first lady waited for her husband to emerge from the operating room, the nation watched the assassination attempt again and again (often repeated in slow motion) on television. Because President Reagan was on his way to give a speech at the time of the attack, all three networks had correspondents and film crews at the scene, so there was plenty of videotape of the shootings. Images of the president being pushed down into his limousine after being shot, John Hinckley being overwhelmed by the Secret Service, and the president's press secretary, James Brady, lying on the pavement were broadcast sixteen times by CBS alone.[76] Even worse, the early reports of the shooting were often confusing. The first broadcasts stated that Ronald Reagan had not even been shot. Once the networks verified that the president had indeed been hit, reports varied as to the severity of his injury. Confusion reigned over whether he was undergoing surgery, whether the surgery was on his heart, and how long the surgery would take.[77]

Once President Reagan moved into the postoperative and recovery stages, news coverage of the assassination attempt gave way to hospital briefings about the nature of his wounds and the prognosis for his recovery. The George Washington University (GWU) spokesman in charge of the briefings furnished detailed medical reports about their newest patient. Mrs. Reagan was not pleased at the volume of information that the hospital provided about the president's recovery and treatment, and her father was outraged. Dr. Davis was so incensed that he called Dr. Daniel Rudge, his former associate and the current White House physician, to complain that the press briefings were much too explicit. Dr. Rudge, in turn, ordered the GWU doctors to limit the details released on the president's condition.[78]

During President Reagan's recovery, a University of Pennsylvania student wrote in the school newspaper that he hoped the president would die from his wounds. Mrs. Reagan, already unnerved by the shooting, was so upset by the student's comments that she asked Attorney General William French Smith to inquire whether the student could be punished. Smith, an old family friend, was sympathetic to Mrs. Reagan's concerns, but informed her that there was nothing the Justice Department could do.[79]

Mrs. Reagan almost seemed more emotionally scarred by the assassination attempt than her husband. The already slender first lady lost more than ten pounds (dropping from one hundred and twelve pounds to under one hundred pounds) in just a couple of months following the shooting. Her rapid weight loss gave rise to speculation that she was ill. Because Mrs. Reagan could not adequately explain to the press the level of anxiety she felt whenever the president left the White House or Camp David, she could not dispel the rumors about her health. To the public Mrs. Reagan remained stoic, but in private she was terrified as she slowly came to grips with the fact that she could not always safeguard her husband.

That realization didn't mean that she would give up—merely that she would have to redouble her efforts. After the assassination attempt, Mrs. Reagan became even more protective of her husband's schedule. If she felt that his aides were planning too many meetings or events, she forced them to cut back on the demands on the president's time. Her calls to the chief of staff to modify President Reagan's agenda became even more frequent. She insisted on changing times and dates for the president's speeches, trips, and public appearances, and even when Air Force One would land. She now considered it a critical part of her job to ensure that the president was well rested and healthy. Clearly, the first lady had reason to be distracted from the political criticism swirling around her. The press and the public might be calling her Queen Nancy, but Mrs. Reagan had more important concerns.

In light of the heavy criticism that Mrs. Reagan received, the White House staff began discussing the "Nancy problem," focusing on the possible negative effect she might have on the president's reelection chances in 1984. Even Michael Deaver, Mrs. Reagan's closest confidant on the president's staff, felt that she might be hurting the administration's overall image. Richard Wirthlin, the president's pollster, saw in his numbers that all the negative news stories on redecorating, the new china, and Mrs. Reagan's lavish lifestyle were beginning to affect the president's popularity.[80]

Mrs. Reagan's image problems stemmed in part from a national debate about the role of first ladies. During the 1980s, it seemed as if the nation could not make up its mind about what kind of first lady it desired. Some Americans clearly sought an activist first lady, such as Eleanor Roosevelt, Betty Ford, or even Rosalynn Carter. To them Mrs. Reagan, with her emphasis on style rather than substance, was a disappointment. Other Americans wanted a first lady who supported her husband but stayed out of politics, limiting herself to "safe" causes and hosting White House affairs. No matter how Nancy filled the role a large segment of the public would be disappointed.

Eventually, a Camp David meeting was held to work out a strategy for dealing with the first lady's image. Most of the president's image shapers, including Richard Wirthlin, Michael Deaver, Joseph Canzeri, and Stuart Spencer, attended the meeting. One of the proposed solutions was to have Mrs. Reagan adopt an essentially nineteenth-century hostess role. Such a change would take advantage of her natural talent for entertaining, but would also keep her out of the public eye. Deaver and Wirthlin strongly disagreed with the strategy, arguing that under the right circumstances, Mrs. Reagan could become a considerable asset to the administration.[81] Their persuasiveness resulted in a three-part plan to improve the first lady's image.

Part one of the plan required Mrs. Reagan to limit contact with her fun-loving California crowd and tone down the parties, designer dresses, and traveling hairdressers. In the second part of the plan, Mrs. Reagan would make an effort to cultivate the press. She took her first step in this effort on 29 March 1982 at the annual Gridiron Dinner (an occasion for humorous exchanges between politicians and the press). After one reporter appeared on stage singing new lyrics to the song "Second Hand Rose," poking fun at Mrs. Reagan's love of fine clothes, Mrs. Reagan slipped away from the dinner table. While the lights were down, she changed into old, ill-fitting, ragged clothes and then appeared on stage (surprising even the president, which was part of the plan) to sing her own self-deprecating version of the song:

I'm wearing second-hand clothes,
Second-hand clothes.
They're quite the style
In spring fashion shows.
Even my new trench coat with collar
Ronnie bought for ten cents on the dollar.

Second-hand gowns
And old hand-me-downs.
The china is the only thing that's new.
Even though they tell me that I'm no longer
Queen,
Did Ronnie have to buy me that new
Sewing machine?
I sure hope Ed Meese sews.[82]

Mrs. Reagan ended her act by throwing a plate that resembled the new White House china on the floor. The plate was supposed to break, but unfortunately did not. It was the only glitch in an otherwise flawless performance.

The response to Mrs. Reagan's appearance was extraordinary. She was called back to the stage for an encore, with shouts of "Bravo" and thunderous applause (this time the plate broke). Mrs. Reagan presented a new aspect of her personality—the ability to laugh at herself—one that the press had not seen before, and of which they approved. The reviews of her act were exceptional and marked the beginning of a thaw in the relationship between the media and the first lady. Although Mrs. Reagan's press relations would always suffer from ups and downs, a lot of the nasty tone of the coverage dissipated after this performance.[83]

During her first year as first lady, Mrs. Reagan showed little interest in improving her press relations. She routinely turned down requests for interviews from foreign media, and even declined local media requests.[84] Mrs. Reagan's press office did not provide daily press briefings, nor did she hold regularly scheduled press conferences. The first lady believed that only those in policy-making positions should hold press conferences.[85]

After her success at the Gridiron Dinner, Mrs. Reagan agreed that cultivating members of the elite Washington press corps could improve her image. Soon Washington insiders such as columnist George Will; Katharine Graham, owner of the *Washington Post*; Roone Arledge, head of ABC News and Sports; and Frank Reynolds, television anchor, became regular visitors to the White House. Mrs. Reagan and Mrs. Graham would become close friends.[86]

For the third phase in rehabilitating her image, Mrs. Reagan was to focus on a cause that would showcase the serious and caring side of her personality. When she was asked about adopting a cause during the 1980 campaign, Mrs. Reagan responded that her husband was her cause, and that she would continue to focus on his needs. Once the first lady was convinced that the president's interests were at stake, she reconsidered. She realized that the practical limits of the Foster Grandparents program required her to develop an additional policy interest. The drug problem seemed a viable alternative. In fact, during the 1980 campaign, she had already begun to gather information about drug abuse, meet with experts in the field, and tentatively speak out on the subject.

During the first six months of the administration, a variety of factors slowed the emergence of drug abuse as a major cause for the first lady. The administration had not yet appointed a national drug czar, and Mrs. Reagan's own staff was still not fully in place. In the early days of the administration closed-door meetings were held with the many parties involved in setting drug policy. In the course of these meetings Mrs. Reagan settled on the particular aspect of drug abuse she wanted to address: preventing drug use among children.[87]

The president's advisors went along with Mrs. Reagan's idea for an antidrug campaign, but many were not enthusiastic. Ann Wrobeski and Frank Ursomarso from Mrs. Reagan's staff had worked at developing an antidrug program since the summer of 1981, but it still lacked a clear focus and theme.[88] Many of the president's men felt that an antidrug campaign would be too negative. As a result, staffers even suggested that as a more positive alternative, Mrs. Reagan champion unspecified public–private-sector initiatives to address social problems. As late as 2 December 1981, it was suggested that Mrs. Reagan host a weekly television program dealing with a historical aspect of the White House with thirty high school seniors serving as her audience.[89] Sheila Tate responded that Mrs. Reagan has "repeatedly expressed her desire to me to concentrate on the two areas she wishes to pursue—the Foster Grandparent program and drug abuse."[90] Mrs. Reagan remained adamant in her choice.

One of the exceptions among the West Wing skeptics was Richard Wirthlin, whose most recent polls identified drug abuse as one of American's most important concerns.[91] Another of the president's men noted that "drug abuse among children—like kid pornography—has no supporters, only suppliers. It is a safe issue." He also argued that it was too late to limit Mrs. Reagan's involvement with drug abuse, since "she talked about it all over the country during the campaign. The time to stop her was then—by the time she moved here, it was too late—expectations had been raised."[92]

What neither staff realized was that Mrs. Reagan had already developed a strong interest in an antidrug program. As first lady of California, she had arranged meetings between recovering teenage addicts and young students, telling parents that their children would be more convinced by their peers than by adults. She also realized that her own daughter, Patti, had experimented with drugs, and that even Nancy's own earlier use of prescription pills to help her sleep and to calm her held the potential for abuse.[93] Mrs. Reagan's own informal medical experience provided another reason for adopting drug abuse as her cause. As a child, she had often accompanied her father on his hospital tours, even watching as he operated on patients. In college she earned extra money working as a nurses' aide. As a result, she knew that she could be at ease with those suffering from medical problems. When it came time for her to focus on a cause, it was natural for her to choose something in the medical field.[94]

Mrs. Reagan's interest in drug abuse as a cause had been heightened by some of her encounters during the 1980 campaign. While campaigning for her husband in New York, she scheduled a stop at Daytop Village, a drug abuse rehabilitation center for youths, and was moved by experiences they shared. She also had intimate, lengthy conversations with comedienne Carol Burnett, whose teenage daughter was then suffering from drug addiction, and with television personality Art Linkletter, whose daughter had died from an overdose of LSD.[95] Yet few of the reporters covering the Reagan presidential campaign seemed to notice Mrs. Reagan's interest in drug abuse, let alone asked her in-depth questions on the subject.

In the early 1980s, drug abuse was not just a major social problem—it was an epidemic. According to the National Institute on Drug Abuse, 43 million people, or 20 percent of the population of the United States, were believed to have tried marijuana. Sixteen million (about the population of Pennsylvania at the time) had used marijuana in the previous month. Cocaine use was growing almost as fast: approximately 10 million Americans had tried the powerful stimulant. Seven million Americans were estimated to have tried angel dust, the highly addictive street drug made from animal tranquilizers. Increased drug use had even spun off a new industry—drug paraphernalia. The paraphernalia industry, with its smoking papers, ivory pipes, gold spoons, and straws for snorting cocaine, was making $350 million in profit a year.[96] The problem was particularly acute among the nation's young. According to the 1981 National Survey on Drug Abuse, there were 4.5 million drug abusers and 8.7 million alcohol abusers among children aged 12 to 17.[97]

Drug use was rampant even in the military. In 1981, the Pentagon estimated that 36 percent of military personnel used marijuana and other drugs. The military drug problem was so pervasive that the Pentagon was spending $100 million a year in its campaign against alcohol and drug use.[98] On 18 June 1981 a committee of the House of Representatives heard testimony that traces of marijuana were found in the bodies of six of the fourteen men killed in a May crash of a jet on the deck of the aircraft carrier *Nimitz*. The amount of marijuana found was sufficiently high to suggest that the men had been smoking while on duty before the crash.[99]

Nowhere was the problem greater than in the nation's capital. By the first week in August 1981, seventy-two people had died of drug overdoses, ten more than for all of the previous year. The Washington police reported that the improved quantity and quality of the heroin supply (the best it had been it years) worsened the capital's drug problem. Heroin was so plentiful that the price had fallen dramatically. One street dealer was reportedly giving away free samples and encouraging addicts to get their friends addicted.[100] If Mrs. Reagan was concerned about drug abuse, she certainly didn't have to go far to see its effects.

The primary drug prevention policy was interdiction. In 1979, government agents seized drugs with an estimated street value of $2.5 billion in the United States and abroad. But authorities estimated that drugs worth about $35 to $45 billion a year were changing hands.[101] Prevention campaigns were just beginning, with a focus on the young. The Drug Enforcement Agency urged young people through the media to make informed decisions about drug use.

The press noncoverage of Mrs. Reagan's interest in the drug abuse problem continued after the election. When asked about causes that interested her, Mrs. Reagan stated that she was considering drug abuse among children. Despite uncertainty about the exact direction such a campaign should take, the first lady felt that although it was often easier for parents to say "yes," what they should do more often is "just say no." Nevertheless, the topic received almost no media comment.

As part of reshaping her image, Nancy Reagan agreed to the appointment of a new East Wing chief of staff. However, she insisted that she make the final selection. Chief of Mrs. Reagan's staff had turned into a position that was difficult to keep filled. Peter McCoy initially held the position, but he was blamed for the first lady's negative public image and was transferred to the Commerce Department.[102] Another staff director, Lee Verstandig (hand-picked by Michael Deaver), lasted only four weeks. He left when he was asked to fill in temporarily at the Environmental Protection Agency after Anne Burford resigned.[103]

With Michael Deaver's help, Mrs. Reagan selected James Rosebush from the Commerce Department. Rosebush also had an interest in drug abuse. He proved to be the longest lasting and the most successful of Mrs. Reagan's chiefs of staff. He assisted the first lady in setting in motion the antidrug campaign, which proved to be one of the keys to redefining her image.[104] Rosebush was also the first East Wing chief of staff to be appointed to the president's staff and to regularly attend senior staff meetings. His dual appointment was another major reason for the improved relations between the East Wing and West Wing staffs.[105]

Once the Rosebush appointment was complete, Mrs. Reagan took a planeload of reporters on a two-day trip to Florida and Texas to observe various approaches to the problem of drug abuse. In Florida, they stopped at a grammar school to see an example of the ALPHA program, a motivational program designed to steer fifth-grade students away from drugs. They also visited a confrontational "therapy" session between parents and their children that lasted for over three hours, during which Mrs. Reagan and the accompanying reporters were startled by the stories told. Mrs. Reagan spoke with great eloquence, telling the parents that the greatest pain humans experienced was between parents and their children, and how much she respected them for their courage.[106] While in Texas, they met with Governor William Clements and a citizen action group representing a war on drugs effort spearheaded by Ross Perot. The Reagan administration's emphasis on private-sector involvement in solving social problems meshed nicely with Perot's plan to denote $1.2 million of his own money to the antidrug effort.[107]

The phrase "Just say no" (replacing the original slogan, "Drugs are dumb") originated in a visit to an Oakland, California, school, where Mrs. Reagan told a student that if he were approached to try drugs, he should "just say no!"[108] Although some doubted the effectiveness of this approach, few could question Mrs. Reagan's commitment to the program. During her years as first lady, she received and read thousands of letters from schoolchildren, many of them telling gruesome tales. One letter from a fifteen-year-old girl imprisoned for parole violation and drug possession told of growing up with a father who fed her pills so he could laugh as she stumbled and tried to speak. Despite the obvious public relations benefits to her image, Mrs. Reagan chose not to exploit the children's suffering and never released most of the letters to the media.[109]

The East Wing worked with a wide variety of drug abuse programs to promote Mrs. Reagan's cause, including rehabilitation groups such as the Phoenix House. In 1984, her staff enlisted traditional groups such as the Girl Scouts and the Kiwanis Club International in the antidrug campaign. The Girl Scouts introduced a Drug Free merit badge, and the Kiwanis put up over two thousand billboards with the first lady's likeness and the phrase "Just Say No." In addition, over five thousand "Just Say No" clubs were founded in the United States and abroad. Another group Mrs. Reagan worked with was the National Federation of Parents for a Drug–Free Youth, a parent group begun from a local Parent Teachers Association in Sacramento, California. Over time, the group had grown into a national organization committed to stopping drug abuse among children.[110]

By the autumn of 1985, Mrs. Reagan had appeared on twenty-three talk shows to discuss drugs and her "Just Say No" program, co-hosted an episode of the television show *Good Morning America* focusing on the drug problem (the first presidential spouse to cohost such a show), and starred in a two-hour documentary on drug abuse for PBS. She had also traveled 55,000 miles to forty-four cities in twenty-seven states in her efforts to combat school-age drug and alcohol abuse.[111] That same year, she used her international connections to invite first ladies from seventeen other countries to a drug summit in Washington and Atlanta. The conference provided first ladies with an opportunity to hear speakers on a variety of topics, and also to meet for informal discussion about the drug problem in their respective countries.[112] Also in 1985, the Nancy Reagan Drug Abuse Fund was established through the tax-exempt Community Foundation of Greater Washington as a vehicle for raising revenues to fight drug abuse.[113] Once the fund was established, worthwhile antidrug organizations asked Mrs. Reagan to intervene with the Community Foundation on their behalf.[114]

When speaking before various groups, the first lady would occasionally be asked to lobby for increased funding for drug abuse programs. Her standard reply was that she was responsible for raising awareness, not funding. Throughout her years in the White House, Mrs. Reagan made a heroic effort to fulfill her responsibility.

There is some evidence that drug abuse significantly declined during the Reagan years. A study by the Institute for Social Research at the University of Michigan showed that more young people were saying no to drugs. The research reported that the percentage of high school seniors using marijuana dropped from a peak of 50.1 percent in 1978 to 36 percent in 1987. The percentage of students using other drugs showed a similar downward trend. The use of hallucinogens dropped from 11 percent to 6 percent, cocaine from 12 percent to 10 percent, and heroin from 1 percent to .5 percent. Even alcohol use dropped from 88 percent to 85 percent.[115] Mrs. Reagan's speaking forcefully against the use of illegal drugs undoubtedly increased public awareness of the problem. It is, however, impossible to connect the declining trend in drug usage directly to Mrs. Reagan's "Just Say No" program. Still, the first lady was aware that a change in attitude was occurring and increasingly urged individuals not just to say no, but also to become active in their community in the fight against drugs.[116]

The antidrug campaign also improved Mrs. Reagan's public image. Her press coverage became much more positive—including a cover story in *Time* and an hour-long special on NBC, both very favorable to the first lady. An even more significant change took place in public opinion. A *New York Times*/CBS News poll in January 1985 found that the first lady's popularity was even greater than the president's (72 percent favorability for Mrs. Reagan versus 62 favorability for President Reagan). An NBC News poll found her approval/disapproval ratio at nearly eight to one (69 percent to 9 percent). When respondents were asked what they most admired about her, the most frequent response was that she supports the president and *acts like a first lady should* (emphasis added).[117] James Rosebush felt that her adoption of the antidrug cause did much to improve her standing with the press. Traveling with the first lady as she logged all the miles in the first year of the antidrug campaign, the press became better acquainted with her and saw that she "had a large heart, caring feelings, and a good sense of humor."[118]

The members of the press accompanying the first lady were especially moved during a 1982 visit to Straight Ivey, a drug rehabilitation center in Orlando, Florida. Mrs. Reagan listened to youngsters tell how they had prostituted themselves for drugs, burned crosses on their arms, taken insecticides, and even turned younger siblings and pets on to drugs. As Rosebush recalled:

> Mrs. Reagan was asked to talk to a group of about three hundred. With no prepared speech and puffy eyes, red from crying, she turned to the parents first and told them how she knew no hurt could be as painful as the hurt between parent and child and that she admired them for acknowledging their family problems and for getting help. Next, fighting back more tears, she turned to the children and told them she loved them, and she wanted them to fight hard to be drug free, and that the world needed them.[119]

Even the most hardened of cynics were touched by the raw emotion of the event. In just three years, a very well organized public relations campaign emphasizing Mrs. Reagan's more compassionate and caring qualities had managed to eradicate her earlier elitist image. As a result, she seemed much more in touch with the concerns of average Americans. Her involvement in the antidrug campaign also provided the first lady with some gravitas, overcoming the common criticism of Mrs. Reagan as a political and intellectual lightweight.[120] By 1983, most of the vestiges of Queen Nancy were gone. When she hosted an opulent dinner at a movie studio for Britain's Queen Elizabeth with movie stars as guests, attended Prince Andrew's royal wedding, and referred to Prince Charles as "family," hardly a murmur was heard from the press. By the end of the president's first term, Mrs. Reagan had successfully remade her image to more closely fit the public's perception of a first lady. In fact, she seemed to have a better sense of how to rehabilitate her image than many of the president's own image-makers. It was, after all, the first lady who doggedly insisted on the drug problem as being worthy of her attention, while members of the president's staff argued that drug abuse was much too negative to have the desired effect.

During her husband's first term, Mrs. Reagan's experience as an actress proved useful in several ways. Initially, her Hollywood background could be seen most clearly in her love of style, which was so frequently on display early in the Reagan administration. The White House dinners requiring white ties and gloves, with stars such as Frank Sinatra providing entertainment, were pure Hollywood productions. In terms of style, Mrs. Reagan successfully merged Hollywood and Washington, although not always to her own advantage.

Mrs. Reagan's aptitude for shaping her public image was also pure theater. She learned a great deal in her acting years, including how to stand and present herself for the best possible effect. While much has been made of the "gaze," it is only one of the looks that Mrs. Reagan used effectively while first lady. There was also the smile of delight from the top of the stairs of Airforce One, and the look of concern at drug addicts as they told their story. What was most remarkable was her ability to recreate each look time after time, without the expression changing by a millimeter. Such perfection of effort represents practiced skill, not spontaneity.[121]

With Michael Deaver's help, Mrs. Reagan also became expert at managing photo opportunities. As a former actress, she was experienced at manipulating how she appeared on camera. She knew that when shaking a person's hand, she should open her mouth just slightly to give the impression in the photo that she was deep in conversation with the other person. It has been said that while first lady, Mrs. Reagan never had a bad picture taken. The public, however, never realized the amount of preparation that went into those photographs. Mrs. Reagan's advance staff would check the color scheme of sites she would visit so that the shade of her clothes could be chosen to coordinate with her surroundings. For "spontaneous" photos, staff members would often set down pieces of tape as a mark for her to toe for the picture to be perfect. Finally, before White House photos were released to the press, Mrs. Reagan frequently went through dozens of shots taken by her official photographer, looking for just the right one. She would initial the backs of those she wanted to use and tear off the right corner of the ones that should never be seen again.[122] Mrs. Reagan's staff also instructed the networks on how best to film her, noting that "Mrs. Reagan is extremely difficult to light with deep set eyes and fair skin."[123]

Although Mrs. Reagan spent much time arranging her image, there was substance behind that image. If the public became convinced that Mrs. Reagan really cared about the drug abuse problem, it was because she did. Although there is disagreement about the long-term effectiveness of the "Just Say No" program, there is little debate that Mrs. Reagan took it seriously. She argued too hard about the value of the cause, traveled too many miles, appeared before too many groups, and read too many heart-wrenching letters for it all to have been just a publicity campaign.

Mrs. Reagan realized that to effectively redo her image, she needed a cause of value and significance not only to the American public, but also to herself. It is important to remember why she undertook the campaign to reshape her image. Prior to being approached by the president's advisors with evidence that her public image was hurting her husband's presidency, Mrs. Reagan had resisted her staff's efforts to get her involved in a serious cause. Although she had dabbled in the antidrug campaign, she did not put much effort into it—until her husband needed her to. Mrs. Reagan, for all her glamour and style, was still the dependable supporting actor in the production of the Reagan presidency, always looking out for the star's best interest.

CHAPTER 3

NANCY REAGAN, CASTING DIRECTOR

As a good supporting actress, Mrs. Reagan always looked for ways to make the show better. By all accounts, the first lady devoted considerable effort to surrounding the president with just the right advisors and staff. Her innate ability to read people combined with the president's excessive feelings of loyalty and his resulting difficulty in firing members of his staff placed Mrs. Reagan at the center of many important personnel decisions.

Her involvement in West Wing staff matters became one of the most controversial aspects of the first lady's tenure. During President Reagan's first term, his wife's influence in personnel issues was an open secret within the Washington Beltway, but not widely known outside of the capital. By the end of the second term, Mrs. Reagan's feud with White House Chief of Staff Donald Regan had created a media firestorm that in the middle of the Iran-Contra scandal exposed her involvement to the public eye.

Nancy Reagan was compared to Edith Wilson, who dominated the White House during her husband's prolonged illness. Dubbed the "Dragon Lady," Mrs. Reagan seemed to be another example of a pushy first lady becoming deeply involved in White House affairs. In reality, she was simply continuing her long-standing role in her husband's public life. She was the loyal supporting actress and sometime casting director whose primary concern was always the success of the main production—the presidency of Ronald Reagan.[1] Mrs. Reagan believed that her participation served her husband's best interests. She knew that he needed a calm environment to give his best performance. As a former actor, Mrs. Reagan knew that disapproval from critics was something all actors learned to deal with. Doubts from the wings, however, undercut an actor's ability to perform. Garry Wills noted that Mrs. Reagan's famous run-ins with the president's aides were almost always "over things they did to throw him off stride, wreck the mood, get him down."[2] During the 1984 campaign Reagan noted that disagreements in the campaign were "giving him knots in his stomach."[3] Mrs. Reagan understood that that in order to give his best performance, the president needed support. Those members of his staff who had their own agenda soon found themselves replaced.

Michael Deaver wrote, "She has made him her career, and the White House did not change or enlarge her methods or motives."[4] Because her husband tended to avoid conflict, Mrs. Reagan often felt the need to act on his behalf. Her involvement in his life made things happen. Jimmy Stewart, one of Mrs. Reagan's pre-Hollywood friends (and a pretty good actor himself), put it best: "If Nancy Reagan had been Ronald Reagan's first wife, he would have never gone into politics. Instead she would have seen to it that he got all the best parts, he would have won three or four Oscars and been a real star."[5]

Mrs. Reagan's involvement in personnel decisions affected the direction of policy and influenced the ideological composition of the president's staff. Mrs. Reagan and her allies, James Baker, Michael Deaver, and later Secretary of State George Shultz, favored moderate and more pragmatic Republicans. But Mrs. Reagan was less concerned with ideology than their ability to get things done on behalf of the president. She felt that more practical Republicans would be better able to work with Congress in passing the president's programs. Of course, as Helene Von Damm, a deputy assistant to the president, noted, personnel decisions also affect policy: "It wasn't just about patronage. It was a matter of which direction the Administration would move in."[6]

Mrs. Reagan's preference for moderates helped shape the administration from the very beginning. Two days after the 1980 election, the president-elect asked James Baker to serve as his chief of staff. Two weeks earlier, Nancy Reagan, Michael Deaver, and Stuart Spencer had strongly suggested that Baker would be the best man for the job.[7] The group viewed Ed Meese, one of the president's California cohorts, as too conservative and too inflexible to be chief of staff. Mrs. Reagan also preferred James Brady to the rumpled Lynn Nofziger as press secretary. Together with her supporters, the first lady prevented the conservative Meese from becoming chief of staff and helped the more moderate James Brady become the president's press secretary.[8] In both cases, Mrs. Reagan's preference was the more moderate and pragmatic Republican.

During the transition, Mrs. Reagan extended her influence to other personnel choices. When financier and former Ford administration official William Simon met with president-elect Reagan, the feisty Wall Streeter stated in no uncertain terms his conditions for becoming Secretary of the Treasury. Mrs. Reagan attended the meeting, said nothing, but listened intently. Another participant recalled the effect of Simon's pushiness: "Bill Simon walked out of the President's life that day, I mean he couldn't get a phone call through after that."[9] The first lady simply pointed out to the president that "you don't hire people who make demands before they have the job."[10]

Later in the Reagan administration, Mrs. Reagan helped oust Raymond Donovan as Secretary of Labor because she felt his legal problems had become an embarrassment (even though he had been cleared of all charges). She also eased Margaret Heckler out of her post as Secretary of Health and Human Services because of what Mrs. Reagan saw as Heckler's personal problems and her limitations as an administrator. In return for losing her cabinet position at Health and Human Services, Heckler was appointed ambassador to Ireland. Her new assignment prompted Helene Von Damm to remark, "if living well is the best revenge, Margaret Heckler got it." Mrs. Reagan was also instrumental in the removal of Alexander Haig as Secretary of State and James Watt from the Department of the Interior.[11]

Another of Mrs. Reagan's targets during the first term was William Clark, who had replaced Richard Allen as national security advisor in January 1982. An old friend of the president's from California, Clark lacked foreign policy experience and was perceived in Washington as more of a technician or facilitator. Much to everyone's surprise, during his tenure Clark enhanced the size and reach of the national security advisor's office. He soon became a prominent figure in the administration's foreign policy, with initiatives on Central America, arms control, and the controversial Strategic Defense Initiative.[12]

Mrs. Reagan thought that Clark was pushing the administration's foreign policy in an ever more conservative direction. She was especially concerned with his involvement in the sensitive area of American-Soviet relations. The first lady believed that Clark was too abrasive toward the Soviets and that his tough stand against the Communists would hurt her husband politically. Mrs. Reagan's problem with Clark also stemmed from his recommendation that President Reagan go to the Philippines to bolster the government of Ferdinand Marcos. Mrs. Reagan felt that the trip was too dangerous, and she never forgave Clark for his willingness to put her husband in harm's way. [13]

Mrs. Reagan and her allies set to work undercutting Clark. She let members of the administration and her friends in the press know that Clark was not a team player and did not get along with the Baker-Deaver faction. Mrs. Reagan poisoned the well against Clark, hoping that the president would be less inclined to take his advice. She elaborates her case against Clark in her memoirs, writing that his selection was "a bad choice" because he wasn't qualified to be Deputy Secretary of State, let alone national security advisor: "He struck me as a user—especially when he traveled around the country claiming he represented Ronnie, which wasn't true. I spoke to Ronnie about him, but Ronnie liked him, so he stayed around longer than I would have liked."[14]

Mrs. Reagan found support for her moderate position on the Soviets with Secretary of State George Shultz. He replaced Alexander Haig, the president's first, but ultimately unsatisfactory, choice for that position. Shultz shared Mrs. Reagan's interest in better U.S.-Soviet relations, and the two soon became allies. As the first lady explains, "I trusted George completely; if he said it was raining, I didn't have to look out the window."[15] Mrs. Reagan noted that the Soviet leaders felt much the same way about Shultz, and she thought that it was one reason they worked together so well. The first lady and Shultz even arranged for the Soviet ambassador to the United States to have a private meeting with the president, one not announced to the media, in 1983.

Administration conservatives were upset about the exclusion of other foreign policy advisors from the meeting with the Soviet ambassador. National security advisor Clark was particularly annoyed at being left out. He realized that the combined efforts of Mrs. Reagan, Michael Deaver, and George Shultz were limiting his effectiveness. Clark blamed the first lady and Deaver in particular for the meeting: "Mike and Nancy were anxious for the outbreak of world peace. They thought that by getting Dobrynin into the East Wing, peace would prevail."[16]

By the end of 1983, some in the administration were beginning to warm to the idea of resuming negotiations with the Soviets. The suddenly robust economy and the billions of dollars poured into national defense had strengthened the American bargaining position. Secretary Shultz in particular thought the time was ripe for negotiation. Deputy national security advisor Robert McFarlane agreed with Shultz; James Baker and Michael Deaver, who were thinking about the 1984 election, were also on board, as was Mrs. Reagan. Shultz maintained that even President Reagan was eager to restore negotiations, telling his associates, "Every meeting I go to . . . the President talks about abolishing nuclear weapons. I cannot get it through your heads that the man is serious."[17]

According to Ed Meese, Clark had become concerned about the constant leaks of sensitive information to the press. He felt that the leaks undermined his position in the administration and, worse, that they damaged national security. Clark proposed that the Justice Department investigate the matter, using lie detectors to determine if members of the president's staff were responsible for the leaks. James Baker and Michael Deaver resisted the proposal, as did George Shultz, who said he would take the test, but only once. If he were asked a second time, he would resign. After Baker and Deaver went to the president and expressed their concerns about the constitutionality of the testing, the plan was withdrawn.[18]

Before the rift between William Clark and the first lady widened, circumstances intervened. Secretary of the Interior James Watt was forced out of office because of some indiscreet public comments, and Clark agreed to take Watt's place. Clark had grown tired of coping with the pressures of his job, including the problems of coordinating the various elements of the national security community and the efforts of some of his colleagues to undermine him. When William Clark resigned, moderates within the administration conspired to increase their influence. Baker, Deaver, and the first lady suggested to the president that James Baker should move into Clark's post as national security advisor, with Michael Deaver then assuming Baker's position of chief of staff. Their plan did not sit well with administration conservatives and was shelved. Robert McFarlane, whom Mrs. Reagan liked a great deal, was named national security advisor.

Mrs. Reagan's fondness for Bud McFarlane stemmed from his unassuming nature. She was convinced that he was one of the few members of the administration who was not trying to bolster his own reputation at the president's expense. McFarlane and the first lady were also in agreement on the need to take a softer line with the Soviet Union. Mrs. Reagan found McFarlane "good looking, closed mouthed, and one of the few people in the administration who had not overplayed his hand."[19] To solidify McFarlane's relationship with the president, Michael Deaver arranged for the Reagans and the McFarlanes to get together socially. How the president felt about McFarlane is not known, but the first lady was obviously impressed.

The Clark affair illustrates Mrs. Reagan's strategy for influencing policy through personnel appointments. When the first lady decided that a particular policy direction would increase the president's stature or popularity, or contribute to his legacy, she worked to place a person who shared her views in a position where he or she could help Mrs. Reagan achieve her goals. The president gave her a great deal of latitude on tactical issues because he respected her political instincts. He often deferred to her advice regarding political maneuvers or personnel decisions. Family friend C. Z. Wrek made an interesting comparison between the president and the first lady, stating that, "She's micro and he's macro. He's the big picture in terms of the whole country, while she's good with the people closest to him."[20]

During the second term, Mrs. Reagan's influence on the White House staff grew even greater. She continued to believe that the administration's success depended on the production's star performer. In the first term she had discreetly intervened to determine who would best serve the president. In the second term her involvement became more visible and controversial. She became the de facto White House casting director. She also became known as the Dragon Lady—the feared power behind the throne—and her actions came under intense, and often unfriendly, scrutiny.

Before there could be a second term, of course, there had to be an election, and before there could be an election, the first lady had to be convinced that her husband should run. Mrs. Reagan had a number of reservations. She was concerned about her husband's physical safety. She couldn't forget the assassination attempt of early 1981. She also noticed subtle physical changes that had occurred in him— a loss of hearing and a small but, to her, noticeable decrease in his energy.[21] As of February 6, 1984, her husband was seventy-three years old, and she was afraid that he might not survive another term.

She was also concerned about his legacy. At the end of Ronald Reagan's first four years as president, the economy had rebounded from the recession and was surging ahead at a record-setting pace. The country's armed forces had been rebuilt and, although the world was still not a safe place, the United States' position in it seemed much stronger. Mrs. Reagan had been involved in enough theater productions to know that it was infinitely better to leave your audience wanting more than to wear out your welcome. Also, the first lady had not really enjoyed the first term. The questions about her lifestyle, the prying press, and the negative caricature of her as Queen Nancy had all left scars.[22]

When the Reagans discussed the possibilities of a second term, Mrs. Reagan expressed her reservations. However, the president noted that there was still much unfinished business and that it had been too long since the United States had a two-term president. While Mrs. Reagan was still wavering, stories surfaced that President Reagan would not run again because the first lady was ill. As a result of the rumors, the stock market tumbled sharply. Mrs. Reagan was appalled that reports about her health could have such major consequences. Ever the trouper, she decided that the show must go on.

Mrs. Reagan was soon demonstrating her burgeoning political skills. In a meeting with Stuart Spencer preceding the 1984 Democratic primaries, Mrs. Reagan predicted that Senator John Glenn would not get the Democratic nomination. She also foresaw that Senator Gary Hart would provide the stiffest competition to former vice-president Walter Mondale, who would ultimately win the Democratic nomination.[23]

The 1984 campaign was much easier than the 1980 campaign. This time the Reagans had the power of incumbency. The economy was humming along nicely. Each quarter brought new increases in economic growth. President Reagan was able to bask in the glow of "morning again in America."[24] Vice-President Mondale's ties to the Carter administration kept him from becoming a strong opponent. Public opinion polls reflected both President Reagan's strength and Mondale's weakness, showing a twenty-point differential between the two candidates.

The only worrisome moment in the campaign came during the debates. Vice-President Mondale easily won the first debate. President Reagan seemed flustered and at times unable to articulate coherent answers to the questions. The president seemed old, and for the first time in the campaign the gap between the two candidates began to narrow (although it never got tighter than ten points).[25] After the debate, Mrs. Reagan went on the offensive, accusing the president's staff of brutalizing him with too many facts during the debate preparation. The first lady saw the president as a star performer whose failure was caused by poor preparation, for which she blamed his staff and his campaign directors.[26] Supporters remarked that the president's handlers wouldn't let Reagan be Reagan.

The charge that the president was brutalized by the facts—overprepared—was later refuted by those involved in the debate preparation. The president's briefing books were actually very slim, and were nothing more than he had mastered in previous campaigns. However, Mrs. Reagan's real point was not that her husband was overprepared, but rather that his staff had gone about preparing the president in the wrong way. David Stockman, who played Walter Mondale in the practice debates, had pummeled the president with detailed knowledge of the issues and in the process had planted a seed of doubt in the president's psyche. The result was that the president lost the first debate badly; he needed to score a clear victory in the second debate.

The preparation for the second debate initially went no better. The president seemed apathetic and dispirited. He muffed his lines, forgot important points he was supposed to emphasize, and had difficulty concentrating. Hearing that the rehearsals were going badly, Mrs. Reagan decided to intervene. The first lady strode into the briefing room clad in an oversized coat. She walked up to the president's podium. Then, much like a flasher, she threw open her coat to reveal her sweater imprinted with the words "4 more in 84." When he didn't respond as expected, the first lady flashed him again. The second time was the charm: her husband broke into a hearty guffaw and then doubled over in laughter. When the president finally got his breath he said, "All right, okay, let's take it from the top."[27]

In addition, with Mrs. Reagan's urging, the numbers of practice sessions were cut from five to two, old friends were brought to the White House to keep the president company, and a pep rally for the president was held prior to the second debate.[28] The revitalized president won the second debate easily. He handled the dreaded age question with a seemingly offhand opening remark, in which he pledged not to use his opponent's youth and inexperience against him.[29] From that point on, the race was over, and Reagan won in a landslide.

It would be an obvious oversimplification to credit the 1984 victory to Mrs. Reagan's flashing of the president. However, her actions once again demonstrated that Nancy Reagan understood her husband much better than did his aides. She realized that what her husband needed was to be built up, not beaten down, before his big performance. The first lady knew that an unhappy or disgruntled Ronald Reagan was not really Ronald Reagan at all. The president wasn't asking the voters to give him a second term because he knew more facts than his opponent; he was asking for a second term because of his vision for America. He was at his best when talking in broad outlines, not in details and numbers. If the president was out of sorts, he could not project his infectious optimism to the American people. Mrs. Reagan was once again drawing upon the notion that the success of the production depends on the star. If the star is not feeling happy and secure, then the whole production suffers.

Another incident from the 1984 campaign demonstrates how well Mrs. Reagan understood her supporting role. During an impromptu press conference at the Reagan ranch, a member of the press asked the president what could be done to bring the Soviets to the bargaining table. President Reagan paused, lost in thought for a full five seconds. Taking a quick look at her husband, Mrs. Reagan whispered to him, "Doing everything we can." After a short interval, President Reagan said, "Doing everything we can."[30]

Although both the first lady and the president denied that she had prompted him with the correct response, a similar situation had occurred in 1980. During a campaign stop, the president was asked if people might smoke fewer cigarettes if they smoked marijuana. The first lady immediately poked the president and whispered, "You wouldn't know." The president quickly responded, "I don't know."[31] The press was eager to present this event in a sinister light. Mrs. Reagan was portrayed as a Svengali who manipulated the president to her will. In essence, however, Mrs. Reagan did nothing more than help out a fellow actor who was in trouble by feeding him a line. She often had done this. In her starring role in her high school play, *First Lady*, she memorized both her own lines and those of all the other parts, feeding the rest of the actors their lines throughout the play. The only difference in this case was that Mrs. Reagan was in the supporting role.

Over the years, Ronald Reagan returned the favor many times. When Mrs. Reagan's frustration with the press threatened to boil over, President Reagan would often interject a joke to break the tension. It was a natural response for them both: just one actor helping out another. The president and the first lady related to each other not just as husband and wife, but also as actors. They were members of the same troupe, able to sense when their fellow performer was in trouble and willing to intervene to save the performance.

Marlin Fitzwater, the president's press secretary after Larry Speakes, noticed as they prepared to meet Soviet President Mikhail Gorbachev how well the president and first lady worked together. "He walked directly to Nancy, as always. They did not like to work separately on these occasions. They preferred to work as a team. The president and Mrs. Reagan were always in their own world, always attached by an invisible string, always aware of each other's presence, even if both were working a handshake line or visiting at a reception. Today was their favorite kind of event, working together as two performers in the same play."[32]

At the start of the second term, there was significant staff turnover, particularly in the president's inner circle. During the inevitable turmoil, Mrs. Reagan was at the center of decision-making. Her office was in the center of the White House, halfway between the East Wing and the West Wing. Her most important tool was the telephone. She had a special line installed with an unlisted number, which allowed her to maintain private conversations, dial people directly, and receive calls without their being tracked and recorded by White House operators. She used her phone so often that she sometimes quipped that when she was buried, a telephone should be placed in her coffin.[33]

The most significant personnel change in the new term occurred when Chief of Staff James Baker and Treasury Secretary Donald Regan switched jobs. Baker was exhausted from the first term, at least partially because of the first lady's constant demands. Several of his close friends reported that the chief of staff had been worn down by the steady stream of complaints and suggestions from the East Wing.[34] Baker realized that he had reached his limit after the first debate between President Reagan and Vice President Mondale. He was convinced that Mrs. Reagan considered White House staff members merely hired hands. A senior aide expressed Baker's frustration when he stated that the first lady "viewed us all as servants—some were house servants and some were field hands—but we all had dirt under our fingernails."[35] As a result, Baker was determined to leave his position.

Donald Regan, for his part, had performed admirably at the Treasury Department and had a reputation as a good manager. The move made sense, and at first it seemed to work well. In her regular meetings with Richard Wirthlin, Mrs. Reagan saw that her husband's poll numbers remained high. Since the first lady generally judged success by the president's popularity, Regan seemed to be serving the president well.[36] Unfortunately, Mrs. Reagan and the president's new chief of staff were soon at odds with each other.

Their first serious clash occurred during the summer of 1985, during the president's recovery from surgery for colon cancer, during which his doctors removed almost two feet of his large intestine. Fortunately, the cancer had not spread to other organs. Mrs. Reagan foresaw potential problems when Regan scheduled a White House helicopter for one of his visits to the hospital. The first lady, who was traveling to the hospital by car, called the chief of staff and asked him if what she had heard was true. When he said that it was, Mrs. Reagan pointed out that, by tradition, the landing pad on the south lawn of the White House was reserved for the president. Regan's using it was a major breach of protocol. Regan got the hint and began traveling to the hospital by car.[37]

Mrs. Reagan was always protective of her husband's time and energy, but during his recovery she was more determined than ever to shield him. She thought that while the president was hospitalized, no one besides herself and his doctor should be allowed to see him. Donald Regan disagreed, and ruled that he also would be allowed to see the president. The first lady felt that Regan was insensitive to her concerns. She also resented his constant presence in her husband's hospital room, disturbing his rest and pressing him to discuss policy matters.

Mrs. Reagan had her own plans for the president after he was released from the hospital. Once the president was back at the White House, she planned to have veto power over her husband's appointments. She also had the president's duties cut down to the bare minimum and moved up the date for their California vacation.[38]

The first lady carefully stage-managed the photo of her hospitalized husband that was released to the press. The picture showed Nancy bending over to kiss the president. What it did not show was that Mrs. Reagan was carefully obscuring his breathing tube from view. To the general public, President Reagan looked remarkably strong and fit for someone who had just undergone major surgery.[39]

The first lady again demonstrated her keen sense of public relations. She realized that part of her husband's appeal was based on his image of vitality. Pictures of the President with a throat tube would make him appear feeble. Some of the clash between Mrs. Reagan and the chief of staff occurred because Donald Regan never fully understood that as he took over more and more responsibilities for the president, he made her husband seem ever weaker.

Regan also didn't comprehend the significant political role that Mrs. Reagan played. The chief of staff had come from a corporate background, where very few women had risen high enough to be treated as equals. One close friend of Ronald Reagan's said, "Regan didn't understand how important Nancy was and how much she had to offer. Regan was almost incapable of understanding this relationship, which was so different from his own marital relationship or the marital relationships he knew about. He was a victim of his generation."[40]

Donald Regan's actions led Mrs. Reagan to believe that he almost welcomed the president's absence. She was concerned that he was using the opportunity to demonstrate that he was the chief executive officer of the administration by taking on the burdens of the Oval Office. When Regan was quoted in the *Washington Post* as saying, "We'll try to spare him [the president] as many of the details as possible,"[41] Mrs. Reagan's worst fears seemed confirmed. Such talk violated the informal code of loyal Reaganites, who were determined to conceal the president's detachment from the specifics of the policy process. This kind of posturing at her husband's expense infuriated the first lady, and she did not hesitate to let the chief of staff know exactly how she felt. There was only one star in this White House, and his name was Reagan, not Regan.

However, the chief of staff did not respond as Mrs. Reagan anticipated. After their exchange, Regan delegated the job of "handling" the first lady to one of his aides. When Nancy Reagan found out that he had cut her off from direct access, she exploded. Regan remembers their telephone conversation:

> "There should be somebody on the President's staff you can call on," I explained. "Dennis [Thomas] will be very good at the job."
>
> A silence gathered on the other end of the phone line. Finally, Mrs. Reagan said, "I don't think you need a deputy, Don. I think you can handle this yourself."
>
> "Well," I replied, "I thought that somebody should be attentive to your needs in the way that Mike was."
>
> "When I need something, I'll call you directly," the first lady said. "I don't see the need for an intermediary."[42]

After the storm had passed, Ed Rollins, deputy chief of staff for political and governmental affairs, jokingly told Regan that one of his "burdens" in life would now be "to take Mrs. Reagan's shit."

Regan responded in a fury, shouting, "I've never let any broad push me around before, and I'm not about to start now."[43]

By this point, a serious feud had developed between the first lady and the chief of staff. For over a year they barely spoke. When Mrs. Reagan did address Donald Regan, it was with great disdain and only to inform the chief of staff of changes to be made in the president's schedule.

What Regan found most frustrating was Mrs. Reagan's unwillingness to approach her husband directly. It seemed to Regan that she preferred to maneuver around him by pressuring his advisors. Regan considered the approach odd, thinking that Mrs. Reagan believed either that her husband could not be counted on to take decisive action or that the president would not take her views on policy and personnel seriously. Either way, he did not like being placed in the middle. The chief of staff thought that Mrs. Reagan was too deeply involved in the president's affairs, explaining, "If the First Lady was not always wrong in her recommendations, the correctness of her exercising what were clearly the prerogatives of the President was less obvious."[44]

Conflict between two such strong personalities was perhaps inevitable. An additional factor that probably exacerbated the problem was Michael Deaver's departure from the White House to start a consulting firm. Mrs. Reagan and Deaver shared a sense of what reflected well upon the president, and they had given each other invaluable advice throughout the first term. Taking care of Mrs. Reagan was a full-time job. As deputy chief of staff during the first term, Deaver often received as many as six to eight phone calls a day from the first lady. By handling her concerns, Deaver buffered Chief of Staff James Baker from Mrs. Reagan while providing her with direct access to the president's staff.

According to both Mrs. Reagan and Deaver, the only serious disagreement between them arose over the infamous Bitburg visit. The White House dispatched Deaver to Germany to do advance work for the May 1985 economic summit. He agreed to Chancellor Helmut Kohl's suggestion that President Reagan accompany Kohl to a cemetery in Bitburg to lay a wreath honoring the dead of both countries. Deaver thought that such a visit would make a good photo op for the president. In mid-April, German newspapers broke the news that the cemetery included the graves of forty-nine members of the Waffen SS, a branch of the Nazi guards who ran World War II concentration camps. They were the most notorious symbol of Hitler's regime. The outcry over an American president laying a wreath at a cemetery that contained the Nazis' remains was immediate and bitter. The White House had a public relations nightmare on its hands.[45]

Mrs. Reagan blamed Deaver for the debacle, which she was sure would tarnish the president's image. She demanded that the trip be canceled and railed that Deaver's poor advance work had ruined her husband's presidency. The first lady tried, to no avail, to convince the president not to go. Ronald Reagan said he would visit the cemetery because he had given his word to Chancellor Kohl. He told the first lady, "I simply do not think you are right, and I am not going to change my mind."[46] Knowing her husband would not be pushed any further, Mrs. Reagan backed off; but she did not stop worrying. In fact, she was so concerned that on the first part of the trip she was physically ill.[47] As a result of his mistake, Deaver found himself, for one of the few times in his tenure, on the opposite side of an issue from the first lady.[48]

Once Deaver left the administration, there was no one to screen the chief of staff from Mrs. Reagan's frequent calls. In fact, before leaving the White House, Deaver warned Regan that, as Regan put it, "the First Lady would place demands on me and my time that I could not foresee."[49] The new chief of staff thus could not have been totally unprepared for the first lady.

Mrs. Reagan thought that Donald Regan was building a staff that was loyal only to him, not the president. Regan's administrative style was not to bother President Reagan or pull him into the decision-making process unless it was necessary. He informed the president that the staff could handle various problems for him. Regan also felt free to sit in on cabinet meetings and at press encounters, where he sometimes joked that it was now permissible to mispronounce President "Reagan" as "Regan." When Frank Carlucci, a candidate to replace William Poindexter as national security advisor, visited the Oval Office, he asked only four questions during his interview. Donald Regan, rather than the president, answered all four.[50] Mrs. Reagan felt that the chief of staff's management style played to the president's worst trait: passivity. It also allowed Regan to consolidate even more power in his own office. She felt that Regan had forgotten that the president, not the chief of staff, was the star.

Mrs. Reagan found it particularly galling when Regan emerged as the president's alter ego. The president and chief of staff spent a great deal of time together, and gales of laughter could frequently be heard coming from the Oval Office as they traded ribald stories.[51] The first lady thought that Regan was taking advantage of her husband's good nature. As the president became more isolated, Mrs. Reagan was sure that the chief of staff was serving him poorly.

In the autumn of 1986, the cold war between Mrs. Reagan and the president's chief of staff turned white hot with the emergence of the Iran-Contra scandal over trading arms for hostages. His handling of the affair convinced the first lady that Regan had assembled a second-rate staff, and that he was more interested in making himself look good than in protecting her husband. She was particularly incensed when the chief of staff told the *New York Times,* "Some of us are like a shovel brigade that follow a parade down Main Street cleaning up."[52] Mrs. Reagan felt that his comments demonstrated Regan's lack of loyalty to the president and set a bad example for the rest of the White House staff.

Mrs. Reagan was especially angry that Regan had supported the policy of arms sales to Iran, which was at the heart of the Iran-Contra affair, but now seemed to want to shift the blame elsewhere. She also worried that impeachment was a real possibility. Her fear of a disastrous second term seemed to be coming true. In an administration in which the new policy suddenly seemed to be every man for himself, she felt that she was the only one who still placed the president's survival above everything else.[53]

Donald Regan has since expressed his opinion that he was made a scapegoat for the Iran-Contra affair and that Mrs. Reagan orchestrated a campaign to have him removed from his position.[54] While the first point was not strictly true (there were plenty of other scapegoats), the latter certainly was. By the early spring of 1987, the first lady was convinced that firing Donald Regan would work to the president's political advantage. At a time when the president needed to appear strong and in charge, the chief of staff's management style made Ronald Reagan look weak. Given the president's obvious dependence on Regan, firing the chief of staff would make Reagan look strong. Relieving Regan of his duties would appear as a decisive and painful necessity, the type of choice made by a chief executive determined to clean house.

Ironically, Mrs. Reagan was hindered in her attempts to remove Regan from the White House by the perception she had carefully fostered that she had no real influence. She could not openly confront the chief of staff; instead, she had to work behind the scenes. In fact, the first lady was still perpetuating the myth of her having no influence while she was orchestrating Donald Regan's departure. When the first lady met with reporters, she informed them that a decision about the chief of staff's future had nothing to do with her. Her claim that she was not involved in personnel decisions was never true, and it would be exposed as such over the next several months. That Mrs. Reagan could, at this late date, maintain the fiction that she had nothing to do with administrative decisions was a tribute to how successful she had been in creating the image of the supportive, but not political, wife. Her ability to keep up the facade suggests that even more than the president, she had held onto her training as an actor. Anne Edwards writes that Mrs. Reagan was "adept at playing two roles simultaneously—the-weaker-than-her-husband-and-must-be-protected-wife and the authoritative woman staunchly taking on the tough world of power politics."[55]

Ronald Reagan's good personal relationship with Donald Regan and his general reluctance to fire members of his staff made a direct appeal to the president impossible. Therefore, Mrs. Reagan decided that an indirect approach would be the most effective. Her first move was to bring in Michael Deaver to persuade the president that Donald Regan had to go. Early in December 1986, Deaver and Stuart Spencer paid a visit to the president to lay out the case against his chief of staff. The crucial part of their meeting went as follows:

> *Deaver:* Mr. President, I just want to tell you and Stu here agrees with me that you ought to consider firing Donald Regan.
> *Reagan:* (slamming his pen down in rare rage) Listen, I'm not going to sacrifice anybody's ass to save my ass.
> *Deaver:* It's not a question of anybody's ass. You were elected to serve the country—it's the country that you should worry about.[56]

The president was not convinced, and argued that Regan was getting a "bum rap" for his handling of the Iran-Contra affair.

Mrs. Reagan's next move was to bring in two administration outsiders whom President Reagan respected—Robert Strauss of the Democratic National Committee and former Secretary of State William Rogers. Mr. Rogers was not particularly helpful to the first lady's cause, telling the president that he should just ride out the affair. Mr. Strauss told President Reagan that the chief of staff could not help him politically with the Iran-Contra affair because he had no allies on Capitol Hill and no friends in the press. Again, Ronald Reagan refused, stating that Donald Regan had been loyal to him and that he would return his loyalty.[57]

The first lady continued to push for Donald Regan's ouster through more indirect methods. She even turned to the press for assistance. With the first lady's blessing, Joseph Canzeri, a former White House aide and friend of Michael Deaver's, began spreading the word that top members of the administration wanted the chief of staff to resign. At a Washington party, Canzeri dropped the hint to R. W. Apple, Jr., the chief Washington correspondent for the *New York Times*.[58] As a result, a story about the chief of staff's plight, with an accompanying picture of a downcast Donald Regan, appeared on the front page of the *New York Times* on 11 December 1986. The story spread to the *Washington Post* on 12 December, along with a recounting of Rogers and Strauss's visit to the White House.[59] Mrs. Reagan also used her connections to plant negative stories about the chief of staff with the California newspapers that the president liked to read.

Even as all this was going on, Mrs. Reagan needed occasionally to meet or talk on the phone with Donald Regan on topics such as upcoming trips, or would bump into Regan in the halls of the White House. The first lady would often feign surprise and greet the chief of staff by saying, "Hi, Don, are you still here?"[60] During one of their phone conversations, the first lady and Regan quarreled, and the conversation ended with Regan slamming down the receiver hard in her ear. The first lady was upset with the chief of staff's rudeness, but she realized that her husband had heard enough from her on the Regan issue. Again instead of approaching the president directly, she mentioned Regan's behavior to friends, who soon passed the information to the press.[61]

Both the first lady and the president were also disturbed by a rumor that the chief of staff's office had leaked an unflattering story about a quarrel between the couple. Reportedly, the first lady had reminded the president, "I was right about David Stockman. I was right about Bill Clark. Why won't you listen to me about Donald Regan?" and her husband had responded by telling the first lady to "get off my god damn back."[62] Although their argument was actually quite mild, both of the image-conscious Reagans were upset to read about it in the papers.

At a press conference soon after the leak, a reporter asked President Reagan whether the chief of staff should resign. Reagan's response—that it was Donald Regan's decision to make—fell far short of the endorsements he had previously given to his chief of staff. Afterward, the president called Regan into the Oval Office to discuss the situation and urged him to resign. Regan responded by shouting, "I thought I was chief of staff to the President, not to his wife."[63] Regan ultimately agreed to resign, effective 1 March 1987.

The final report of the Tower Commission's investigation into Iran-Contra was released on 27 February 1987. Although the commission was hard on the administration, the report only briefly mentioned the chief of staff. Regan suggested to the press that since he was cited in only fifteen lines of the report (representing a mere 2.5 percent of the total), then he would accept only 2.5 percent of the blame.[64] The chief of staff's logic was flawed. Although the Tower Report only briefly mentioned Regan, its criticism of him was severe, saying:

More than any other chief of staff in recent memory, he asserted personal control over the White House staff and sought to extend his control to the national security advisor. He was personally active in national security affairs and attended almost all of the relevant meetings regarding the Iran initiative. He as much as anyone, should have insisted that an orderly process be observed. In addition, he especially should have ensured that plans were made for handling any public disclosure of the initiative. He must bear primary responsibility for the chaos that descended upon the White House when such disclosure did occur.[65]

Mrs. Reagan ensured that Donald Regan's efforts to save face as he eased his way out the door would be frustrated. While he was busy discounting his involvement in the Iran-Contra affair, Mrs. Reagan had staff members spreading the rumor that Howard Baker, former U.S. senator from Tennessee, would become the new chief of staff. By mid-morning, reporters were calling the first lady for verification. She politely wished Regan well and welcomed Howard Baker aboard. The only problem was that Regan had not yet officially submitted his letter of resignation. When Regan returned to the White House after having a haircut, reporters asked him about the rumors that the East Wing had announced his resignation. Ignoring the questions, Regan paid an unplanned farewell call on the president and abruptly left the White House.[66]

In the temporary vacuum created by Donald Regan's exit, Mrs. Reagan served as the de facto chief of staff.[67] She supervised the search for Regan's replacement and organized the White House effort to react to the Tower Report. Because her distrust of the White House staff was so deep, Mrs. Reagan recruited Landon Parvin, a speechwriter from outside the administration, to write the president's official answer to the report. When the press asked the East Wing staff if the first lady planned to edit the response, they indicated that she and Landon Parvin would share responsibility. Mrs. Reagan was also thought to have vetoed a planned Reagan press conference to respond to the charges leveled in the Tower Report. When the president's aid to the Nicaraguan Contras was defeated, she helped broker a compromise aid package with Speaker of the House Jim Wright.[68]

Even before Regan's departure, Mrs. Reagan exerted influence over the administration's response to the Iran-Contra affair. She consulted a private attorney to help plan the administration's legal strategy. She also urged President Reagan to call upon the Senate Intelligence Committee to give Colonel Oliver North and Admiral Richard Poindexeter immunity, so their testimony could not be used against them in a trial.[69] A junior White House aide who questioned this idea was surprised to get a call from the first lady, informing him that the decision had been made in the East Wing, not the West Wing of the White House.[70]

Mrs. Reagan was especially worried about the upcoming State of the Union address and the president's need to appear strong and in command. She insisted that Kenneth Khachigian, one of President Reagan's most trusted speechwriters from California, be brought into the White House to write the speech. The first lady discussed the address with Khachigian, and the two agreed that the president had to demonstrate that despite newspaper reports to the contrary, he was strong, vigorous, and in charge. They decided that the best way for him to appear in control was to assert that he had no plans to abandon his bold foreign policy initiatives.[71]

Mrs. Reagan has never denied that she thought that Donald Regan was not serving the president well. She also admits recommending to the president that the chief of staff be replaced. She has stated, however, that she did not have the kind of power within the White House to have Regan removed. She has argued that firing Donald Regan was the president's decision to make, maintaining that if it had been up to her, Regan would have been gone much sooner. She claims to have only given the president the kind of supportive advice a husband should expect from his wife. In actuality, of course, the first lady did much more.

Donald Regan's removal touched off a mini-firestorm of controversy, with the *New York Times* publishing an essay by William Safire entitled "The First Lady Stages a Coup." In the essay, Safire referred to Mrs. Reagan as an "incipient Edith Wilson, unelected, and unaccountable, presuming to control the actions and the appointments of the executive branch." Safire went on to write: "On matters of patronage, she has been a powerhouse. Through her first friend, Mary Jane Wick, she controls jobs, trips, and honors at USIA and is arranging a post administration presence in Washington by replacing Roger Stevens with Charles Wick as the head of the Kennedy Center. She has been all too interested in the appointments of U.S. ambassadors, and suspected manipulation of these positions by Michael Deaver for his private benefit is presumably under grand jury review."[72]

The day after the Safire piece appeared, the *New York Times* published a related lead story by Bernard Weinraub. In "Nancy Reagan's Power Is Considered at Peak," Weinraub argued that Mrs. Reagan now exercised more power and was more involved in her husband's administration than at any time in the past.[73] The ABC news program *Nightline* even held a debate about the extent of the first lady's power.

Some members of Congress pointed out that the Regan affair, coming on the heels of the Iran-Contra scandal, served to further paint a picture of a president who was disengaged both from policy-making and from the personnel process of his own administration. William Richardson, a New Mexico Democrat, asked from the floor of the House of Representatives, "What is happening at the White House? Who is in charge? A constituent of mine asked, 'How can the President deal with the Soviets if he cannot settle a dispute between his wife and the chief of staff?' "[74] In her attempts to protect her husband's image, the first lady may have made the president appear even more distracted and less in control while simultaneously shattering the myth of her own noninvolvement.

Mrs. Reagan did have some supporters, many of whom pointed out that her detractors were the very people who had been calling the loudest for Regan's ouster. Joseph Hersch, writing in the *Christian Science Monitor,* argued that the "weight of Mrs. Reagan's influence when added to that of the leaders of the party and Congress, produced a quicker result than would otherwise have been the case. . . . Nancy Reagan speeded the inevitable change and helped the healing process begin. And why not?"[75] Anna Quindlen wrote in her *New York Times* column, "Certainly, if she told him [Ronald Reagan] that Donald T. Regan had to go, she would only have been reflecting an opinion held by many others. And if she felt that Mr. Regan's presence could harm the President, no one should be surprised that she did her best to hasten his departure." Quindlen went on to suggest that there was an element of male chauvinism in the criticism of Mrs. Reagan, that the first lady's critics were proposing that she should "stick to your knitting, lady.[76] Mrs. Reagan's long-time friend Nancy Reynolds suggested that Mrs. Reagan was being told to adhere to the traditional first lady's role: "If Mrs. Reagan has influence on her husband's decisions, it is because he values her opinions and political instincts. Why if we insist on scrutinizing first ladies' every action, must we insist that they give up their opinions as well as their privacy? Mrs. Reagan has earned her influence, and she has the right to her opinions even on issues once chauvinistically thought of as men's concerns."[77] Supporters pointed out that the first lady's role in Regan's dismissal was not a sudden grab for power or a sign of weakness on the president's part. Instead, the first lady was simply trying to protect her husband in a time of crisis, just as she had always done.

The Regan affair demonstrated the limits of Mrs. Reagan's influence over personnel decisions. She could not directly convince the president that Regan had to go, even though many Republican members of Congress were also calling for his removal. Ronald Reagan was loyal to those who served him and had a bit of a stubborn streak. The first lady organized the forces against Regan to lobby for his removal. She also brought in political outsiders whom President Reagan respected to help make her case. The first lady achieved her goal only after months of effort and some major missteps by Regan.[78] Of course, the first lady was also short on allies during this time. Michael Deaver and James Baker were both gone from the White House. She had to fight this battle alone.

During the Reagan White House years, the first lady played a major role in personnel decisions. She also strictly regulated the president's schedule. Those in the administration recognized that the first lady had continuously exerted a great deal of control over the president's time. It did not simply begin when President Reagan was recovering from major surgery. She determined the scheduling of major trips, such as the Bitburg trip (in 1985) and the Geneva and Reykjavik summits (in 1985 and 1986 respectively). Mrs. Reagan always believed that she knew her husband's needs better than anyone else. She thought the best way she could help him was by supervising his schedule.

The impact of Mrs. Reagan's acting background was particularly visible in President Reagan's second term. Although the first lady had long been involved in personnel decisions, the influence she wielded was not generally recognized outside of the White House until she crossed paths with Donald Regan. Mrs. Reagan saw the chief of staff as a supporting actor who was attempting to steal a scene from the star. Every show has only one star, and Mrs. Reagan was determined that it be her husband, not Donald Regan.

As Ronald Reagan's second term wound down, Mrs. Reagan was increasingly concerned about the president's legacy. She feared the success and popularity the president had enjoyed in his first term would be marred by events during the second four years. For the first lady, the Iran-Contra affair was a bad dream come true. Less than two and a half years away from the end of Ronald Reagan's second term, his legacy seemed threatened by an unwise policy decision. Given her background and experience, the first lady realized that one's exit was as important as one's entrance, and suddenly the president's graceful exit from office was threatened. Thus, Mrs. Reagan felt compelled to become even more aggressive in the president's defense. Unfortunately for the first lady, as her actions became more visible, the president came to seem even more passive and detached.

Mrs. Reagan's efforts to remove Donald Regan from his position as chief of staff differed from her previous involvement in personnel matters only in terms of visibility. She had long played a prominent role in surrounding the president with staff who would put his interests ahead of their own. Those staff members who attempted to push their own ideological interests or burnish their own image soon crossed swords with the first lady. Mrs. Reagan knew from experience that a successful play or movie depended on the lead actor's performance, not the bit players. The true responsibility of the rest of the cast was to make the star shine. A good casting director, she sought out those supporting actors who would put the well-being of the star before their own. That was all Mrs. Reagan demanded of the president's staff.

Nancy with her mother, Edith, January 1931.

Newlyweds Ronald and Nancy Reagan cut their wedding cake.

Happy times in the Reagan family—
Ronald Reagan, Ron, Jr., Nancy, and Patti.

Nancy Reagan with President Reagan
as he recuperates from the assassination attempt.

Nancy Reagan at the annual Gridiron Dinner, where she brought down the house with her performance of "Second Hand Rose."

Vice President and Mrs. Bush, and Mrs. Reagan and President Reagan at the 1984 Republican convention.

President Reagan and former Vice President Walter Mondale at the crucial second 1984 presidential debate.

Mrs. Reagan addresses the United Nations about the problem of drug abuse.

*President and Mrs. Reagan with Soviet President Mikhail Gorbachev
and his wife, Raisa, at the Washington Summit.*

Former President and Mrs. Reagan approaching the helicopter to leave Washington, D.C., after the inauguration of President George H. W. Bush.

CHAPTER 4

LIVING UNDER
THE LIGHTS

All modern first ladies lead their lives in the glare of the spotlight, and Mrs. Reagan was no exception. As the mass media have evolved, presidents and their wives have become national celebrities.[1] Every action they take and all that happens to them is fodder for the national news and radio talk shows. With the advent of cable news, they are now in the public eye twenty-four hours a day.

The rapid growth of broadcast media brought major changes in American life. In 1950, only 9 percent of Americans owned television sets. By the time the Reagans came to Washington, 98 percent of Americans had television, and 50 percent of homes were wired for cable. Over the same time period, the percentage of households receiving a daily newspaper dropped from 37 percent to 27 percent. By 1988, television was the major source of most news for 64 percent of the public; only 34 percent preferred newspapers. By a plurality of almost 20 percent, Americans considered broadcast news to be more reliable than newspapers (51 percent to 29 percent).[2]

Although the mere growth of broadcast news does not ensure its impact, its pervasiveness and speed increase its influence, allowing the news to reach so much of the public so quickly. Although the broadcast media often set the agenda for politics, however, they rarely follow the policy process to its conclusion. Presidents and, to a lesser extent, their families have become the stars of media coverage.

Everything a president does both professionally and privately has become newsworthy. The president's health, a vacation, even a pet can be a major story.[3]

As a result, the relationship between the media and politics changed dramatically. The public and private lives of public figures have become increasingly blurred, and the press has expanded its coverage to all aspects of the first family. Medical problems and familial relations—topics that would have been off limits just decades ago—are now front-page stories. At the same time public figures, including first ladies, have become more adept at using the media to mold and shape their image. President's wives now have their own press secretaries to handle the overwhelming demand for interviews and to help present the first lady in the best possible light.

Compared with their predecessors, President and Mrs. Reagan seemed well equipped to deal with the heightened attention. The Reagans were not only political celebrities, they had also been Hollywood celebrities. However, they were actors from a Hollywood of a different era. When the Reagans walked the motion picture lots, actors' lives were controlled—and protected—by the movie studios. During the 1930s and 1940s, actors were a studio's exclusive property. Each studio had a vested interest in promoting a particular image for their actors and shielding them from a prying press. Mrs. Reagan's studio, MGM, was particularly adept at guiding and protecting its stars. MGM told its actors how to dress and whom to date. When their players were threatened with scandal, the studio even interfered in police cases. It carefully guarded the secret backgrounds of stars such as Joan Crawford and Clark Gable.[4] As Hollywood actors, President and Mrs. Reagan were skilled in the art of shaping and presenting a particular image, but they had very little experience dealing with the media.

After leaving Hollywood, Mrs. Reagan disappeared from public view. As the mother of small children, busy running a household, she attracted only occasional attention. While Ronald Reagan remained in the spotlight by traveling the country making speeches for General Electric and eventually becoming the host of TV's *Death Valley Days,* Mrs. Reagan remained in the shadows.

When her husband became governor of California, Mrs. Reagan reemerged as a public figure. She seems to remember most the negative press she experienced as first lady of California.[5] In fact, however, during their California years, the press rarely intruded into their private lives.

Thus, when the Reagans came to the White House, there was little in their acting careers or their prior political experience to prepare them for the intrusiveness of the Washington press corps. Once Ronald Reagan became president, everything about their lives was fair game: the medical procedures they underwent, their relations with their children, their personal beliefs, and their interactions with other political leaders. Mrs. Reagan explains how the invasiveness of the press was one of the most surprising aspects of her new position: "The experience of having not only your public appearances but your private life scrutinized and examined by the entire country, by the entire *world,* is almost too intense to describe. Although I lived with it for eight years, I still have trouble believing it."[6]

As described earlier, Mrs. Reagan ran afoul of the press early in her tenure as first lady. She was often portrayed as caring only about fancy clothes, shopping with her California friends, and redecorating the White House. Although she was eventually able to use skills honed by her acting career to gradually improve her image, there were times when her reputation as a dilettante came back to haunt her.

As a result, some members of the national press were not inclined to take her seriously. Such a situation arose during the 1985 Geneva summit, when they were prompted to make comparisons between Mrs. Reagan and Raisa Gorbachev. Mrs. Gorbachev came to the summit prepared to talk about serious issues, while Mrs. Reagan was prepared to talk about families and lifestyles, leaving the serious issues to the husbands. In her book *My Turn,* Mrs. Reagan discusses in great detail the differences between the two first ladies.

From the moment we met, she talked and talked and talked—so much so that I could barely get a word in edgewise or otherwise. Perhaps it was insecurity on her part, but during the dozen encounters in three different countries, my fundamental impression of Raisa Gorbachev was that she never stopped talking, or lecturing to be more accurate. Sometimes the subject was the Soviet Union and the glories of the Communist system. Sometimes it was Soviet art. More often than not, it was Marxism and Leninism.

Once or twice, she even lectured me on the failings of the American political system. I wasn't prepared for this, and I didn't like it. I had assumed we would talk about personal matters: our husbands, our children, being in the limelight or perhaps our hopes for the future.[7]

Mrs. Gorbachev would undoubtedly put her own spin on their encounters, but she would surely agree with Mrs. Reagan about their differences. The contrasts between the two first ladies were emphasized by the press in their coverage of the summit. Those interested in style noted the distinctions in dress between Mrs. Reagan and Mrs. Gorbachev, and declared Mrs. Reagan the clear winner. Other commentators, however, noted that while Mrs. Gorbachev might have lost the fashion competition, she was plainly more comfortable in dealing with matters of substance. In comparison, the first lady seemed shallow. According to Mrs. Reagan, the constant press coverage made it difficult to develop a relationship with Mrs. Gorbachev. Mrs. Reagan noted, "If Raisa and I had been left alone, without any press, we would have had an easier time of it. But even before our first meeting in Geneva, there had been so much talk about the two of us that we were enormously self-conscious."[8]

Mrs. Reagan's personal life also came under close scrutiny by the press. The first lady faced a traumatic experience in August 1982 with the passing of Loyal Davis. Mrs. Reagan was only the second woman in the twentieth century to have her father see her assume the position of the first lady of the United States (the first being Nellie Taft).[9] Since Christmas 1981 she had known her stepfather was dying, and in January 1982 she went to Arizona to celebrate his eighty-sixth birthday. After returning to Washington, she called Dr. Davis and her mother individually almost every day.

On 9 August, when it became clear that her stepfather had only a few days to live, Mrs. Reagan flew to her parents' home in Phoenix. She spent the next ten days in a hospital suite adjoining his so that she could be with him, holding his hand as he died. Mrs. Reagan was devastated, but she had an additional task to do. After her emotionally wrenching experience at the hospital, Mrs. Reagan rushed to tell her mother the bad news before Edith heard it on television or the radio.[10]

When her beloved "Bopa" died, Mrs. Reagan lost perhaps the most significant role model of her youth—a man who was crucial in the formation of her character. Dr. Davis taught her discipline, respect for authority, and his basic principles of life. One of his rules was that food should be thoroughly chewed before swallowed in order to aid in digestion. To this day, Mrs. Reagan chews each bite of food thirty-two times.[11] In her memoirs, Mrs. Reagan remembers her stepfather: "Loyal Davis was a man of great integrity who exemplified old fashioned values: That girls and boys should grow up to be ladies and gentlemen. That children should respect and obey their parents, that no matter what you did, you should never cheapen yourself, and that no matter what you worked at—whether it was a complicated medical procedure, or a relatively simple act like sweeping the floor—you should do it as well as you could."[12]

Loyal Davis provided young Nancy with more than a set of values. He gave her back her mother, who after marrying Dr. Davis quit the stage and moved to Chicago, where the three could be a real family. He also provided access to a prestigious world that Nancy could only have dreamed of when she lived with the Galbraiths. For all of these reasons, Mrs. Reagan was deeply loyal to her stepfather. In her book *Nancy*, Mrs. Reagan called Dr. Davis her father; whenever she was asked by reporters about her adoption she always insisted that he, not Kenneth Robbins, was her father. Lou Cannon recounts an episode when a reporter noted that *Who's Who in America* said she was adopted. Mrs. Reagan replied that she didn't care what a book said, Dr. Davis was her father.[13]

Dr. Davis's death led to a heated disagreement between Mrs. Reagan and her stepbrother, Richard. Dick Davis, also a physician, felt that Mrs. Reagan had made medical decisions regarding their father's treatment that he was better equipped to handle. The night before the memorial service they argued over the burial and Mrs. Reagan's management of the estate. Her stepbrother was so angry, he took a plane back to the East Coast and missed his father's service.[14]

The president, who also thought highly of his father-in-law, was deeply affected by his passing. In fact, many felt that Dr. Davis played an important role in Reagan's conversion from liberal Democrat to conservative Republican. Throughout his political career, Ronald Reagan denied Dr. Davis's influence, saying "he was most tactful—we didn't talk politics."[15] Michael Deaver agrees that the president and Dr. Davis rarely discussed politics, saying that they were more likely to discuss medicine. According to Deaver, even years later, someone could mention a disease and Ronald Reagan would be able to recall what Dr. Davis had said about its progression.[16]

When President Reagan underwent major surgery, first for colon cancer and later for a basal-cell cancer on his nose, the first lady had to manage her fears while overseeing the president's recovery, coordinating his schedule, stage-managing his image, and keeping her own commitments. She also had to deal with a prying press. Mrs. Reagan often saw details of her husband's operations and prognosis for recovery spread across the front page of newspapers or as lead stories on the nightly news. Worse, some of the "news" was far from reassuring. One physician discussing the president's colon cancer operation gave him only four months to live. As the commentaries on her husband's health became increasingly explicit, Mrs. Reagan's frustration grew. She writes in her memoirs:

> For me the biggest shock of all was that even the most intimate details of our medical treatment became a matter of public discussion. I agree that the public has the right to know in some detail about the president's health, especially after several previous presidents have concealed important information. But when the right to know clashes with the president's right to privacy and dignity, the situation calls for discretion—and some limits. As far as I am concerned, those limits are violated when the news media show diagrams of the president's insides, or finds it necessary to inform the country how much he urinated during his first day in the hospital.[17]

Another area of public controversy for President and Mrs. Reagan was their relationship with their children. Although the Reagans liked to project the image of a traditional 1950s couple, in many ways they were thoroughly modern. As Michael Deaver, who knew both the president and the first lady very well, describes them:

> I always find it strange that the Reagans came to be regarded as such a traditional couple, a throwback to another era. Ronald Reagan was America's first divorced president, a dad who, like

lots of divorced dads, had plenty of problems with the kids from his failed marriage. One of the most spiritual people I ever met, he attended church periodically at best. Unlike most politicians, though, he didn't worry what people would think about that. Nancy herself was a product of a broken home until her mother remarried. As a mother herself, Nancy never claimed to be perfect—and the Reagans were collectively anything but the perfect family, but it wasn't for lack of trying.[18]

Even before President Reagan's 1980 election, there was considerable strain within the family. From the beginning, Mrs. Reagan had trouble developing a close relationship with her two stepchildren, Maureen and Michael. Both children felt their loyalties divided between their stepmother and their birth mother, Jane Wyman. Once Ronald and Nancy Reagan were married, Maureen and Michael often felt unsure of their place in the family.[19]

Difficulties between a stepmother and her stepchildren are not all that unusual, but they are also not generally subject to public scrutiny—unless, of course, your husband is president of the United States. The national press criticized both the president and Mrs. Reagan for not being closer to their children or seeing their grandchildren (Michael Reagan's children) on a regular basis. Throughout the White House years, there were extended periods of tension between Michael and his stepmother and father. As a result, the president and first lady rarely saw their grandchildren. In 1984, the press revealed that the Reagans had never seen their youngest grandchild at all.[20] When asked about the relationship at a press conference, Mrs. Reagan replied, "No, there is an estrangement right now. We are sorry about it and we hope that it can be resolved, but we don't believe in discussing family matters in public."[21] His stepmother's response surprised Michael, who was well aware that he had not seen his father and stepmother in a year, but hadn't realized they were "estranged."[22] The first lady had been badgered by reporters shouting out numerous questions about their relationship, and had blurted out the first response that came to mind.

An accusation by a member of the Secret Service detail assigned to guard Michael and his family also contributed to the problems between Michael and his parents. An agent claimed he witnessed

Michael stealing several small items from local drugstores. The accusation was reported to the president and first lady, along with a recommendation that Michael receive psychiatric treatment for kleptomania.[23] When confronted by his parents, Michael denied the charges and demanded to see a list of items he was accused of stealing. His parents stonewalled, insisting that he seek treatment. When Michael asked his father why he took the word of the Secret Service over that of his son, Ronald Reagan replied, "Because the Secret Service saved my life, and I trust them more than you because your past history leaves a lot to be desired."[24] President Reagan's response was understandable, given the attempt on his life in 1981. However, the president's retort devastated his son. It was not until Michael was able to clear his name (which he was able to do once he knew the specific charges) that the tensions diminished.[25]

The stresses and strains of two presidential campaigns also contributed to the estrangement. In his autobiography, Michael Reagan recounts how hard he and Maureen worked in his father's presidential campaigns, and how little recognition they received for their efforts. In 1976, Michael campaigned for his father mostly in California, but in 1980 he quit his job and campaigned across the country.[26] He made more than twenty campaign trips to Iowa alone during the Republican primaries. Yet because he and Maureen were visible reminders of the candidate's divorce and remarriage, overeager staff members consistently relegated them to the background during public events.[27] Up to that time, no divorced candidate had ever won the U.S. presidency.

Another cause for the rift in the family were Michael's feelings of inadequacy and subsequent identity problems resulting from a camp counselor's sexually molesting him when he was young. At the time, Michael was unable to tell either his father or his stepmother about the molestation and as a result felt guilty not only about the event, but also about having kept it hidden for so many years.[28]

Mrs. Reagan's relationship with her stepdaughter, Maureen, avoided many of the pitfalls that might have been created by the Reagans' marriage. While Maureen remained loyal to her mother (who was clearly not one of her stepmother's favorite people), she and her stepmother enjoyed each other's company from the very beginning.[29] Mrs. Reagan fondly remembers Maureen when she was only ten years old, coming to visit her in her apartment. Maureen often brought her Victrola, and they spent afternoons listening to her records.[30]

Years later, however, Maureen's decision to run for the Republican nomination for a U.S. Senate seat from California tested their relationship. As a Republican president, Ronald Reagan felt that he should not endorse any Republican in the primary, even his own daughter. Maureen was aware of her father's position, and did not expect his political support: "Since his first run for governor in 1966, Dad has judiciously avoided giving primary endorsements, choosing instead to help unify the party for the general election ahead. . . . Any support he might give his daughter's candidacy would be a slap in the face to all of the others who had hoped for his support in the past."[31]

The press had a field day with the president's refusal to endorse Maureen. While she was deciding whether or not to run in the primary, reporters asked President Reagan his opinion on whether she would launch a campaign. His response—"I hope not"—was widely reported, but also misinterpreted. What the president meant was that he wasn't sure that Maureen was ready for a life of politics. However, many in the press construed his response as a lack of faith in his daughter.[32] The president realized his mistake immediately and called Maureen to explain that what he meant was that the rigors of a statewide California campaign were not something that he would wish on his daughter. By discussing his remarks directly with his daughter, the president was able to smooth over any ruffled feelings.

Later, when Mrs. Reagan was facing cancer surgery and the death of her mother, she and Maureen became closer. By the time the first lady published her memoirs, she referred to Maureen not just as her stepdaughter, but also her friend.[33]

Aside from some of the usual tensions between parents and sons, the Reagans' relationship with Ron, Jr., remained fairly close. Both the president and the first lady were supportive of (although surprised by) Ron's decision to join the Joffrey Ballet and to perform with the Joffrey II dancers. Because of their busy schedules, it was difficult for the president and Mrs. Reagan to attend Ron's performances. However, they read the reviews of his performances with pride. Mrs. Reagan responded to a favorable review that was mailed to her by writing, "Thanks so much for sending the review of Ron's performance. Being a typical mother, I was very pleased as you can imagine."[34]

When Ron, Jr., performed at the Metropolitan Opera House in New York City on 16 March 1981, the Reagans were in attendance. Ron danced in four of the five ballets scheduled and earned positive reviews for his performance.[35] His parents also attended a performance of the Joffrey II dancers at George Washington University's Lisner Auditorium. In fact, the White House reserved 300 seats for the performance. Afterward Mrs. Reagan hugged her son, saying, "I never knew you could do that."[36] President Reagan also seemed quite pleased, remarking that his favorite was "Threads from a String of Swing," which had been performed to Glenn Miller music.[37]

Even so, Mrs. Reagan was happy when Ron left the Joffrey and became a freelance journalist. She always thought that he had exceptional writing talent and was thankful that he would be able to put it to use. When Ron, Jr., married his wife, Doria Palmieri, however, his parents were not at the ceremony. The first lady explained that it was the suddenness of Ron and Doria's decision to marry, not a family quarrel, that kept President and Mrs. Reagan from attending.[38]

The Reagans' relationship with their daughter, Patti Davis, was much more troublesome and more widely reported. Patti changed her name from Reagan to distance herself from her father's political views and career. Mrs. Reagan notes that she and Patti had a difficult relationship from the start. Patti was a headstrong child, and Mrs. Reagan was an inexperienced first-time mother who tried to control her children's lives.[39]

When Patti published a thinly veiled autobiographical novel entitled *Homefront* (1986), the most difficult period in her relationship with her parents began. Her main characters were an ambitious television star and his superficial wife, who sacrificed their family for political success.[40] The novel became an immediate topic of newspaper stories, and the president and first lady were repeatedly asked to comment on their daughter and her book. The Reagans claimed not to be bothered by the novel, saying publicly that after all, it was fiction. In reality, they were hurt by Patti's portrayal of them. Their response to her was silence. Neither parent contacted Patti—which may have ruined her intent in writing the book, but also validated her portrait of a dysfunctional family. In her memoirs, Mrs. Reagan described how deeply wounded she was by her daughter's portrayal of her family. She also recalls how hard it was to attempt to reconcile their differences while in the White House and squarely in the public eye.

The conflict between the first lady and Patti was exacerbated by Patti's second book, *The Way I See It*, published in 1992. In this memoir, Patti portrays Ronald Reagan as a genial but detached father, who did not really want to know the inner workings of his family. She was not nearly as charitable toward her mother. She accused Mrs. Reagan of spending most of Patti's childhood being strung out on drugs (tranquilizers and sleeping pills) and hitting her on an almost daily basis—including once across the face with a hair brush. One incident Patti related demonstrated both her mother's compulsive neatness and her lack of compassion. One day, Mrs. Reagan refused to let their hot and exhausted gardener into their house for a drink of water. She was afraid he would track mud on their floors. The gardener had to stagger next door for water, where he collapsed, not from thirst, but from a heart attack.[41] The only participants in most of the stories Patti relates are her mother and herself, so most of them cannot be verified. The picture that Patti Davis paints in *The Way I See It* is nonetheless disturbing, as it portrays a relationship between mother and daughter that seems almost beyond repair.

Contributing to the intense press scrutiny of the Reagans' familial relationships was a perceived hypocrisy in the values the president and the first lady espoused and the life that they led. Ronald Reagan's presidential campaigns made the notion of a return to "traditional family values" a centerpiece of both the 1980 and the 1984 elections. When candidate Reagan gave his acceptance speech at the 1980 Republican convention, he stood under a banner reading "Family, Neighborhood, Work, Peace, Freedom" and spoke of "Democrats, Independents, and Republicans from all economic conditions, walks of life bound together in the community of *shared values of family*, work, neighborhood, peace, and freedom" (emphasis added). He went on to encourage Americans "not simply to 'trust me' *but to trust your values—our values*—and to hold me responsible for living up to them" (emphasis added).[42]

The press questioned whether the Reagans lived up to those values. To some columnists the answer was a resounding no. Judith Mann, writing in the *Washington Post,* referred to the hypocrisy of the profamily administration as "breathtaking."[43] United Press International White House reporter Helen Thomas noted that the "Reagans see less of their children than any other first family that has lived in the White House in twenty years."[44]

While the Reagans' difficulties with their children were widely reported by the press, neither the president nor the first lady suffered politically. Families across the United States constantly dealt with a variety of issues, and more than a few parents were estranged from their children. Whatever their problems, none of the Reagan children were addicted to drugs or alcohol or involved in serious crime. To many, the Reagan family situations probably seemed minor. Mrs. Reagan's improved public image, resulting from her hard and very visible work on the drug issue, undoubtedly also helped her overcome the negative publicity associated with her family situation.

Mrs. Reagan has identified 1987 as her most difficult year in the White House, saying that it was "terrible, terrible" and that "next year has to be better."[45] In addition to the many political problems of the second term, Mrs. Reagan had to deal with some very troubling personal problems. One concern was for her husband's health. In January 1987 the president underwent yet another serious operation, this time on his prostate. In March 1985, he had had surgery for colon cancer, and in July of that same year he had his skin cancer surgery. Because of the intense press scrutiny of the president's previous medical problems, steps were taken to keep the 1987 surgery secret. The biopsy was submitted to a lab under a White House secretary's name, and the first lady insisted that the precise nature of the president's problem be kept from the press (over the objections of President Reagan's press secretary, Larry Speakes). The media, however, eventually found out. The result was a confrontational press briefing, during which reporters demanded to know why they had been misled and Speakes had to defend a policy he didn't support. At one point, when a member of the press asked who he was fronting for, the press secretary replied that if they "had two grains of salt for sense, they could figure it out."[46]

During her husband's recovery, Mrs. Reagan once again tangled with Donald Regan. The first lady thought that because of the president's relatively advanced age and previous cancer surgery, he should not attempt to deliver a State of the Union Address. The chief of staff, however, felt that in the face of the Iran-Contra affair, President Reagan needed to resume his official duties as quickly as possible. Although Regan won that particular point, he would soon lose the larger war. Because of the president's Iran-Contra problems (which called into question his strength and virility) and her experiences with her husband's previous hospitalization, Mrs. Reagan soon declared a complete embargo of detailed discussion of the president's condition.[47]

In October 1987 Mrs. Reagan faced her own medical crisis when a routine mammogram found a malignant tumor in her left breast. After her doctors apprised her of her options, Mrs. Reagan decided to undergo a modified radical mastectomy. The surgeons would remove the breast, but not the surrounding muscle and tissue, during a fifty-minute operation. To avoid the kind of publicity that accompanied the president's colon surgery and to allow her to complete her scheduled activities, the White House did not announce the first lady's hospitalization until the very day of the procedure.[48]

The night before the operation, Mrs. Reagan was just as adamant about her choice of treatment. When her surgeon questioned whether she was still confident of her decision, she replied with a bit of her husband's bravado, "Look, please don't wake me to have a conversation about it. Just do it. It shouldn't take you long, because there isn't much there to take off. Dolly Parton, I'm not."[49]

Maureen Reagan was sure that the media would debate the first lady's decision. She warned her father the night before Mrs. Reagan went into the hospital, "If you hated the graphic displays on the colon cancer or prostate surgery, then wait until you see what they do with breast surgery."[50] Unfortunately, Maureen was correct. Mrs. Reagan's decision was soon subject to public debate.

The airways were full of "experts" arguing that Mrs. Reagan should have had a lumpectomy combined with either radiation treatments or chemotherapy, which would have allowed her to keep her breast. Some critics even suggested that by choosing a mastectomy, Mrs. Reagan might have scared away other women from seeking treatment.[51] The director of the Breast Cancer Advisory Center was quoted as saying that the first lady had set the treatment of breast cancer back ten years.[52]

Mrs. Reagan deeply resented this criticism, arguing that the choice of treatment for breast cancer is a decision each woman must make for herself. The first lady, aware of her tendency to worry compulsively, felt that she made the choice that would give her the most peace of mind. She was not recommending that every woman make the same decision. She also argued that either radiation treatments or chemotherapy would have left her too weak to carry out her responsibilities as first lady.[53] Mrs. Reagan's doctors were also criticized for not prescribing chemoprevention, a newly developed procedure in which a once-a-day estrogen blocking pill is administered to prevent the reoccurrence of cancer.[54] Critics argued that had her physicians recommended such a course of action, it would have raised women's awareness and saved thousands of lives.[55]

Although Mrs. Reagan's position that treatment is a matter of individual choice is certainly correct, for first ladies it seems not to apply. The debate over her treatment for breast cancer (much like President Reagan's treatment for his colon and skin cancer) is another example of the degree to which the first family had become a focal point of the American press and public. If you live in the White House, there is no longer any such thing as a private decision about health care.

Mrs. Reagan felt that the detailed media coverage of her cancer surgery was just as intrusive as the coverage of the president's colon surgery. In *My Turn,* she writes, "I didn't like it any better, by the way, when diagrams of my 1987 breast surgery were shown on television. Was that really necessary?"[56] In her view, the media had gone too far in their invasion of personal privacy, all the while justifying the intrusion in terms of the public's right to know.

Just four days after Mrs. Reagan's own surgery, her mother died of a stroke. Although Edith had been ill for some time, her death was still difficult for the first lady. With the exception of the president, there was no one to whom she was closer or who had been more supportive of her needs. While Loyal Davis taught his stepdaughter the virtue of hard work, Edith Davis made her life fun. As a former actress, Edith always had a wealth of stories to tell (some of them slightly off color), and she loved people and entertaining. Her connection to the theater world had brought scores of interesting people into Nancy Reagan's life. President Reagan shared his wife's love for her mother. In the eulogy the president delivered, he said that "meeting her was like opening a bottle of champagne" and that she "gave wit and charm and kindliness throughout her life."[57] Her mother's death forced Mrs. Reagan to deal with both her own recovery from surgery and her grief, all while in the public spotlight. Making matters worse, Patti did not attend her grandmother's funeral; instead, she phoned Elaine Crispen, Mrs. Reagan's former personal assistant and press secretary, and asked her to tell her mother that she was out of the country.[58]

The following year, 1988, also proved to be difficult for Mrs. Reagan. The president continued to be dogged by accusations about Iran-contra. Questions about the scandal even came up in Mrs. Reagan's meeting with the press about her drug-abuse programs. Worse, Donald Regan's memoirs, which painted an unflattering portrait of the first lady, were published in May 1988. Regan's most devastating revelation was that Mrs. Reagan had fallen under the influence of a West Coast astrologer named Joan Quigley. The former chief of staff revealed that Mrs. Reagan frequently used the astrologer in planning the president's activities. He portrayed Mrs. Reagan as depending on Quigley to provide detailed advice for arranging President Reagan's time—so much so that the president's schedule was often thrown into chaos. Regan describes in some detail the difficulty the White House staff had in trying to arrange the president's speaking schedule around the optimal astrological dates provided by Mrs. Reagan's astrologer.[59]

Regan wrote that Joan Quigley's advice was not used only in planning minor public activities or appearances. He claimed that a number of major presidential events hinged on Mrs. Reagan's astrological readings. According to Regan, the first lady's astrologer even influenced the scheduling of the Reagan-Gorbachev Washington summit. After preparing the astrological charts for both men, the astrologer determined that 2:00 p.m. on 8 December 1987 was the most advantageous time for them to sign the intermediate-range nuclear force (INF) treaty.[60] According to Regan, other events

planned around Joan Quigley's advice included the Reykjavik summit, the Bitburg trip, and the president's 1985 polyp operation.[61]
Quigley herself contends that her influence extended even further
than Donald Regan realized. She claims that the president was not
only aware of her advice, but actively sought it out before making
major decisions. According to the astrologer, the president would
ask his wife, "What does Joan say?" when he wanted guidance on the
space shuttle *Challenger* investigation or Irangate.[62]

According to Joan Quigley, ever since she met Mrs. Reagan on the
Merv Griffin television show during the 1970s, she had provided her
with periodic consultations. Reportedly, she had even contributed
free astrological advice to the Reagan presidential campaigns in 1976
and 1980.[63] After Ronald Reagan won the presidency in 1980, Joan
Quigley's influence increased even more—she became a paid con-
sultant to the first lady.

Given the extraordinary scrutiny of first ladies generally and of
Mrs. Reagan in particular, it's remarkable that the first lady's reliance on astrology remained secret for as long as it did. The press and
the public didn't learn of Mrs. Reagan's astrological interests until
late in the final year of the Reagan presidency. Donald Regan's memoirs made one of the East Wing's most closely guarded secrets
public. The first lady's use of an astrologer to plan the president's
schedule became the hottest political topic of the summer of 1988.
The media seized on the issue, and for several weeks Washington
and the press talked of little else. National newspapers suggested
that the entire White House had fallen under the control of a West
Coast astrologer. Rumors abounded that Joan Quigley was helping
the president develop and implement public policy.

The astrology flap caused tension between the first lady and some
of the president's most ardent supporters—the Christian Right. Television evangelist James Kennedy stated in one of his sermons, "A belief in astrology and a belief in Scriptures are antithetical."[64] Los Angeles broadcasting executive George Otis traveled to the White House
carrying suitcases packed with 25,000 petitions signed by conservative Christians, calling on the president to "just say no" to astrology.[65]

Mrs. Reagan seemed stunned by the uproar in the press. Given that
millions of Americans believe in astrology and that most newspapers
carry a daily horoscope, it seemed ludicrous to her that her use of an

astrologer could become such a huge story. Part of the reason for the uproar may have been that in her disdain for the press, the first lady decided not to speak publicly on the issue. She hoped that the story would blow over in a day or two. Ironically, the longer Mrs. Reagan kept quiet, the more validity there seemed to be to the story. After all, if the story weren't true, why wouldn't she speak out?

In her memoir, Mrs. Reagan attempts to clarify her stance on astrology. She claims that although she met Joan Quigley as far back as the 1980 presidential campaign, it was not until after President Reagan was shot in 1981 that Mrs. Reagan began to rely on her advice. Joan Quigley demonstrated to Mrs. Reagan that her astrological charts predicted that the period around 30 March 1981 would be an extremely dangerous time for President Reagan. Emotionally shaken by the attempt on the president's life, Mrs. Reagan began depending on Quigley's readings to ensure that no further harm would come to her husband. Mrs. Reagan writes:

> After March 30, 1981, I wasn't about to take any chances. Very few people can really understand what it is like to have your husband shot at and almost die, and then have him exposed all the time to enormous crowds, tens of thousands of people, any one of who might be a lunatic with a gun. I have been criticized and ridiculed for turning to astrology, but after a while I reached a point where I didn't care. I was doing everything I could think of to protect my husband and keep him alive.[66]

Mrs. Reagan adamantly argued that at no point during the Reagan administration were political or policy decisions influenced by astrology, and that only the president's schedule was affected, writing: "I want to state one thing again and unequivocally: Joan's recommendations had nothing to do with policy or politics—ever. Her advice was confined to timing—to Ronnie's schedule, and to what days were good or bad, especially with regard to his out-of-town trips."[67]

In hindsight, Mrs. Reagan may be correct in feeling that the story was overplayed. However, the first lady has never been completely forthcoming about her interest in astrology. While Mrs. Reagan's reliance on Joan Quigley may have greatly increased after the attempt on the president's life, she actually sought the astrologer's advice much earlier than she admits.

Mrs. Reagan's confidants have noted that she has been interested in astrological readings since at least 1967, when she was the first lady of California. At first, Mrs. Reagan relied on noted astrologer Jean Dixon; she later turned to Joan Quigley. Even as far back as his acting days, Ronald Reagan was known to have had his astrological charts done regularly. There is, however, little to suggest that he took astrology as seriously as his wife. As former actors, it was not unusual for the Reagans to have superstitions and astrological beliefs. Hollywood supports a number of well-paid astrologers. President Reagan often referred to the psychic abilities of one of his former teachers, as well as those of his mother, Nellie. He also discussed in interviews his and Nancy's friendship with astrologer Carol Richter.[68]

President and Mrs. Reagan were always superstitious, observing the usual harmless rituals of knocking on wood and walking around, but never under, ladders. Actors are traditionally a rather superstitious group. Some commonly held superstitions of the theater world are that it brings bad luck to have three lit candles on stage or in a dressing room, to receive flowers before a performance, for an actor to wear blue, to be knitting on stage, or to whistle anywhere in a theater.[69]

The first lady also subscribed to other superstitions. When her hairdresser handed Mrs. Reagan a letter opener, she told the hairdresser that it was bad luck for a knife to pass directly from one person's hand to another. If the first lady inadvertently put an article of clothing on inside out, she was reluctant to take it off because of the bad luck that was supposed to result. Mrs. Reagan also thought it bad luck for shoes to be stored above eye level, and even wore her trademark red because she thought it was a lucky color.[70] Mrs. Reagan's mother is a likely source for some of these superstitious beliefs. Edith was of course a stage actress and introduced her daughter to the theater at a very young age. It is possible, therefore, that the first lady was exposed to many of these superstitions as a child.

Once in Hollywood, she found belief in superstition and astrology to be quite common. Many of Nancy Reagan's contemporaries had career-guiding relationships with astrologers. Ronald Colman, Tyrone Power, Susan Hayward, Robert Cummings, and even Grace Kelly were devotees of astrology.[71] Many of them were clients of Carol Richter, the same astrologer the Reagans visited.

President and Mrs. Reagan very likely brought a belief in astrology with them from Hollywood; they didn't come to it after they had arrived in Washington.

Like first ladies Mary Lincoln and Edith Wilson, Nancy Reagan was also interested in the metaphysical. At first she was skeptical of her husband's belief that Abraham Lincoln haunted the White House. But after she noticed that a picture in Lincoln's bedroom kept slanting after she straightened it, she began to believe that her husband might be right.

During her husband's two terms in office, Nancy Reagan displayed a great deal of fortitude in coping with the many challenges she faced. Her background as an actor may have helped her put forward the best possible image as she dealt with her husband's and her own medical problems, the rifts within her family, and the death of her mother and father; but it could not have given her the strength she needed.

The genesis of her strength can more likely be found in her background and upbringing. One need only recall the determined fourteen-year-old setting out to New York by herself to convince her birth father to sign adoption papers to realize that Mrs. Reagan's grittiness was not a recent development. Separated from her parents by their divorce and her mother's return to the stage, young Nancy learned to rely on herself at a very early age. In addition, the most significant role model of her youth, the towering figure of Dr. Davis, preached self-reliance and self-discipline to Nancy and anyone else who would listen. His stepdaughter clearly took his lessons to heart.

In light of those early experiences, Mrs. Reagan's inner strength is not surprising. What is remarkable is how often she seemed to be caught off guard by the press's intrusion into her private life. One might expect a Hollywood actress to be more familiar with and more adept at handling the media. But Mrs. Reagan came from an earlier generation of contract players whose studios sheltered them from a prying press. Although in many ways the first lady's experience as a Hollywood actor was helpful, in at least this one area it left her ill prepared for her role as the president's wife.

CHAPTER 5

NANCY REAGAN, SCREENWRITER

Nancy Reagan's role in her husband's administration remains a matter of heated debate. Was she simply a "china doll" who emphasized only ceremonial events and vague programs such as "Just Say No"? Or was she, in Howard Baker's phrase, a "dragon lady" who wielded considerable behind-the-scenes influence? The reality is more complicated than these two characterizations would suggest. In some areas Mrs. Reagan had a significant impact. In others, she deferred to her husband's political agenda. Nonetheless, Nancy Reagan was more of an activist first lady than many realized during the years she and her husband occupied the White House.

Given Mrs. Reagan's involvement in personnel matters, it was only natural that questions about her impact on policy would be raised. If the first lady could arrange the resignation of the president's chief of staff, she might also help shape the administration's foreign and domestic policies. Mrs. Reagan became her husband's "screenwriter" in several policy areas, first carefully plotting the steps that would lead to his reelection in 1984 and then, during the second term, pushing for policies that would assure his place in history. But politics is not the movies, and Mrs. Reagan could not craft every nuance of her husband's administration. If she could, Donald Regan would have been written out of the scene much earlier. Instead, she concentrated on developing broad themes to make her husband's administration a success.

Although the first lady's acting experience did not include writing, she followed some of the best-known rules of scriptwriting. Screenwriter Lawrence Konner feels that the most important rule is to keep your focus on the main character. The best movies are character driven, rather than plot driven. Konner also suggests that characters must have flaws or weaknesses that will make it harder for them to accomplish their goal, as well as obstacles that they must overcome. Finally, there must be real villains to make the main character's actions seem more heroic.[1]

Nancy Reagan followed these guidelines for most of her husband's political career. Her own Hollywood experience had taught her that people watch a movie for the lead actor. If the actor is not believable, then the situations that the star faces will not seem real. The first lady was devoted to keeping the focus on her husband and his goals. The attack on the president's life and his remarkable recovery (as well as the ease with which he handled major cancer surgery) made him appear heroic. Mrs. Reagan played her part in fashioning the president's image, choosing his clothes, convincing him to change his hairstyle, and sorting through hundreds of photos for just the right ones to release to the press. Mrs. Reagan's influence extended well beyond image, however—she even helped her husband begin negotiations with his nemesis, the Soviet Union.

In many ways, then, Mrs. Reagan scripted various aspects of her husband's presidency, but she never acted in her own interest. According to longtime friend Nancy Reynolds, the first lady "has only one agenda, and that's Ronald Reagan and his happiness," and that is measured through his health, his popularity, and his legacy.[2] Richard Neustadt also recognized the same quality in Mrs. Reagan, writing that "she was utterly devoted to his person, his practice, and his eventual place of renown in history. As such she evidently could and did police his policies and personnel, ever alert to threats against his personal public standing."[3]

A number of President Reagan's staff recognized the first lady's influence. They realized that she was concerned with all aspects of her husband's presidency and would do what she needed to do to secure his place in history. One administration insider noted:

> There was more than pillow talk between the Reagans or wifely interest. Nancy was always concerned with what Ronnie's place would be in history. She wanted to be sure that he would be revered, respected, one of the great presidents that every school child grows up learning about. One can't fault her for that. But very often it was as though she were *writing the script and directing the action* [italics added]. She was kept fully apprised of his schedule and knew where he was and with whom he was talking every minute he was not with her.[4]

Michael Deaver recalled how the first lady operated: "She will wage a quiet campaign, planting a thought, recruiting others of us to help push it along, making a case: foreign policy will be hurt . . . our allies will be let down." Deaver knew that the first lady wasn't always successful. Mrs. Reagan couldn't convince the president to limit U.S. involvement in Nicaragua or reduce military spending and increase funding for social programs.[5]

Sometimes Mrs. Reagan failed because a group of advisors united in support of a policy. On other occasions the president's commitment to a policy was ideological, while Mrs. Reagan was urging more pragmatic considerations. President Reagan also had a stubborn streak, particularly when it came to supporting those who had helped him. The first lady had to know how far she could push her husband and when she needed to back off. Of course, it was much easier for her to guide the president when he was already inclined to move in the direction she was urging.

In her public posture on specific issues, Nancy Reagan seemed apolitical. Unlike Betty Ford, who not only publicly supported the ERA but also lobbied state legislatures for its passage, Mrs. Reagan avoided causes. She rarely took a stand on a political issue and, as a result, her policy preferences were a mystery. Many in the administration and in the press thought Mrs. Reagan was more moderate than the president on abortion, for example, favoring choice in cases of incest, rape, and protecting the mother's life. Some also thought she favored equal pay for equal work. But she was hesitant to address these issues publicly. Therefore, few could be sure of the first lady's position on any issue.[6]

When Mrs. Reagan was asked questions about her pet project, the "Just Say No" program, she stated that her only goal was to raise public awareness and to encourage greater individual responsibility from parents and children. Even as the administration was cutting funding for drug treatment programs, the first lady made it very clear that she would not lobby for budget increases or changes in administration policy. During the Reagan administration, drug policy emphasis shifted from treatment and public education to interdiction. In the 1970s, two-thirds of all federal appropriations for drug abuse went to treatment and education, but a decade later interdiction consumed 80 percent of federal drug funds.[7] Funding, however, was not the first lady's concern. She remained focused on the goal of increasing families' awareness of the danger of drugs.

During President Reagan's first term, the first lady kept an especially low profile on policy issues. She was battling her own image problems, and was particularly careful not to give the appearance of exerting undue influence within the administration. Still, the press constantly reported that she was quietly campaigning behind the scenes for changes in various policy areas. In foreign affairs, Mrs. Reagan was said to be pushing for improved relations between the United States and the Soviet Union, and in domestic policy she was urging caution on social issues such as school prayer and abortion.[8]

The first lady's interest in such policy matters stemmed from her desire to protect the president—the same reason for her involvement in personnel issues. Mrs. Reagan understood that her husband's popularity, success, and place in history would be determined by his policy decisions. She wanted to ensure that his legacy would be substantial. Achieving this goal might mean that staff members who were not fully committed to the president's program would have to leave. If so, Mrs. Reagan would gladly show them the door. And if establishing the president's place in history required her to lobby on behalf of certain policies or to use her influence to relegate others to the back burner, she would be happy to oblige.

During the 1980 campaign and throughout Ronald Reagan's White House years, Mrs. Reagan allied herself with a group of the president's advisors referred to by the press as the "pragmatists," or nonideologues. The group included James Baker, Michael Deaver,

George Shultz, Ken Duberstein, and later Howard Baker. She helped promote these people within the president's staff (in fact, were it not for Mrs. Reagan's assistance, James Baker might never have been the president's chief of staff).[9] She was drawn to this band of men not because of ideology, but because, as one commentator put it, they seemed more "politically adroit, more adept, better at image making, and better for her husband's political persona."[10]

Mrs. Reagan thought that at times the president needed to be protected from his more conservative instincts and advisors. Richard Wirthlin's polling numbers convinced her that the public approved of the moderate Reagan, who cooperated with Democrats in Congress to solve problems. Mrs. Reagan, ever mindful of her husband's image, sought to steer him in a more moderate direction. She was particularly concerned about his conservative allies, who often seemed more focused on their own agenda than the president's well-being. A friend of the Reagans was quoted as saying, "She has been the force to say, 'this is too strident, this too difficult for people to follow, it's politically not doable. . . . ' When the antennae go up, and she spots somebody trying to use Ronald Reagan for the benefit of his own philosophy, she'll fight like a tiger."[11]

That Mrs. Reagan advised the president on issues did not surprise those who knew them. Nancy Reynolds noted that Mrs. Reagan "is the president's closest confidante and his most trusted advisor."[12] Martin Anderson, President Reagan's domestic policy advisor, acknowledged the first lady's political skills, commenting that "her judgments on public policy issues, political strategy, and personnel were superb. . . . Reagan recognized a good mind when he encountered one." Anderson went on to say that "Reagan consulted her constantly on just about everything. It was done in a restrained, low-keyed manner. He would never hesitate to overrule her, although he seldom did because she was usually right."[13]

Mrs. Reagan acknowledged her influence while delivering a speech in New York City in 1987. Describing her role as a president's wife, Mrs. Reagan said, "I'm a woman who loves her husband and I make no apologies for looking out for his personal and political welfare," and then added, "I see the First Lady as another means to keep a president from being isolated. I talk to people. They tell me things. They pass along ideas. And sure I tell my husband. And if someone else is about to become a problem or fall between the cracks—I'm not above calling a staff person and asking about it."[14]

One of the most obvious and least recognized ways Mrs. Reagan affected the administration's policy was by influencing the choice of people who worked for her husband. She helped determine not only who made up the president's staff, but also the overall ideological composition of his advisors. As stated earlier, Mrs. Reagan and her allies favored moderate rather than conservative Republicans. Helene Von Damm, a deputy assistant to the president (and a committed conservative), understood the relationship between policy and personnel, and in her memoir, *At Reagan's Side*, she described Mrs. Reagan's influence: "Mrs. Reagan always said that she was interested in 'people not policy,' but what is the distinction? People are policy. That is why personnel struggles became so fierce. It wasn't just about patronage. It was a matter of which direction the Administration would move in."[15]

After the 1980 election, the most important policy decision facing the new administration was whether to move quickly on the president's economic program or to make social issues the top priority. The decision was difficult. It involved not just a choice of policy direction, but also a choice between the two major wings of the Republican Party.

Republicans were clearly divided into two factions. Economic conservatives saw the election as a mandate for the Reagan economic program (reducing government spending, taxation, and regulation). Social conservatives viewed the election as a mandate for constitutional amendments to ban abortion and reinstitute school prayers, legislation to restrict pornography and drug use, and opposition to the Equal Rights Amendment.[16] No matter which policy the administration chose to emphasize, it risked alienating an important wing of the party and a major part of its winning electoral coalition. By early 1981, Republican strategists who had once hoped that Reagan's victory would usher in a new Republican era in the country were openly worrying that the party would be split over issues of personal morality.[17]

Mrs. Reagan helped influence her husband's decision to give his economic agenda a higher priority than social issues. A lack of enthusiasm for abortion limits permeated the administration, particularly among those closest to the president. Many of the Californians who surrounded President Reagan clearly lacked zeal for this battle. Presidential counselor Ed Meese, although conservative on many other social issues, shared with the first lady a middle-of-the-road position on abortion. Others, such as Lynn Nofziger, were pro-choice. Most of the president's advisors (including the first lady) considered economic issues to be more important and urged him to make them his top priority. To strengthen their position, economic conservatives such as James Baker cited public opinion polls showing that people who had voted for Ronald Reagan were very enthusiastic about his economic program, but much less concerned about social issues. A clear majority of Americans still supported legalized abortion. A *Washington Post*–ABC News poll taken in June 1981 showed that Americans continued to support legalized abortion by a wide margin and that two out of every three Americans rejected any law that would make abortion murder.[18]

In 1980, candidate Reagan insisted that the Republican Party platform call for a constitutional amendment banning abortion, while admitting the diversity of viewpoints on abortion within the party and the electorate. The platform stated, "While we recognize differing views on this question among Americans in general—and in our own Party—we affirm our support of a constitutional amendment to restore protection of the right to life for unborn children. We also support the Congressional efforts to restrict the use of taxpayers' dollars for abortion."[19] Ronald Reagan stressed his anti-abortion position by declaring in his acceptance speech, "My answer as to what kind of abortion bill I could sign was one that recognized an abortion is the taking of a human life."[20]

Evidence of the abortion issue's personal importance to President Reagan is mixed. Abortion may have been more important to the president as a campaign issue than as a centerpiece of his administration's domestic program. While governor of California, Reagan signed a permissive abortion bill that resulted in over a million abortions during his tenure. While President Reagan consistently voiced support for a constitutional amendment banning abortion, the administration invested little political capital in gaining its passage and did not work particularly hard at trying to change abortion laws.[21] In 1982, abortion foes were surprised at the administration's lackadaisical lobbying effort on a Senate bill that would have greatly reduced a woman's right to an abortion.

Ronald Reagan's opposition to abortion may have increased over time. When he signed the abortion bill in California, he scarcely gave it any thought. His staff had assured him that the legislation would make very little difference in the number of abortions. After abortions did increase, however, Reagan suggested that he regretted signing the legislation.[22] While President Reagan did not push hard for a legislative end to abortion or a constitutional amendment outlawing abortion, he supported the Supreme Court's efforts to shift decision-making authority on abortion back to the state governments. He also advocated parental consent laws and imposed a gag order on family planning clinics.[23]

By 1983, the number of abortions had more than doubled in the ten years since abortion had been legalized, to 1.5 million a year—a quarter of all terminated pregnancies.[24] As a result, some in the right-to-life movement openly criticized the administration's lack of emphasis on abortion limits. Richard Doerflinger of the National Conference of Catholic Bishops Committee stated, "We're still waiting for the president to do something on an amendment."[25]

The administration's lack of emphasis on the abortion issue was not accidental. Mrs. Reagan worked with the James Baker–Michael Deaver White House team and the Republican Senate leadership to ensure that the new right's social agenda was confined to the rhetorical realm.[26] They managed both to moderate the President's image, making him more appealing to the political mainstream, and keep the Reagan coalition from being split apart before the 1984 campaign.

During his first term, President Reagan never addressed the annual Washington, D.C. pro-life rally in person, instead communicating to them by speakerphone. Many in the anti-abortion movement attributed the president's reluctance to Michael Deaver's attempts at image making. However, the practice continued after Deaver left the administration, and it became obvious that it was the first lady who had convinced the president not to appear.[27] Very few conservatives recognized the impact that Nancy Reagan and her moderate allies had on their cause. Paul Weyrich, a leader of the New Right, was one of the few who did, and later complained about the first lady's impact: "She considers virtually all conservative ideas as a liability. She operated at the level of imagery, but with policy objectives. She would intervene and say, you shouldn't do this; your image will be affected. Without her intervention or Deaver's, the Reagan presidency would have been 30 to 40 percent more conservative than it turned out to be."[28]

Mrs. Reagan understood that abortion was a divisive issue. Few Americans favored the complete outlawing of abortion, and equally few favored abortion on demand. By 1984, a fringe element of the anti-abortion movement had begun using violence against abortion providers—a tactic of which most Americans did not approve. As a result, President Reagan offered encouragement to pro-life demonstrators assembled in Washington, D.C., but never met with organizers of the event or appeared at their rally. In this way the president managed to maintain his pro-life credentials while avoiding having photos appear in the national media connecting him too closely with the movement.

Ronald Reagan retained his popularity with those in the anti-abortion movement by communicating his admiration for their commitment through White House correspondence. In one letter to the members of the National Right to Life Committee, for example, the president wrote, "I cannot commend too highly the dedication of citizens like you who have worked, struggled, and prayed for years to save the unborn and to give crucial help to mothers."[29]

A controversy erupted in September 1984, when Mrs. Reagan seemed to suggest that there were circumstances in which she could endorse a woman's right to an abortion. During a newspaper interview, the first lady was asked if she would have an abortion or recommend one to her daughter or stepdaughter if one of them became pregnant as the result of a rape. Mrs. Reagan replied, "I don't know." She went on to say that such a decision could not be made in the abstract, but that if it happened, it would have to be faced.[30]

When the interview appeared, Mrs. Reagan's position aroused interest. The first lady seemed to have adopted a more liberal position on abortion than her husband. President Reagan supported a complete ban on abortion except to save the life of the mother, a stance less flexible than the one his wife appeared to advocate. Sheila Tate explained that the first lady was only responding to a hypothetical question and answered without thinking through her response. Subsequently, a member of the press asked for clarification of Mrs. Reagan's actual point of view. Tate answered that the issue was one that the first lady "really did not want to get involved in" and that she "had no obligation to explain her position further, because she is not an elected official or a person seeking office."[31] Of course, that had not prevented Mrs. Reagan from speaking out on drugs and other issues. She used the role of first lady to advocate policies when she wanted to do so and hid behind her nonofficial status when it suited her.

In President Reagan's first term there was little movement on abortion; what movement there was flew below the political radar. The administration was accused of "packing" a panel of advisors for the Food and Drug Administration with pro-life supporters who didn't have the sufficiently strong medical credentials; instead, they had ties to the president's family, the Republican Party, and the anti-abortion movement. A right-to-life activist was even recommended for a committee that oversaw contraception and abortion drugs, and Mrs. Reagan's stepfather, Dr. Loyal Davis, was listed as a reference for another.[32]

President Reagan also made a record number of appointments to the federal judiciary. By the end of his second term, he had appointed 368 judges to the federal court system (the most of any modern president), and 94 percent of them were Republicans, the vast majority of whom were conservative on social issues.[33] Few Americans, however, notice appointments to bureaucratic commissions or to the federal judiciary, even though such appointments have major policy implications.

The administration also sought to limit the impact of *Roe v. Wade* through executive orders and laws quietly passed through Congress. Changes included a decision that federal dollars could no longer be used for abortion unless the mother's life was threatened. Private employers were no longer responsible for providing health insurance coverage that included abortion. Legal aid lawyers were prohibited from providing legal assistance for nontherapeutic abortions. Finally, private organizations would lose federal funds if they engaged in abortion-related activities abroad, including offering abortion services, counseling, and referrals, even if these were financed with money from private, non-American sources (this last development was known as the international gag rule).[34] These were significant changes, but the average American barely noticed.

In other areas of social policy, the administration was more openly aggressive. The Justice Department halted enforcement of affirmative action goals and timetables and discontinued class-action suits brought on behalf of women discriminated against in employment hiring or promotion.[35] At the Equal Employment Opportunity Commission, lawsuits on behalf of women being paid less than men for equal work were halted, and the agency no longer pursued cases against employers for sexual harassment of one employee by another, even though they were liable under the law.[36]

The administration's efforts on behalf of school prayer were consistent with the social conservatives' stance. In 1984, with reelection looming, the administration introduced into Congress a constitutional amendment permitting spoken, organized prayer in America's public school classrooms. The administration's insistence on spoken, rather than silent, prayer doomed the amendment's passage. However, just having the issue raised invigorated social conservatives within the party. Direct-mail specialist Richard Viguerie claimed, "The prayer issue will be our Panama Canal issue in the 1984 campaign."[37]

As the election drew closer, the president's rhetoric on social issues heated up. Speaking at the National Religious Broadcasters convention, Reagan denounced abortion, saying, "This nation cannot continue turning a blind eye and a deaf ear to the taking of some 4,000 unborn children's lives every day."[38] The president went on to pitch his constitutional amendment permitting school prayer, winning thunderous applause and two standing ovations from those in attendance.

The 1984 Republican Party platform was much more direct in its abortion language than it had been four years earlier. In 1980, Ronald Reagan had insisted on a tempered document that recognized differences of opinion on abortion within society and the Republican Party. However, in 1984 the party's social conservatives wrote the abortion plank. It stated, "The unborn child has a fundamental individual right to life which cannot be infringed. We therefore reaffirm our support for a human life amendment to the Constitution, and we endorse legislation to make clear that the Fourteenth Amendment's protections apply to unborn children."[39] The plank went on to commend President Reagan for appointing right-to-life judges to the federal judiciary. As the abortion plank made clear, social conservatives were now firmly entrenched in the Republican Party.

Mrs. Reagan had great difficulty sitting by while the rhetoric on abortion heated up. The first lady realized that in the upcoming election, social conservatives would strongly support the president because there would be no candidate that came as close to their views. She felt that to attract more voters, her husband should move to the center of the political spectrum, not farther to the right. At one point during the campaign, Mrs. Reagan called one of the president's advisors and told him, "I want you to tell him he has to stop talking about abortion. It's turning everybody off. He already has those people, it is doing him no good."[40]

Having given social conservatives a free hand with the party platform, President Reagan took a posture more in line with the first lady's thinking in his acceptance speech. Playing to the millions of Americans watching at home, he emphasized many of his standard themes, such as cutting taxes, reducing the size of government, and peace through strength. In the 5,297 words of his speech, there was only one sentence on school prayer and no specific reference to abortion.[41] Evidently, the president was heeding the advice of the administration's moderates (including Mrs. Reagan) to solidify his conservative base and then to reach out to the vast middle of the electorate, who were decidedly mixed on social issues.

Mrs. Reagan's opposition to the president's strong rhetoric on abortion continued through her husband's second term. According to Donald Regan, the first lady instructed him to have the president's speechwriters remove all references to abortion from the 1987 state of the union address, saying that she didn't give a damn about the right-to-lifers.[42]

The first lady affected another area of social policy—AIDS, which had become a major public health issue during President Reagan's first term. By 1984, the Centers for Disease Control (CDC) had confirmed 3,700 AIDS-related deaths. By the time Ronald Reagan left office, the CDC had confirmed 82,764 AIDS cases and 46, 344 deaths from the disease.[43] In the early years of the outbreak,

President Reagan viewed the disease as a self-inflicted disease that would eventually fade away. He was therefore reluctant to address the issue.

Three factors combined to change his mind. First was the death of actor Rock Hudson, an old Reagan friend. Hudson's death deeply shook the president and raised public awareness about the disease. Second was the persistence of Dr. C. Everett Koop, President Reagan's Surgeon General. On 26 October 1986, Dr. Koop delivered a summary report on AIDS that estimated that 179,000 Americans would die of the disease and another 145,000 AIDS patients would require hospitalization by the end of 1991.[44] Clearly the disease was not going to just fade away.

Third was Nancy Reagan's insistence that her husband begin to speak out on the issue. After Dr. Koop's report, the president was convinced that AIDS was the most important public health issue facing the nation. However, he was still reluctant to use the bully pulpit of the presidency to discuss AIDS prevention, particularly the use of condoms. The first lady had several close male homosexual friends, but she was fearful of the political consequences if the president were to speak out on the disease. Eventually she convinced her husband to substantially increase funding for AIDS research. By 1987, Mrs. Reagan realized that an even stronger effort was needed. At her request, the president agreed to address the issue in a speech delivered at a fund-raising dinner for the American Foundation for AIDS Research.[45]

Earlier, during his first term, Mrs. Reagan also influenced the president on several foreign policy issues. The first lady was concerned about her husband's growing image as a hard-line, bomb-wielding cold warrior. She felt that the media accounts were flawed: "I would read reports that he was a man who was going to start World War III at the drop of a hat. I know that he is not that kind of a man and that's not what he wants. It bothered me. You just don't like that said about somebody you love, knowing that it's not true. I may have said in conversation (to aides) that perception in the press is portraying him in an unfair, harsh light that I don't think he deserves."[46]

Mrs. Reagan was concerned not only about the accuracy of the image, but also about the problems it might cause for the president's reelection. Richard Wirthlin's polling data worried her. Polls showed that women especially were fearful about the direction of U.S.-Soviet relations. More than men, they wanted improved relations between the two superpowers. As the only woman among the president's closest advisors, Mrs. Reagan was sensitive to the impact of these fears on the women's vote. Political strategist Stuart Spencer further advised the first lady that while President Reagan could be reelected, he was vulnerable on the Soviet issue.[47] Wirthlin's polls and Spencer's political analysis confirmed what Mrs. Reagan's common sense and political instincts told her: that it was ridiculous and dangerous for the United States and the Soviet Union to continue their confrontation.

Once convinced of her position, Mrs. Reagan acted to solve the president's "Soviet problem." The first lady insisted that her husband tone down his "evil empire" rhetoric. She also urged him to avoid appearances at military-related events, such as ship dedications and visits to military bases. President Reagan respected his wife's political instincts, and followed her advice. She also helped bring about a change in national security advisors and attempted to start a dialogue between the administration and the Soviets by quietly bringing Soviet ambassador Anatoly Dobrynin into the White House through the East Wing. According to Michael Deaver, it was Mrs. Reagan "who pushed everybody on the Geneva summit and who would buttonhole the Secretary of State and the Head of the National Security Council to make sure that everyone was headed in the right direction."[48]

Just prior to the 1984 election, Mrs. Reagan convinced the president to invite Soviet foreign minister Andrei Gromyko to the White House. Upon Gromyko's arrival, Mrs. Reagan was the usual charming host, but at one point she one-upped the foreign minister in their verbal exchange. When Gromyko asked the first lady, "Does your husband believe in peace or war?" Mrs. Reagan replied without hesitation, "Peace." Gromyko then said, "Well then, whisper peace in his ear every night." Mrs. Reagan shot back, "I will. I'll also whisper peace in your ear."[49] Although this exchange is interesting as an example of the first lady's quick thinking, it is, perhaps, more significant as evidence that the foreign minister recognized the first lady's importance in building a lasting relationship between the two countries and actively sought her out.

Mrs. Reagan suggests much the same point in her memoirs: "When the President returns each afternoon from the West Wing, it's only natural that he'll talk things over with the person he's closest to, and that he'll take her viewpoint into consideration."[50] Of course, because this type of persuasion is exercised behind closed doors, it's the most difficult aspect of any first lady's influence to assess. Given Mrs. Reagan's efforts to shape personnel and build alliances among the president's staff in order to move the U.S.-Soviet policy to a more cooperative level, she likely also lobbied her husband for the same policy changes in private. Comparing her own efforts at changing the president's mind on U.S.-Soviet relations to her efforts to convince him not to go to Bitburg, Mrs. Reagan modestly suggests that "I was somewhat more successful in encouraging Ronnie to consider a more conciliatory relationship with the Soviet Union."[51]

While the president's acceptance speech at the 1984 Republican convention barely mentioned social issues, U.S.-Soviet relations were thoroughly covered. Absent from the speech were any of the standard references to the evil empire. President Reagan emphasized the need for cooperation between the superpowers in reducing their stockpiles of nuclear weapons, saying, "There are only two nations who by their agreement can rid the world of those doomsday weapons—the United States of America and the Soviet Union. For the safety of this Earth, we ask the Soviets—who have walked out of our negotiations—to join us in reducing and, yes, ridding the Earth of this awful threat."[52] With his wife's help, the longtime cold-war militant had metamorphosed into a man of peace. The Republican platform was in full agreement with the president, stating, "Americans, while caring deeply about arms control, realize that it is not an end in itself, but can be a major component of a foreign and defense policy which keeps America free, strong, and independent."[53]

As the administration rolled into its second term, the first lady found herself in an unusual position. Her closest allies from the first term were either gone or would soon be leaving. James Baker had moved over to the Treasury Department, and Michael Deaver had taken a public relations job. Other staff changes also took place. Presidential counselor Edwin Meese III had become attorney general, replacing President Reagan's old friend William French Smith. William

Clark left the Department of the Interior and was also headed back to California. As a result, most of the Californians who had surrounded President Reagan during his first term would be gone. While the first lady would miss the support of Baker and Deaver, her own influence seemed likely to grow. A White House aide was quoted in the *New York Times* as saying "Reagan will rely more and more on her as the second term progresses. Many of the Californians are going, and he won't have the old timers with him."[54] Not only was Mrs. Reagan now first among presidential advisors, she had her own priority for the second term—arms control. An arms control treaty involving significant reductions, not just caps on production, was the foreign policy breakthrough that would secure President Reagan's legacy. As a result, the first lady became the president's guide and mentor on arms control.

Mrs. Reagan's efforts on arms control were made easier by President Reagan's deeply held religious beliefs, which led him to favor the complete elimination of both U.S. and Soviet nuclear stockpiles. The president was fascinated with the biblical account of Armageddon—the end of the world. His interest in the topic was first sparked in 1968 when his pastor, Donn Moommaw, and the evangelist Billy Graham visited him in the hospital. During their visit, the three men discussed biblical prophecy, including Armageddon. In 1971, while attending a dinner for James Mills, president pro tem of the California state legislature, Ronald Reagan startled Mills by informing him that the end of the world was near. During a 1980 appearance on Jim Bakker's PTL television network, Reagan said, "We may be the generation that sees Armageddon."[55] President Reagan was appalled by the nuclear doctrine of mutually assured destruction (MAD). Under the doctrine, the United States and the Soviet Union deterred each other from a first strike by holding each other's populations hostage to a retaliatory nuclear strike. The president believed that a failure of MAD was the most likely source of a nuclear holocaust that would one day mark the end of the world.

In the second 1984 presidential debate, Marvin Kalb, chief diplomatic correspondent for NBC news, raised the question of Ronald Reagan's belief in Armageddon. The president responded that although he believed in Armageddon, it didn't affect the administration's policies. To the relief of his campaign advisors who thought the story had "legs," both the press and the Mondale campaign dropped the issue. In a later interview with Washington reporter Lou Cannon, a puzzled Stuart Spencer mused, "Why do they spend so much time in the media worrying about horoscopes and astrologers? It seems to me Armageddon has much more depth and meaning. It's rooted in the Bible [and could be related to] international relations, nuclear war. Nobody ever pursued Armageddon."[56] The Washington press and the Mondale campaign did not pursue the issue, but approximately one hundred mainstream Protestant, Roman Catholic, and Jewish leaders signed a statement of concern. The letter maintained that Armageddon theology is a false reading of the Bible and that belief in it diminishes concern about the possibility of nuclear war.[57] However, after limited media coverage, the religious leaders' concerns were forgotten.

Ronald Reagan's beliefs on Armageddon led him to attempt to shield the United States from the damages of a nuclear conflict. National Security Advisor Robert McFarlane thought that the president's views were crucial in the establishment of the Strategic Defense Initiative (SDI). If an all-out nuclear exchange between the United States and the Soviet Union was to be the most likely cause of Armageddon, the president saw SDI as the best method for delaying or diverting such a catastrophe. According to McFarlane, "From the time he adopted the Armageddon thesis, he saw it as a nuclear catastrophe. Well, what do you do about that? Reagan's answer was that you build a tent or bubble to protect your country."[58]

Against the backdrop of her husband's belief in Armageddon, the first lady pursued her goal of establishing his legacy through arms control. Encouraging him to aggressively pursue arms reductions with the Soviets (the "evil empire") could have been difficult, but Mrs. Reagan wisely portrayed arms control as a solution to the president's desire to avert nuclear Armageddon. As usual, the first lady found it easier to guide President Reagan in the direction she knew he really wanted to go.[59]

Mrs. Reagan developed an ally in her quest for arms reductions in Secretary of State George Shultz when she realized that they had a common goal. Shultz also saw an arms control agreement with the Soviet Union as the way to achieve a lasting impact for the president in foreign policy.[60] As a result, he was one of the few cabinet members whom Mrs. Reagan held in high regard. She also felt that the Soviets trusted Shultz and that this allowed him to work well with Soviet diplomats in representing President Reagan's interests.[61]

Once Mikhail Gorbachev came to power, Mrs. Reagan redoubled her efforts to convince her husband to meet with the Soviets. The first lady thought Gorbachev represented real change. His push for *glasnost* (candor with regard to discussion of social problems and shortcomings) and *perestroika* (restructuring of the Soviet economy and bureaucracy) made her think that he might be willing to discuss significant arms reductions. At the same time, though, others in the administration, such as Secretary of Defense Caspar Weinberger, were counseling President Reagan to get tougher on the Soviets. Mrs. Reagan kept after the president to make some kind of overture to the new Soviet leader. The "other woman" in her husband's life, British Prime Minister Margaret Thatcher, joined the first lady in her efforts. President Reagan had enormous respect for Thatcher, and her describing Gorbachev as "a chap we can do business with" carried a great deal of weight.[62] When Reagan and Gorbachev finally agreed to meet, it appeared that Mrs. Reagan was well on the road to securing the legacy she desired for her husband.

At the Reykjavik summit in 1986, President Reagan and Premier Gorbachev came very close to reaching an arms control agreement that would have removed all strategic nuclear weapons from Soviet and American arsenals by 1996. The deal breaker was Ronald Reagan's refusal to include SDI in the agreement (or, from the president's perspective, Gorbachev's insistence that SDI be part of the agreement). As a result, President Reagan's dream of completely eliminating nuclear weapons and forestalling the advent of Armageddon died. According to Mrs. Reagan, it was one of the few times that she had seen her usually even-tempered husband angry. "I was watching on television when the two leaders came outside. I knew from Ronnie's expression that something had gone wrong. He looked angry, very angry. His face was pale and his teeth were clenched. I had seen that look before, but not often—and certainly not on television. You have to push Ronnie very far to get that expression."[63]

Thus, Mrs. Reagan's own dream, of achieving her husband's legacy through dramatic breakthroughs in arms control, also died in Iceland. Her hope that he would win a Nobel Peace Prize evaporated too. There would be other significant agreements on nuclear weapons during the Reagan presidency (such as an INF treaty in 1987), but both sides recognized the missed opportunity. Still, President Reagan made a substantial contribution to the end of the cold war by meeting and negotiating with the Soviets on nuclear arms control, which itself would be a lasting legacy. In a discussion with Jim Wright, then Speaker of the House of Representatives, President Reagan left no doubt that the first lady deserved much of the credit for his foreign policy achievements: "Nancy is determined that I go down in history as the President of Peace."[64]

The first lady's foreign policy impact was not limited to arms control. Earlier in the Reagan presidency, Mrs. Reagan was reported to have fought against an agreement that would have allowed General Manuel Noriega, the military ruler of Panama, to give up his position in return for the dismissal of a federal drug trafficking indictment against him. Mrs. Reagan opposed the deal because it would have undermined the credibility of her own campaign against drugs and possibly damaged her husband politically. The president was also said to have requested Mrs. Reagan's approval of the agenda for the 1985 Geneva summit.[65] In addition, after the defeat of the administration's aid package to the contras in Nicaragua in early 1988, the first lady reportedly worked with Howard Baker to broker a compromise package with Speaker of the House Jim Wright.[66]

Mrs. Reagan also contributed diplomatically to the Reagan administration. At the time she was the most widely traveled first lady, making solo trips to Mexico, Italy, the Vatican, Sweden, Thailand, Malaysia, Indonesia, Monaco, and England.[67] When traveling with the president, she immersed herself in the culture of the country, whether it be flamenco dancing in Spain or acupuncture treatments in China. She was provided briefing books before her trips, but preferred to find her own reading, or consult friends who had recently visited her destination and who could provide firsthand experiences. Mrs. Reagan was also a master of the state dinner, hosting sixty-one dinners for foreign heads of state, more than any other first lady.[68]

While the administration pursued arms control in foreign policy, a dramatic shift was taking place in social policy. During the president's first term, under Mrs. Reagan's watchful eye, the administration had emphasized economic policy and paid only lip service to social issues. During President Reagan's second term the administration moved substantially on the conservative social agenda. Through the more aggressively conservative leadership of new attorney general Edwin Meese, many of these efforts were initiated by the Justice Department. Without the tempering effect of moderates such as James Baker and Michael Deaver within the White House, and with Mrs. Reagan preoccupied with her husband's health and her own personal and political problems, the attorney general had much more freedom to push a conservative agenda. After winning a tough confirmation battle in 1985, Ed Meese took steps to limit the effectiveness of a presidential executive order on affirmative action hiring for minorities and had Justice Department lawyers file a brief with the Supreme Court seeking to overturn the landmark abortion decision of *Roe v. Wade*.[69]

In 1987 the administration moved on a number of fronts to satisfy one of their strongest supporters, abortion foes. When Justice Lewis Powell resigned from the Supreme Court, the White House had the opportunity to appoint someone who could be the decisive conservative vote. The Reagan administration had previously appointed to the Supreme Court Sandra Day O'Connor and Anthony Scalia. Justice O'Connor was more moderate in her decisions than the administration would have preferred, but her appointment fulfilled a 1980 campaign vow to nominate a woman to the Supreme Court. Justice Scalia was named to the court when President Reagan promoted William Rehnquist from associate justice to chief justice in 1986. Subsequent Supreme Court decisions confirmed the administration's faith that Justice Scalia would be a strong conservative voice on the court.

With several important Supreme Court decisions looming, particularly on abortion, Ronald Reagan named Judge Robert E. Bork from the U.S. Court of Appeals for the District Court of Columbia Circuit as his nominee for the Supreme Court. Bork, who believed the 1973 abortion decision in *Roe v. Wade* was "wrongly decided," could have been the decisive conservative vote. However, after a bruising and bitter confirmation battle, the U.S. Senate rejected Bork by a vote of fifty-two to forty-eight. President Reagan's second nominee for the position, Douglas Ginsburg, was forced to withdraw his nomination because of past marijuana use. The president's third nomination for the position, Anthony Kennedy, was confirmed. Members of the administration hoped that Justice Kennedy would ultimately provide the conservative vote on the Supreme Court that they sought. Kennedy, however, has proven not to be nearly as ideologically conservative and more willing to compromise than Bork would have been.

At the same time the Reagan administration was looking to tilt the Supreme Court in a more conservative direction, it was also launching an assault on Title X of the Public Health Service Act, which provides for the government's family planning services. In 1987, over four million women were counseled in Title X programs, which were funded at $142 million. Since 1970, Congress had prohibited Title X dollars for paying for either abortion counseling or abortion. As a result, clinics had to use private funding for abortion services.[70]

Having unsuccessfully sought legislation to completely eliminate Title X in the past, the Reagan administration decided to seek to change the rules governing the program. Three specific rule changes were implemented. First, family planning counselors would no longer be allowed to mention abortion as a family planning option or to refer clients to abortion service providers. Second, organizations that were using federal dollars for family planning services and private donations for abortion services, such as Planned Parenthood, would be required to have separate sites for each service. Finally, no federal money could be used for "any program that encourages, promotes, or advocates abortion."[71] The Department of Health and Human Services, which oversees the Public Health Service, defended the new rules, saying, "There is no absolute imperative upon physicians to counsel or refer for an abortion."[72]

Would the script on social policy for the administration's second term have read the same if Mrs. Reagan had been more involved? Attempting to secure her husband's legacy through arms control, facing various medical emergencies (including her own breast cancer surgery), and fighting Donald Regan certainly took up a great deal of the first lady's time and energy. Mrs. Reagan was not happy about many of the actions taken on the social-policy front. She was one of the first members of the administration to realize that Bork could not win confirmation and urged that his name be withdrawn from consideration.[73] Mrs. Reagan, a dedicated poll watcher, was undoubtedly aware of increasing public opposition to Bork. An ABC News poll taken after the confirmation hearings showed that 52 percent of Americans opposed the nomination, and an *Atlanta Constitution* poll found that 51 percent of white southerners (including white conservatives) also opposed his nomination.[74] Justice Bork's support was dwindling to just a core of conservatives, and the first lady had never been a fan of what she referred to as "jump-off-the-cliff-with-the-flag-flying-conservatism."[75]

Perhaps, however, Mrs. Reagan may not have had the interest to "fight the fight" with the social conservatives in the second term as she had in the first, since the Twenty-Second Amendment barred her husband from running for another term. In addition, because she had lost many of her moderate allies from the president's first term, she may not have been able to influence the direction of policy as effectively.

The absence of the first lady's first-term allies may have also had an effect on aspects of foreign policy. Lynn Nofziger, for example, feels that had the old team of advisors remained in the White House, Iran-contra would not have happened. Ed Meese and William Clark would have convinced the president that swapping arms for hostages made no sense and violated the principles he stood for. Michael Deaver's instincts would have told him that politically it was the wrong thing to do, and he would have enlisted James Baker and the first lady in convincing the president. But by the end of the second term, Nofziger notes, Mrs. Reagan "was left with no one who could effectively add his voice to hers, or keep her on track as she sought to guide the president."[76]

In general, however, Mrs. Reagan had a substantial impact on specific areas of policy. She was a major force behind her husband's moderating his approach to the Soviet Union and aiming for an arms control treaty as part of the Reagan legacy. During Ronald Reagan's first term, the first lady and fellow moderates James Baker and Michael Deaver focused on the president's economic program. Mrs. Reagan was also responsible for putting as much distance as possible (sometimes literally) between President Reagan and social conservatives, whose agenda she viewed as detrimental to his chances for reelection.

The first lady scripted various aspects of her husband's presidency, but never in her own interest. She was concerned not with specific policies, but with her husband's political success. She decided what was best for President Reagan's image, his reelection, and ultimately his legacy, and then convinced the president, often with the help of others, to heed her advice.

Mrs. Reagan's influence didn't stem from any formal or informal policy positions that she held. In fact, she had very little interest in any specific area of policy other than how it related to her husband's success. Unlike some of the president's aides, the first lady never forgot that Ronald Reagan was the lead player and that the role of others was to provide him with support. Her influence was exercised discreetly, out of the public eye. She realized that most Americans wanted first ladies to be active in promoting a cause, but not meddling in policy affairs.

By the end of Reagan's second term, the majority of Americans had come to recognize how important Mrs. Reagan was in her husband's administration, and they expressed their approval of her role. For example, in a 1987 *Washington Post–Newsweek* poll taken between 5 March and 9 March (after Donald Regan's resignation), 1,511 Americans were asked about the first lady's influence: 31 percent said that Mrs. Reagan had "a great deal" of influence in the way the president governs, 26 percent "a good amount," 27 percent "only some," and only 16 percent said "very little." The majority of respondents—62 percent—also felt that Mrs. Reagan had more influence than previous first ladies and a great deal more influence than at the beginning of the Reagan presidency. In addition, 63 percent of the respondents said they had a favorable view of the first lady, with only 20 percent having an unfavorable rating.[77] If Mrs. Reagan was a "dragon lady," she was a popular one.

By the end of the Reagans' years in the White House, Mrs. Reagan had come to the conclusion that first ladies should not be confined to a limited role. Because the first lady knows the president better than anyone else in the administration, she is exposed to perspectives and insights from White House aides and elected officials that the president never gets to hear. According to Mrs. Reagan, it would be far better "if the president's men included the first lady as part of their team."[78] First ladies, she opined, might better support the president and serve their country by not having to pretend that they have no interest in or ideas about the administration's programs and policies, but instead by being part of the process in which decisions are made. At the same time, however, it's important to note what Mrs. Reagan did not say. She did not advocate that first ladies barnstorm the country on behalf of specific programs and policies. That would put her at risk of stealing the spotlight from the president. In Mrs. Reagan's world, there were no copresidencies. First ladies should never distract from the president—he is, after all, the star. But they can bring their unique talents and perspectives to the process of devising the script by which the administration will operate. In Mrs. Reagan's opinion, first ladies can better serve their husbands if they are at the center of this process, working together with the president's staff.

CHAPTER 6

THE CURTAIN FALLS

In reviewing the years of the Reagan presidency, it is clear that Nancy Reagan's contributions as first lady differed from her contemporaries. She was not in the mold of a Betty Ford, who spoke out on public issues, or a Rosalynn Carter, who sat in on cabinet meetings. Unlike Hillary Clinton, she did not lead a presidential commission. Mrs. Reagan's focus was simply on making her husband's presidency successful. Mrs. Reagan did have clout—her influence pervaded the administration. She oversaw the president's schedule, made key personnel decisions, and strongly influenced domestic and foreign policy decision-making. However, Mrs. Reagan used her power not to push her own agenda, but rather to help her husband gain an important place in history.

The key to understanding Mrs. Reagan's tenure as first lady is her background as an actor. During her childhood, she attended a number of her mother's performances and met her mother's many friends from the acting profession. Mrs. Reagan herself became a moderately successful Hollywood actress and an experienced stage actress (she is still the only first lady to have sung in a Broadway production). Nancy Reagan viewed the world through an actor's eyes. When she left her acting career, she took with her the skills she had acquired. She knew how to play a role, how to judge talent, and how to evaluate the response of an audience. She also learned the importance of the ensemble in creating an environment for the star's success. While first lady, she employed all of these skills on behalf of her husband.

Mrs. Reagan is part of a different generation of women from many of her critics. Born in the early 1920s, she came of age at a time when opportunities outside of the home were limited for most women. Acting was one of the few professions in which gender did not diminish a woman's chances of success.

Many women of Nancy Reagan's generation learned to achieve satisfaction through their husbands, and their husbands' success.[1] Mrs. Reagan's mother, who had given up her own moderately successful acting career to marry, was a perfect role model for this approach for women. She often instructed young Nancy in the importance of a good home life, including getting up early to have a hot breakfast with her husband, "because if you don't, you can be sure that some woman who lives around the corner will be perfectly happy to do so."[2]

Like many other women of her generation, Mrs. Reagan defined her own success through that of her husband. When she said that her life began when she met Ronald Reagan, she meant exactly what she said. She fell madly in love with the tall, good-looking actor, and she realized that by combining their talents, they could become a formidable pair. They would complement each other's strengths and compensate for the other's weaknesses. Ronald Reagan was trusting and loyal, sometimes to the point where he would be taken advantage of, while Nancy was generally suspicious of people's motives until they proved themselves true. Ronald Reagan was easygoing and slow to anger, while Mrs. Reagan had a legendary short fuse. But although their lives together made for a true partnership, Mrs. Reagan never forgot that her husband was the star and she was the supporting actress.

During their early years together, Mrs. Reagan helped her husband through the worst period of his life. His movie career was over. His first wife had unceremoniously dumped him. He had two small children dependent on him for their well-being, and his job prospects looked bleak. Nancy convinced him that things would improve and that he could still be a success. She had to persuade the most optimistic man she ever knew that there were still reasons to be optimistic. She recognized even then that optimism was an essential component of her husband's personality. If Reagan was to be Reagan, then he had to be at his best, which meant optimistic and upbeat. Her job was to make sure he was always at his peak.[3]

Mrs. Reagan played a supportive role throughout her husband's political career. When his 1980 presidential campaign faltered in Iowa, Mrs. Reagan intervened by clearing out the deadwood on his staff and making sure that Governor Reagan had the cast he needed to become president of the United States. After the election, her focus on personnel continued. Many advisors fell by the wayside because the first lady concluded that they were not serving her husband well. Among the casualties during the president's first term were Lynn Nofziger (who claims to have been fired by Mrs. Reagan several times), William Clark (who was not fired, but left the White House for the Department of the Interior), Richard Allen, and Alexander Haig. The first lady was not solely responsible for these departures, but she was a major factor in each case. When lobbying the president to have Donald Regan fired in the second Reagan term, Mrs. Reagan argued that she "was right about Stockman, I was right about Bill Clark. Why won't you listen to me about Donald Regan?"[4]

Mrs. Reagan's highest priority was surrounding the president with staff who would put the president's priorities above their own. From the first lady's perspective, Donald Regan didn't understand his role. She has been quite clear why he needed to leave: "Don Regan didn't see himself as one of the president's advisors. He didn't consider himself to be part of the White House staff. He saw himself as kind of a deputy president."[5]

Mrs. Reagan's was not the only voice calling for Donald Regan's departure. In the budget negotiations of 1985, Regan had alienated many Republican members of Congress, and they were also eager to see him leave. However, they were concerned that President Reagan's well-known loyalty to his staff might keep Regan from being let go. To advance their cause, Republican congressional leaders approached Mrs. Reagan about intervening with her husband.[6] Vice-President George Bush also asked the first lady to use her influence to get Regan fired, but she told him that he should approach the president himself.[7]

Mrs. Reagan exerted additional influence in the policy process. She helped convince the president that economics, not social issues, should be the administration's top priority. Her motivation for pushing social issues such as abortion to the back burner had little to do with ideology. She understood that the divisiveness of the New Right's social agenda might threaten the president's chances for re-election in 1984. While the first lady was not sure that she wanted her husband to run for reelection, she wanted him to win if he did decide to run. Numerous accounts suggest that the first lady also used her influence to push for arms control during the president's second term. Mrs. Reagan wanted her husband to have a significant legacy, perhaps even a Nobel Peace Prize. An arms control treaty seemed the most likely way to achieve this goal.

The first lady used her power in very traditional ways. She whispered in the president's ear what she thought he needed to hear. Her husband listened because he respected his wife's political instincts. On the rare occasions when the president resisted her persuasions, Mrs. Reagan teamed with like-minded members of his staff to convince him to take the appropriate measures. If the president needed even more persuading (as was the case in the attempt to get rid of Donald Regan), Mrs. Reagan brought in people he respected from outside the White House.

Nancy Reagan's own legacy will depend on how her influence within the Reagan administration is weighed. Currently, there is significant disagreement over just how important she was in the direction of the administration. Those who worked in the Reagan administration tend to see her as very influential, while most Reagan biographers feel that her impact has been somewhat exaggerated. Longtime Reagan aides Michael Deaver and Lynn Nofziger argue that the first lady had quite a bit of clout. Deaver writes that Mrs. Reagan "lobbied the president to soften his line on the Soviet Union; to reduce military spending and not to push Star Wars at the expense of the poor and dispossessed. She favored a diplomatic solution in Nicaragua and opposed his trip to Bitburg. Nancy wins most of the time. When she does, it is not by wearing him down, but usually being on the right side of an issue."[8] Lynn Nofziger states, "Her influence became more pronounced in the latter years of his presidency. When he was Governor, she would get mad at someone; she tried to have me fired a half a dozen times. . . . She was probably the deciding force on the appointment of James Baker, instead of Ed Meese, as the first chief of staff."[9] Reagan campaign advisor Ed Rollins contends that he once had the opportunity to spar eight rounds with heavyweight boxer Joe Frazier, but that Nancy Reagan beat him up much worse during a one-hour meeting to discuss plans for the 1984 Republican convention.[10]

Assessing the first lady's policy impact, Reagan biographer Lou Cannon disagrees with Deaver: "Reagan went to Bitburg, and he relied more on the contras than diplomacy in Nicaragua. He also vastly increased the rate of military spending, which leveled off only when Congress refused to approve funding requested by the administration. He spent billions on Star Wars and decreased the relative amount of federal spending for the poor. Of the issues cited by Deaver, Nancy Reagan was persuasive only on influencing his approach to the Soviets, admittedly a pretty big only."[11] President Reagan's official biographer, Edmund Morris, also downplays Mrs. Reagan's influence: "Her power inside the Reagan White House has been exaggerated politically and underestimated psychologically. And her much celebrated humanization of Dutch's prejudice against the Soviet Union is hard to prove."[12]

Two of Mrs. Reagan's staff members have a slightly different perspective. Both Sheila Tate and James Rosebush agree that Mrs. Reagan influenced policy, but that her impact was more selective and subtle than Deaver and Nofziger suggest. Tate emphasizes that Mrs. Reagan was active only in those policy areas where she felt she could help the president and that she never pushed an independent agenda.[13] Mr. Rosebush agrees with this assessment, but takes Tate's analysis a bit further by suggesting that Mrs. Reagan created opportunities for the president to move in certain policy directions, adding that ultimately it was his decision to make.[14] For example, the first lady created an opportunity for President Reagan to move toward arms control, while other advisors urged the president to adopt a harder line. The president ultimately chose to pursue arms control.

These disagreements over Mrs. Reagan's impact are the result of the varying perspectives of the commentators, but they also result from the way in which she filled the role of first lady. Mrs. Reagan rarely let her involvement become public. Whispers in the president's ear are difficult for others to hear. Also, the first lady took an interest in certain policies only because of the effect they might have on her husband's presidency. The only agenda she pushed was her husband's success. Perhaps as Mrs. Reagan's personal papers become available, historians and political scientists will be able to form a clearer picture of her role as first lady.

Still, certain conclusions can be drawn. The first lady undoubtedly influenced the direction of certain policy areas—arms control and some social issues. There is too much evidence from those both inside and outside the administration to think otherwise. Her influence was limited in range because her primary concern was simply to ensure her husband's success, not to shape policy by her own lights. Also, though her impact was real, it was also usually subtle. In addition, the first lady rarely went public with her concerns. From a broader perspective, however, Mrs. Reagan's input on personnel decisions ultimately helped determine the direction of the administration's policies; because people make policy, so influencing the selection of personnel influences policy.

The perception of Mrs. Reagan's tenure as first lady will also depend on how the position continues to evolve. Will the model for first ladies be Hillary Clinton or Rosalynn Carter, strong women who openly shared in their husbands' presidency? Or will it be Mrs. Reagan herself, an equally strong woman who worked behind the scenes to enhance her husband's political success? If the former, Mrs. Reagan's contribution as first lady will be discounted; if the latter, her significance will grow.

A few feminist leaders respected Mrs. Reagan for being a strong woman in a world dominated by conservative men. Some even came to her defense when she was accused of inappropriately using her influence in the firing of Donald Regan, arguing that Mrs. Reagan was being pilloried in the media for being a forceful first lady. Yet most feminists, it is probably fair to say, hope that future first ladies do not adopt the Nancy Reagan model.

In general, feminists and Nancy Reagan were not fond of each other. Starting with the Joan Didion interview, Mrs. Reagan felt that feminist writers presented her as a vacuous bubblehead. Didion's interview with Mrs. Reagan in the *Saturday Evening Post,* a two-part series by Wanda McDaniel in the *Los Angeles Herald Examiner,* and an article by Sally Quinn in the *Washington Post* all painted unflattering portraits of the first lady. The writers described Mrs. Reagan as preoccupied with image—of not knowing when to stop acting. Didion wrote, "Nancy Reagan says almost everything with spirit, perhaps because she was an actress for a couple of years and has the beginning actress's habit of investing even the most casual lines with a good deal more dramatic emphasis than is ordinarily called for on a Tuesday morning on 45th Street in Sacramento."[15] All of these negative articles were written by women from a younger generation than Mrs. Reagan's.

The criticism from younger female writers continued throughout the first lady's White House years. Mrs. Reagan has clearly neither forgotten nor forgiven: she devotes a number of pages in her autobiography to detailing the inaccuracies presented in articles about her by these feminist writers. The first lady also explains why she thinks feminists dislike her so intensely. She quotes Katharine Graham, who told her friend that many feminist writers "just couldn't identify with you. You represented everything that they were rebelling against."[16] Mrs. Reagan writes,

I suspect that what may have really bothered some women was my decision to give up my career and devote myself to my husband and our family. Ronnie never asked me do to this; it had been my choice. I could have continued to work in movies. But I had seen too many marriages fall apart in the picture business because both partners had a career. I've always felt that I had the best of both worlds—a career, followed by a happy marriage. Still some women have never forgiven me for making that choice, or for saying that my life really began when I married Ronnie.[17]

Mrs. Reagan is undoubtedly correct in her analysis of how feminist leaders perceived her. To women's rights activists struggling to escape male domination and achieve economic, social, and political equality, the first lady represented the very stereotype they were trying to overcome: a woman who achieved success and influence through her husband, rather than on her own merits.

It is worth remembering that Nancy Reagan was from a completely different generation of women, and that these women were taught to subjugate their own opinions, beliefs, and ideas to those of their husbands. These women grew up thinking that being a presidential spouse was the highest position they could obtain. That was the message that society communicated. More than a decade after women finally gained the vote, the *New York Times* was still suggesting that women should only vote for men and that politics was a male domain: "Just as every American boy may hope to be president, so every girl may hope to be a President's wife."[18]

To women attempting to carve out their own careers in the professions, journalism, or politics, Nancy Reagan seemed as relevant as a dinosaur. When she stated that her life began when she married, she negated the struggle of feminists trying to define their own lives, on their own terms. Mrs. Reagan's life also cast into doubt a central tenet of second-stage feminism in the 1970s and 1980s—that to be truly satisfied, a woman needed to be "liberated." The first lady was clearly a strong and satisfied woman, obviously happy in her traditional role.[19]

Feminist objections to Nancy Reagan were also prompted by the Reagan administration's track record on women's issues. Although Ronald Reagan was generally a popular president, women (particularly liberal women) were less likely to support him than men. The difference between male and female support of a political figure— which became known as the "gender gap"—was first noted in the 1980 presidential elections, when Ronald Reagan did more poorly among female voters than among male voters. The Republicans' unpopularity with female voters continued even after Reagan left office. By the early 1990s, northern white females were 9 percent more likely to vote Democratic than their male counterparts, and southern white females were 13 percent more likely to vote Democratic than white male southerners.[20]

The Reagan administration enacted a number of policies that were unpopular with women activists. The president's general counsel, Bradford Reynolds, instructed the Equal Employment Opportunity Commission to stop pursuing lawsuits initiated by women who argued that they were paid less than men. Reynolds also resisted applying Title IX provisions to employees of federally funded schools. Under President Reagan, the Office of Personnel Management proposed lowering the entry-level salary for librarians with masters degrees (60 percent of whom were women) to $16,659, while the salaries of accountants, chemists, and auditors (fields dominated by men) remained at $20,256. During his first term, the president appointed to the EEOC a substitute teacher who was a state director of ERA opponent Phyllis Schafly's Eagle Forum.[21] There was also Reagan's vocal opposition to abortion. These issues, revolving around equal employment, equal pay for equal work, the Equal Rights Amendment, and abortion rights, were of great importance to feminists of the Reagan era. It is no wonder that supporters of equal rights for women had little enthusiasm for both President Reagan and the first lady. In effect, Mrs. Reagan got caught in the "backlash" of her husband's policies.[22]

These Reagan policies were at the heart of the gender gap. During the 1980s, women generally favored peace, greater equality, and economic security much more than men did. A 1982 poll by the *New York Times* asked voters whether they were afraid that President Reagan would get us into war. Men said no by 57 percent to 36 percent, while women said yes by 56 percent to 36 percent. Given the fact that women voted in equal numbers with men, the poll was cause for concern on the part of the administration.[23]

Some members of the president's administration were disturbed over the electoral implications of the president's lack of popularity with women. In a memo outlining the administration's problem with women, Transportation Secretary Elizabeth Dole noted the possible significance of the gender gap: "While the impact of the women's vote in the 1982 midterm elections is still somewhat inconclusive, the data foreshadow potential problems for Republicans. Polls indicated throughout 1982 that Democratic candidates led by five to fifteen points among women. Network exit polls conducted on November 2 indicated about the same spread, with Democrats leading among women in 73 out of 85 monitored races." Dole also noted that the president's problems were particularly severe among nonmarried working women whom she referred to as the "heart of the gap."[24]

Dole argued that the administration needed to go on the offensive in combating their "anti-women" image and suggested a plan referred to as "the 52 percent solution" (women made up 52 percent of the population). The plan involved economic and legal equity policy initiatives and communication initiatives targeted at disaffected, moderate Republican women, members of potentially supportive women's groups, married women working outside the home, single female heads of households working outside the home, and elderly women dependent on Social Security benefits.[25] Dole also noted that the impending defeat of the Equal Rights Amendment was a major problem, since the president would likely be blamed for its defeat. She suggested that the administration develop a strategy demonstrating that President Reagan took women's issues seriously and that overall the administration had a positive track record on women's issues.[26]

Some prominent women in the administration supported Secretary Dole. Faith Ryan Whittlesey, assistant to the president for public liaison, agreed that the administration needed to develop a higher profile on women's issues and abandon its defensive and reactive position.[27] Others, however, such as Health and Human Services Secretary Margaret Heckler and Nancy Risque from the Office of Legislative Affairs, warned against getting into a bidding war for the support of women that the administration could not win. They thought that the women's issue was primarily rhetorical, with perception being more important than substance.[28]

Michael Uhlman, assistant director for legal policy, argued against a legal strategy, saying that the administration could only bring about incremental changes by prosecuting more gender equity cases and that "we delude ourselves greatly if we think that marginally improved statistics here or there will do much to placate the more severe critics of the administration, much less induce them to support us." Uhlman further suggested that women's groups were not really interested in the administration prosecuting more gender discrimination cases, but instead wanted from the administration "agreement on certain fundamental principles, and in the case of equal pay enforcement, they are upset with us because we reject the premises and remedies associated with comparable worth."[29]

Ultimately, those arguing against the Dole plan carried the day, in part because their position was the dominant one in the administration to begin with. An additional point in their favor was that the gender gap was reversed in regard to male voters. President Reagan's weakness among female voters was offset by his strength among male voters.[30] Thus, in the end the first lady's reputation among feminists would not be improved by the administration's making a more active effort to woo female voters.

For some feminists, the problem was larger than any one first lady. In an age in which women attain ever higher political office and will someday be running for the presidency as the nominee of the Democratic or Republican Party, the position of first lady is increasingly irrelevant. Germaine Greer argues that by its very nature, the position of first lady is an antiquated, sexist institution. According to Greer, the position's primary functions are the same responsibilities women have always had in a male-dominated society. The first lady confirms the president's heterosexuality and sexual prowess (sharing the same bed), as well as his adequacy as a provider (dressing well and spending money wisely), and, together with the president, demonstrates the values of monogamy and family unity. Greer maintains that the position of first lady represents a type of power that is basically undemocratic—that it is not earned, but achieved merely by sharing another person's bed. For Greer, Nancy Reagan represented the position of first lady par excellence, and at the same time was a model of womanhood that runs counter to women's long-term interests.[31]

The 1980s were a period of transition for the feminist movement. Feminist leaders' efforts to turn their daily experience as women into critiques of the repressive sexist institutions and to bring about change through collective action fundamentally had changed women's roles in society. By the late 1980s a conservative reaction was gaining political ascendancy. Some were asserting that many feminist principles (for example, women being able simultaneously to work outside the home and successfully raise and nurture children) threatened the traditional family structure. When summarizing polling data from 1938 to 1985, Rita J. Simon and Jean M. Landis describe the ambivalence about the role of women in the larger culture. Both women and men had come to value women's participation in the labor force, particularly through the 1970s, when two incomes were a necessity. However, Simon and Landis conclude that:

> The majority of both men and women believe the husband's career supersedes that of a wife: a wife should change jobs and

defer career advancement in accordance with the unfolding requirements of her husband's career path. However from 1977 to
1985 a majority of men and women converged in disagreement
with the statement that it is "more important for the wife to help
her husband's career than to have one herself." Perhaps the com-
posite message is one that encourages the married woman to
have a career of her own, so long as it remains within the boun-
daries imposed by the career of her husband.[32]

Thus, perceptions of the first lady mirrored disagreements about
the role of women in society. Those who wanted women to perform
a traditional function saw Mrs. Reagan as a role model, while those
who wanted women to carve out their own political careers and
push their own agendas viewed Mrs. Reagan as an undesirable
throwback to a different era.

Although Mrs. Reagan was clearly wounded by the feminist critique of how she chose to define the role of first lady, her shrewd response was to appear to embrace feminist values while rejecting
feminist dogma.[33] According to Mrs. Reagan, feminism focused on
the right of women to make choices about how they lived, and she
often said she was pleased that women had so many different options available to them. Some women might make their work their
top priority, and they had the perfect right to make that choice.
However, women should not be forced to embrace the workplace, as
so many feminist leaders seemed to her to prefer. Women had an
equal right to make home, family, and their spouses their top priority. Women should be able to choose whatever they wanted, just as
Mrs. Reagan had chosen her marriage and her husband's career over
her own career as an actor. Ironically, Mrs. Reagan's position would
become a central tenet of the next wave of feminism. These later
feminists argue that too often earlier feminists failed to value
women who make traditional choices, embracing home and family
over equality in the workplace.[34]

Although Nancy Reagan saw herself as a supporting player within
the Reagan administration, she will be remembered for a cause that was
uniquely hers: the "Just Say No" program to prevent drug abuse. Having survived the firing of Donald Regan and the Iran-contra scandal,

the first lady increased her efforts on behalf of her antidrug campaign. She seemed to realize that her own place in history would be linked to this cause. In 1988, Mrs. Reagan hosted a weeklong conference on drug abuse as mandated by the Anti–Drug Abuse Act of 1986. She spoke eloquently, with compassion and political sophistication, as she described the effects of drug abuse and noted the relevance of U.S. relations with South American countries for solving the drug problem.[35]

A few months later, Mrs. Reagan became the first incumbent first lady to address a full session of the United Nations. In her remarks, Mrs. Reagan made the argument for supply-side intervention as the most effective way to attack the growing drug problem. She noted that "we will not get anywhere if we place a greater burden of action on foreign governments . . . it is far easier to focus on the coca fields grown by 3,000 campesinos in Peru than to shut down the dealer who can be found on the street corner of our cities. It's often easier to make strong speeches about foreign drug lords or drug smugglers than to arrest a pair of Wall Street bankers buying cocaine on their lunch break. . . . I do not believe that the American people will ever allow the legalization of drugs in their country."[36]

Two decades after the advent of Nancy Reagan's "Just Say No" program, a number of studies have determined that the supply-side approach to the drug problem has not been successful. The largest and best known of the "Just Say No" programs is Drug Abuse Resistance Education—DARE—begun in 1983 by Los Angeles Police Chief Daryl Gates and modeled after an earlier program developed by researchers at the University of California.[37] The DARE program puts police officers into elementary school classrooms to warn students about the dangers of drugs, teaching that experimentation with milder drugs such as marijuana leads to harder drugs such as cocaine and heroin. The program is run almost entirely by public funding, with the federal government contributing about $700 million per year and local governments spending an additional $215 million in the salaries of participating police officers.[38]

Although policy evaluations of the DARE program differ modestly in their conclusions, a consensus seems to be building that it has not been effective. A General Accounting Office report published in January 2003 concluded that the program has had "no statistically significant long-term effects on preventing illicit drug use" and that students participating in the program had "no statistically different attitudes towards drug use than children who did not participate in the program." The report did find evidence of "negative attitudes about drug use and improved social skills" among DARE students, but added that these diminished over time.[39] This "phase out effect" has severely limited the impact of the DARE program. The GAO finding is consistent with other evaluations of the program. For example, in 2001 the U.S. Surgeon General characterized DARE as ineffective, and a 1998 University of Illinois study of 1,798 students found no differences between DARE graduates and nongraduates six years after completing the program.[40] Undoubtedly, Mrs. Reagan's efforts to heighten public awareness about the drug problem in the United States were well intentioned, but there is, sadly, little proof that her approach to educating students about the evils of drug use has had a major impact.

Several differences between Mrs. Reagan's approach and the DARE program, however, are worth mentioning. DARE has no national spokesperson of the first lady's importance. Mrs. Reagan advocated private sector initiatives, while the DARE program relies on government funding. The first lady felt that drug abuse was a family issue and that parents as well as children needed to be educated about the problem. She had been encouraging parental involvement since her televised appearance on *Good Morning America* in November 1981. On that program, she suggested that parents who wanted to join a support group, but were having difficulty locating one, should write to the White House, which would put them in contact with a parent group in their area.[41]

Some felt that Mrs. Reagan's effort to involve parents made her approach to the drug problem of American youth unique for its time. Joseph Califano, former Secretary of Health, Education, and Welfare in the Johnson administration, gave the first lady's program a positive evaluation because of its success in involving parents, and suggested that Mrs. Reagan's "Just Say No" program was one of the most productive projects of any first lady in history.[42] Some evidence indicates that parent education programs such as Project Star and Strengthening Families are more successful than DARE.[43] In any case, Mrs. Reagan will always be associated with her efforts at curbing drug abuse—a laudable goal.

As the end of her husband's term as president approached, Mrs. Reagan reflected on her tenure as first lady. She had come to realize that a bit of self-deprecating humor could disarm even the most hostile press. In 1987, she opened a speech to the Associated Press Publishers' Luncheon by saying, "I was afraid I might have to cancel. You know how busy I am—between staffing the White House and overseeing the arms talks. In fact this morning I had planned to clear up U.S.-Soviet differences on intermediate range nuclear missiles, but I decided to clean out Ronnie's sock drawer instead."[44] She noted that she was completely unprepared for the intense press scrutiny of first ladies. Once she realized that everything she did was news, she tried to channel the coverage to good advantage through her "Just Say No" program. On one point she was adamant: "what nearly every First Lady shares is an overriding interest in her husband's political fortunes and personal contentment."[45]

By the close of 1988, the Reagans were preoccupied with the upcoming election, and of course with their plans to leave the White House. However, the first lady could not slip out the door without one last controversy. In 1982, when Mrs. Reagan was being roundly criticized for conspicuous consumption, she had made a vow never again to accept gifts of clothing. Apparently the promise was easier made than kept: she continued to borrow dresses, jewelry, and furs from some of the nation's top designers. As Mrs. Reagan's new press secretary, Elaine Crispin, said, the first lady "broke her own little rule, which she now regrets."[46] The value of the clothing in question was substantial. Mrs. Reagan "borrowed" sixty to eighty outfits from designer David Hayes of Hollywood, a $10,000 mink from Galanos, and a set of earrings valued at $800,000 from Harry Winston in New York.[47] To make matters worse, the first lady disregarded the advice of White House counsel Fred Fielding. Fielding instructed the Reagans to report the loans on financial disclosure forms even though, in his opinion, they did not constitute gifts within the parameters of the 1978 Ethics in Government Act.[48]

The issue followed the Reagans after they left the White House. The Internal Revenue Service took a hard look at the first lady's practice of borrowing and keeping designer clothes and jewelry. The IRS contended that the apparel constituted taxable income and imposed an estimated $1 million bill for back taxes, interest, and possible penalties on the president and Mrs. Reagan. The Reagans later settled their bill with the IRS. The case was also referred to the criminal division of the IRS, which declined to prosecute.[49]

Another issue facing the Reagans in 1988 was a request for pardons from Oliver North, John Poindexter, and others indicted in the Iran-contra scandal. On his last day in office, the president denied their requests for pardons, saying, "There have been implications of personal gains and so forth. A pardon now before a trial would leave them forever after with that guilt hanging over them."[50] Mrs. Reagan was very vocal in her opposition to pardons for those charged. She felt strongly that not only had they misled her husband, but also that the pardons would raise controversy just as her husband was taking his final bows.[51]

After George H. W. Bush's election as president, the Reagans began the transition to private life. The new president was eager to step out of his predecessor's shadow, and at times the Bushes felt that the Reagans had not wanted them upstairs in the White House family quarters. Despite some obvious friction between the two couples, however, the fact that the president and the president-elect were from the same party and from the same administration made for a relatively easy transition.[52] Mrs. Reagan followed the tradition established by Edith Roosevelt for Nellie Taft, and provided Barbara Bush with a personal tour of the White House. The press also continued its tradition of comparing the incoming and outgoing first ladies, which Mrs. Bush deftly handled with what became her trademark humor: "As you know, we have a lot in common. She adores her husband; I adore mine. She fights drugs. I fight illiteracy. She wears a size three . . . and so is my leg."[53]

Realizing that their time in the spotlight was almost over, the Reagans said their good-byes to official Washington and let the president-elect and Mrs. Bush take center stage. On inauguration day, again following tradition, Mrs. Reagan (in her signature red coat) and Mrs. Bush traveled to the Capitol together for the swearing in. Then it was time for the Reagans to board their helicopter, leaving Washington to begin the rest of their lives together.

Initially, the post–White House years held great promise for the Reagans. They settled easily into their new Bel Air home (purchased for them by friends), and Ronald Reagan once again began to travel the speech-making circuit. As a former president, he was able to earn considerably more than he did in the old days, when he was a spokesperson for General Electric. Mrs. Reagan was elected to the board of Revlon Group Incorporated. Revlon chairman Ronald L. Perelman cited Mrs. Reagan's efforts in the fight against drug abuse in announcing her election to the board.[54] Mrs. Reagan's attempts to stay involved with the antidrug effort, however, involved her in some controversy.

The core of Mrs. Reagan's antidrug efforts while she was first lady was the Nancy Reagan Drug Abuse Fund, originally established under the auspices of the Community Foundation of Greater Washington. When the fund was created, the foundation board stipulated that any money raised was not a trust fund, but was the sole property of the foundation. In the autumn of 1988, community foundation officials were surprised to learn that Mrs. Reagan no longer wanted them to administer "her" fund. She intended to take all the fund's assets back to California to establish her own charitable foundation, the Nancy Reagan Foundation, which would support grants for community-based programs such as Phoenix House and the "Just Say No" program.

The foundation's directors held that, given the stipulations under which the Nancy Reagan Drug Abuse Fund had been created, any revenues from the fund were technically the property of the Community Foundation. They also realized, however, that it was because of the appeal of Nancy Reagan's name that most of the revenue had been raised; in any case, they were reluctant to publicly argue the point with Mrs. Reagan. Therefore, on 6 July 1989, the foundation handed over to Mrs. Reagan's new foundation a check for $3,625,674.76. In just a short time, the Nancy Reagan Foundation, with Mrs. Reagan as its executive director, accumulated assets exceeding $4 million and rented office space just down the hall from President Reagan's office.[55] In 1992, a $50,000 contribution from the Nancy Reagan Fund coupled with a research grant from the National Institute on Drug Abuse was critical in allowing a Prince George's County drug treatment center bearing the former first lady's name to remain open.[56] The foundation has continued to contribute funds to antidrug programs, such as Girls Incorporated, which emphasizes a program called Friendly PEERsuasion, the only national substance abuse program that specifically targets young girls.[57] Keep a Clear Mind, a drug abuse prevention program developed at the University of Arkansas and partially funded by the Nancy Reagan Foundation, was one of only nineteen model programs recognized by the National Registry of Effective Programs in the spring of 2000.[58]

In 1991, celebrity biographer Kitty Kelley's book *Nancy Reagan: An Unauthorized Biography* was published, creating even more controversy for Mrs. Reagan. The biography painted a very unflattering picture of the former first lady, accusing her of everything from infidelity with Frank Sinatra to child abuse. Kelley argued that Mrs. Reagan completely dominated her husband and was responsible for most of the important decisions in the Reagan White House. Although the book was certainly titillating and undoubtedly caused Mrs. Reagan a great deal of embarrassment, the book reviews were for the most part negative.

In 1992, the Republican Party held its presidential convention in Houston, Texas. One of the highlights of the convention was the speech by President Reagan. It would be the former president's last convention appearance. Patrick J. Buchanan's long and divisive speech pushed Reagan's speech out of prime time. In his speech, President Reagan reviewed the successes of his administration and then launched into a vigorous defense of President Bush's achievements. In an unusually reflective passage, the former president stated, "And whatever else history may say about me when I'm gone, I hope it will record that I appealed to your best hopes, not your worst fears, to your confidence rather than your doubts. My dream is that you will travel the road ahead with liberty's lamp guiding your steps and opportunity's arm steadying your way."[59] Ronald Reagan then called for Mrs. Reagan to stand at his side, where for one last time they basked in the glow of their appreciative party.

In 1994, the Reagans' world changed forever when the doctors diagnosed the former president with Alzheimer's disease. Ronald Reagan subsequently revealed his illness to the nation in an open letter. He stated that he hoped by going public, other patients and families struggling with the disease would be helped. Throughout his announcement, the former president dealt with the issue with his characteristic upbeat approach: "At the moment I feel just fine. I intend to live the remainder of the years God has given me on this earth doing the things I have always done. I will continue to share life's journey with my beloved wife and family. I plan to enjoy the outdoors and stay in touch with friends and family."[60]

In the final section of *I Love You, Ronnie,* a collection of romantic letters Ronald Reagan wrote to his wife, Mrs. Reagan recalled the onset of the disease. According to Mrs. Reagan, there were no evident symptoms of the disease until the former president was actually diagnosed. She states her belief that her husband's Alzheimer's was hastened by a 1989 fall he took from his horse that resulted in a concussion and subdural hematoma.[61] After the announcement, the Reagans formed the Ronald and Nancy Reagan Research Institute with the National Alzheimer's Association. The institute's stated purpose is to speed information exchange within the field of Alzheimer's research in order to find promising treatments, preventions, and cures.[62]

Ronald Reagan's announcement raised speculation as to whether he had been affected by the disease while he was in office. His diminishing powers of recall during his last few months as president had raised concern among his staff and the first lady.[63] In particular, his deposition in Admiral John Poindexter's Iran-contra case caused some consternation, as it revealed that the president could barely recall many of the major figures in his administration. Concerns about the president's memory lapses had been raised earlier. Walter Mondale in private used the term "senile" to describe the president after a several-hour, uninterrupted face-to-face meeting during the 1984 campaign.[64] The *New York Times* later reported that those close to President Reagan had noticed a slowing of his ability to react, that his famous anecdotes were increasingly off the mark, that he had become more stubborn, and that he had "on" days and "off" days.[65]

Others, however, reported little change in the president and insisted that although he might have memory lapses, it was just that Ronald Reagan had always had little memory for detail and even less interest in them. The president also had a management style that allowed his aides to deal with many of the details of the presidency. More important, President Reagan had public relations experts—Mrs. Reagan foremost among them—who helped him project an image of strength and vitality to the nation no matter what his actual condition may have been.[66]

Initially, the former president's life after his diagnosis changed little. He continued to spend several hours a day in his Central City office, continued to work out on a regular basis, played golf, and strolled the beach with his Secret Service agents.[67] However, as is always the case with Alzheimer's patients, Ronald Reagan slowly began to lose his memory, which had a devastating impact on his wife. She writes, "You know that it is a progressive disease and that there's no place to go but down, no light at the end of the tunnel. You get tired and frustrated, because you have no control and you feel helpless. We've had an extraordinary life. . . . but the other side of the coin is that it makes it harder. There are so many memories that I can no longer share, which makes it very difficult. When it comes right down to it, you're in it alone. Each day is different, and you get up, put one foot in front of the other, and go—and love; just love."[68]

Mrs. Reagan had always attempted to shield her husband from as many of life's difficulties as possible. In the battle against Alzheimer's, however, the former president was fighting an enemy over which his wife had no control. Instead, like the families of all Alzheimer's patients, Mrs. Reagan had to sit and watch the pieces of their lives together fall away. One important piece fell in 1996, when Mrs. Reagan put their Rancho del Cielo—"our ranch in the clouds"—up for sale. Although former President Reagan dearly loved the ranch, which had served as a quasi-western White House during his administration, he had not been able to visit it for almost two years.[69]

Ronald Reagan's struggle with Alzheimer's affected his entire family, drawing some members closer together and driving others farther apart. Mrs. Reagan and her stepdaughter, Maureen, became even closer. Even though she lived several hundred miles away, Maureen visited the former president and Mrs. Reagan at least once a month, and spoke very highly of the quality of care her father was receiving. When Nancy Reagan occasionally needed time away, Maureen would stay with her father. She would often slip into the room to watch baseball or another sport with him. When asked if he recognized her, Maureen said he was comfortable with her and that was enough. Maureen also became an outspoken proponent for increased funding for fighting Alzheimer's. In March 2000, she appeared before a Senate committee, urging lawmakers to double the Alzheimer's research budget, from $50 million to $100 million.[70]

Alzheimer's research lost an advocate, Nancy Reagan lost a friend, and President Reagan lost a companion when Maureen's five-year battle with skin cancer ended in her death on 8 August 2001.[71] Her death, however, helped move forward a reconciliation between Nancy Reagan and Jane Wyman, which had begun when the former first lady called Ms. Wyman to inform her of President Reagan's illness. At Maureen's funeral, the former and current Mrs. Reagan sat side by side in the same pew as Maureen's husband and daughter.[72] In a press release on her stepdaughter's death, Mrs. Reagan described Maureen's relationship with her father: "Maureen Reagan has been a special part of my life since I met Ronnie over fifty years ago. Like all fathers and daughters, there was a unique bond between them. Maureen had his gift of communication, his love of politics, and when she believed in a cause, she was not afraid to fight hard for it."[73]

Mrs. Reagan's rapport with her other children has been mixed. Her relations with her daughter, Patti, improved as time went by. Patti visited her mother and father on a regular basis and asserted that her father was getting excellent care. When asked to discuss further her feelings about her mother, Patti usually declined, except to say that they have a challenging relationship and that she doesn't speak about her.[74] Mrs. Reagan reported that they reconciled and that the former president sensed the improved relationship.[75] In her book *Angels Don't Die*, Patti writes that "my mother and I have been able to emerge from the tangled brier of her past together, into a clearing where Love was waiting for us to find it." In this book Patti also demonstrates a greater awareness of her mother's role in her father's life. She notes, "My father's nature has never lost its innocence, not because he is a stranger to betrayal or meanness but because he has chosen to look for the good. My mother patrolled the grounds, looking for dark intruders, banishing them if they encroached upon his light."[76]

Michael Reagan has at times been critical of his stepmother. He was clearly displeased with Mrs. Reagan's decision to sell the ranch, complaining that the rest of the family was not consulted. But Michael visited his father and stepmother regularly and was quoted as being concerned about his stepmother's health: "I worry that when Dad goes, Nancy won't be far behind because she lives and breathes for Dad."[77]

Ron, Jr., always a bit of a maverick, managed to stay out of the limelight while he worked as a freelance writer. At times he has criticized his mother's protectiveness. When Mrs. Reagan decided not to have her husband attend his eighty-fifth birthday celebration in 1996 for fear that he would embarrass himself, Ron and Michael both argued that she was being overly cautious. Ron was reported as rarely visiting his parents, but in a May 2003 interview said that he had seen his father in the previous month, and that he didn't seem to be suffering and was well cared for.[78]

As President Reagan's health declined, Nancy Reagan became more active politically. In the fall of 1994, she blasted Senate Republican candidate Oliver North, saying that he "has a great deal of trouble separating fact from fantasy" and that "he lied to my husband and about my husband."[79] North, of course, was one of the major participants in the Iran-contra affair, and Mrs. Reagan never forgave him for casting a shadow over the last few years of the Reagan presidency. Many observers of that close and bitterly fought campaign felt that Mrs. Reagan's intervention may have been the decisive factor in North's defeat. After the first lady's comments, Oliver North dropped six points in the polls. Patrick Buchanan, leader of the most conservative faction of the Republican Party and ally of Oliver North, acknowledged the first lady's impact when he stated, "We took a bullet in the back. We got a match on the bullet. It came from a lady's gun."[80] Campaigners for Charles Robb, North's opponent, immediately realized the impact of the former first lady's words and were described as doing high fives all the way to Richmond. A beaming Charles Robb said that "he wanted to thank the first lady for her assistance."[81]

In 1994, Mrs. Reagan felt free to candidly state her position on abortion, saying, "I don't believe in abortion. On the other hand, I believe in a woman's choice. That puts me somewhere in the middle, but I don't know what we call that."[82] Mrs. Reagan commented that she had previously withheld her view on abortion in deference to her husband. Just a month earlier, former first lady Barbara Bush had made her views public. Mrs. Bush stated that while she had some personal objections to abortion, she also believed that a woman should have the right to choose. Perhaps because both Nancy Reagan and Barbara Bush were *former* first ladies, their announcements were met with a collective yawn from both sides in the abortion battle.

Later that year, Mrs. Reagan appeared before a congressional committee to comment about the current progress of the war on drugs. While testifying, she fired off a few verbal rounds at the Clinton administration, saying, "How could we have forgotten so quickly? Why is it that we no longer hear the drumbeat of the condemnation against drugs from our leaders and our culture?"[83] Privately, members of the administration admitted that Mrs. Reagan's testimony was accurate. Although they had increased funding for the war on drugs, no one in the administration was visibly associated with the cause.

In 1996, Mrs. Reagan addressed the Republican National Convention in San Diego. Her appearance was preceded by a six-minute video tribute to President Reagan, who was missing his first GOP convention since 1964. After the video, the former first lady entered the hall to a three-minute standing ovation, and then said that she had a message from her husband: "Never, never, give up on America."[84] She spoke movingly to a very receptive crowd, many of whom considered her husband to be the greatest living American. Using one of Ronald Reagan's trademark expressions, Mrs. Reagan told the crowd, "I can tell you with certainty that he still sees the shining city on a hill."[85] She went on to speak briefly of her husband's battle against Alzheimer's disease (choking up partway through), and by the time she left the podium there were few dry eyes left in the convention hall.[86]

Since leaving Washington, Mrs. Reagan has been awarded a number of honors. On 16 May 2002 she received the Congressional Medal of Honor, Congress's highest civilian honor. Mrs. Reagan was recognized for her efforts to curb alcohol and drug abuse among the nation's youth. The former first lady was awarded the medal only two years after her husband, who was cited for restoring optimism to the nation and ending the cold war.[87] On 10 July 2002 Mrs. Reagan received the Presidential Medal of Freedom, the highest civilian honor that the country can bestow. In the ceremony, President George W. Bush praised her for her devotion to family and country, her "Just Say No" program, and her work on behalf of servicemen missing in action.[88] Mrs. Reagan has also attended many official events, such as the dedication of the George Bush Presidential Library and the christening and launching of the USS *Reagan,* a $4 billion aircraft carrier named after the former president.

More recently, Mrs. Reagan has demonstrated her awareness that former first ladies have a bully pulpit for life. Mrs. Reagan has used her pulpit to take on George W. Bush's administration over the issue of funding for fetal tissue research. In June 2001, Kenneth M. Duberstein and Michael Deaver hand-delivered a note from the former first lady to the White House, indicating Mrs. Reagan's support for research on embryonic stem cells in searching for a cure for Alzheimer's. The controversy over stem-cell research has to do with using aborted fetuses as a source for the needed stem cells. To obtain the cells, researchers must destroy fetal tissue, usually a five-day-old clump of cells known as balstocyst. Because of the destruction of fetal tissue, many right-to-life groups oppose the procedure. Those who saw the note paraphrased the first lady as saying, "My husband and I believe our legacy should be that no other family should have to go through what our family has been through."[89] President Bush acknowledged the letter, but gave no indication of his position on the research.

The following year Mrs. Reagan upped the pressure on the White House by privately speaking to the *New York Times*, in which she described her husband's condition as deteriorating and said that "a lot of time" was being "wasted" because of the limitations imposed by the Bush administration.[90] In February 2003, Mrs. Reagan pressed her case still more when she sent a letter to Senator Orrin Hatch of Utah in support of cloning for the purpose of medical research. To stress the symbolic nature of her announcement, the former first lady used her husband's ninety-second birthday to endorse Senator Hatch's proposed legislation. The Hatch Bill prohibits cloning for the purpose of creating a person, but would allow cloning to obtain human parts needed for research. The process is controversial because it also involves the destruction of an embryo, and is fiercely opposed by abortion foes. Mrs. Reagan's statement was the first time that she addressed the issue of cloning, which is strongly opposed by the Bush administration. In the letter, Mrs. Reagan made clear the reason for her more aggressive and public stance: "Orrin, there are so many diseases that can be cured, or at least helped, that we can't turn our back on this."[91]

Mrs. Reagan also used a tactic that worked well for her when she was first lady—working the phones. She has a long list of friends and was not shy about enlisting them in her cause. Soon former President Gerald Ford joined the list of those supporting stem-cell research, becoming the first living Republican ex-president to do so.[92]

While attending the 2004 Juvenile Diabetes Research Foundation dinner to accept their caregivers' award, Mrs. Reagan made her most impassioned plea yet for continued stem-cell research. The former first lady said, "Ronnie's long journey has finally taken him to a distant place where I can no longer reach him. Because of this, I'm determined to do whatever I can to save other families from this pain. I just don't see how we can turn our backs on this."[93]

Despite the difficulty of Mrs. Reagan's position, and the energy with which she has pursued this cause, there is a certain tragic irony to her situation, in that in March 1988 the Reagan administration imposed a temporary moratorium on federal funding of fetal tissue research pending an ethical, legal, and scientific study by the Human Fetal Tissue Transplantation Research Panel. After reviewing the panel's report, the advisory committee to the director of the National Institute of Health recommended lifting the moratorium. Despite this recommendation, in 1988 the Department of Health and Human Services extended the moratorium indefinitely.[94] In addition, President George W. Bush is on record as calling for appropriate legislation to protect the unborn from experimentation that does not benefit them directly.[95]

In Ronald Reagan's years of decline from Alzheimer's, Mrs. Reagan was her husband's primary caregiver. The former first lady had always placed a very high priority on her husband's needs, trying her utmost to make his life perfect. As time went by, his need for her assistance became increasingly acute, and no matter what she did, she could not ever make his life perfect again. The Reagans were fortunate in that their financial situation allowed Nancy more professional assistance than is available for many caregivers. The additional help enabled her to insist that her husband remain at home, rather than be institutionalized.[96] Even with professional assistance, however, Mrs. Reagan was reluctant to leave her husband. She only occasionally went out for lunch; most days she spent around their home, taking phone calls from friends, and rarely straying too far from her husband.

Mrs. Reagan was not spared the emotional toll that accompanies being the primary caregiver for an Alzheimer's patient. In *I Love You, Ronnie,* she gives the reader a glimpse into their lives, referring to Alzheimer's as "a truly long good-bye."[97] For a woman who was used to being her husband's supporting player, the feeling of helplessness must have been especially difficult to bear. The burden became greater as the disease progressed. In January 2001 the former president fell in the bedroom of his home and became permanently bedridden. His physical needs were met, but he lost the ability to communicate. Mrs. Reagan soon came to realize that he did not recognize her.[98]

Through it all, Nancy remained in contact with many of her and her husband's friends. Old friends such as Merv Griffin, Betsy Bloomingdale, and Charles Z. Wick have not abandoned her, and a few new friends were drawn into her circle. Charles Wick introduced Mrs. Reagan to author Dominick Dunne when Dunne was covering the O. J. Simpson trial. Mrs. Reagan got so caught up in the news coverage of the Simpson affair that once a week for ten months, Dunne personally briefed her on the trial's developments. Mrs. Reagan also grew close to Casey Ribicoff, the wife of former senator Abraham Ribicoff, who had also suffered from Alzheimer's disease.[99] Many of the former first lady's friends report that she has been dramatically changed by her experience with the illness. Things that once mattered a great deal to her—designer clothes and fine jewelry—became relatively unimportant.[100]

On 5 June 2004, Ronald Reagan died at his home in Bel Air, California. The immediate cause of death was pneumonia, which was complicated by his decade-long fight against Alzheimer's disease. Upon the president's death, Mrs. Reagan issued the following statement. "My family and I would like the world to know that President Ronald Reagan has passed away after ten years of Alzheimer's disease at 93 years of age. We appreciate everyone's prayers."[101] Mrs. Reagan was fortunate to have her daughter, Patti, and son, Ron, present when her husband died. Michael was en route, but arrived after his father died. According to the family, before the former president died, he gave his wife of fifty-two years one last present. As Patti Davis told *People* magazine, "At the last moment, when his breathing told us this was it, he opened his eyes and looked straight at my mother. Eyes that hadn't opened for days did, and they weren't chalky or vague. They were clear and blue and full of love, and then they closed with his last breath."[102] Mrs. Reagan broke down and later told her family, "It was the greatest gift he could have given me."[103]

Once the family was together, funeral plans began to emerge. After a small private ceremony, President Reagan lay in state in California. His casket was then flown back to Washington for the first state funeral for a president since the passing of President Lyndon Baines Johnson. The funeral included a procession along Pennsylvania Avenue, a public viewing in the Capitol rotunda, and a funeral service in the National Cathedral. Reagan's coffin was then flown back to California, where he was laid to rest in a horseshoe-shaped burial site at the Ronald Reagan Presidential Library. President Reagan himself had chosen the site, and Mrs. Reagan plans to be buried there as well.[104]

Nothing was left to chance in Mrs. Reagan's plans for her husband's funeral. The Military District of Washington, which oversees presidential funerals, first approached the Reagans about planning for their funeral in 1989. Their mandatory procedures dictated the general parameters of the state funeral, but many of the specific details were left to the Reagans. Eventually the written plan for the president's funeral exceeded 300 pages. Mrs. Reagan met twice yearly with a small group of former aides to revise the details, to make sure that everything went exactly right. Once it was time to organize the actual funeral, old Reagan hands, including Ken Khachigan, stepped forward to help with the details.[105]

Mrs. Reagan has always been a perfectionist. She planned her husband's funeral with the same attention to detail that she exhibited in her years in the White House. Before state dinners, the first lady often demanded rehearsals, complete with the identical dinner that would be prepared for visiting dignitaries. The dinner would be served days in advance to President and Mrs. Reagan. On particularly important occasions, such as the visit of the Prince and Princess of Wales, more than one rehearsal was required. Just as nothing was left to chance during state dinners at the White House, nothing was left to chance for her husband's funeral. Every moment was scripted, from the placement of the president's riding boots on the riderless horse accompanying his coffin procession, to the climbing of the stairs at the west wing of the rotunda, to the choice of the tenor who sang "Ave Maria" at the cathedral, to the liftoff of the plane to arrive in California in time for a sunset funeral. Mrs. Reagan had taken care of her husband for fifty-two years and as her friend Betsy Bloomingdale said, "she is doing her last thing for Ronnie. She is determined to get it right."[106] She was doing what she had always done, showing absolute devotion to her husband. As Mrs. Reagan herself remarked to Bob Colacello after his appearance on the *Today* show, "You were good, but you left out the most important word . . . Love. Please don't make me sound like some kind of master manipulator. Everything I did, I did for Ronnie."[107]

For Mrs. Reagan, one of the few heartening aspects of her husband's death was the way in which the Reagan children rallied around her. Patti was constantly at her mother's side, often holding her hand and consoling her in her grief. She wrote of her father in *Newsweek* magazine, "My father believed in cycles—the wheel of birth, and life, and death, constantly turning. My hand was tiny when he held it in his and led me to a blackened field weeks after a fire had burned part of our ranch. He showed me green shoots peeking out of the ashes. New life. I let go of his hand for too long, pushed it away, before finally grasping it again."[108] Ron Reagan, Jr., who had once told reporters that he had never had a real conversation with his father, spoke eloquently as his father was laid to rest: "Dad wrote: 'I now begin the journey that will lead me into the sunset of my life.' This evening he has finally arrived." Michael spoke of his father's advice on how to have a long and happy marriage: "You'll never get in trouble if you say I love you at least once a day."[109]

Throughout the ordeal, the eighty-two-year-old Mrs. Reagan's stamina was impressive. To mark the president's passing, she made a cross-country trip and attended four separate ceremonies over several days. While in Washington, the frail-looking Mrs. Reagan met with former members of her staff and received many visitors, including President George W. Bush, Margaret Thatcher, and Mikhail Gorbachev. Dressed in black, Mrs. Reagan rarely gave in to her grief, leaving many Americans with the image of her straightening the folds in the flag that covered her husband's casket, much like she used to straighten his tie or his collar. It was not until she arrived back in California that she finally succumbed to her grief at the graveside ceremony for her husband.

Though it is impossible to guess what lies ahead for the former first lady, some predictions seem likely. The harvesting of fetal tissue clearly is of concern to her. It seems likely that after a period of mourning, she will again take up this issue. In the meantime, Ron Reagan, Jr., has emerged as the most prominent member of the Reagan family backing stem-cell research. He appeared before the Democratic convention in the summer of 2004 to make a plea for support of such research. Although he promised a nonpolitical speech, he told delegates "there are those who would stand in the way of this remarkable future, would deny federal funding so crucial to basic research." He urged delegates to make a choice by casting a vote for stem cell research in November.[110]

Ron Reagan's speech was extremely well received within the convention hall, but he did have his critics. Richard Cohen applauded Reagan's conviction but wrote of his appearance at the Democratic convention, "He is not a well-known ethicist or medical researcher. He will be there just to stick it to the GOP and Bush and to suggest, as do the selfish when they would rather golf than attend a funeral, that they have the permission of the deceased. There is a term for this sort of thing. Grave robbery."[111] Ron, Jr. was also criticized by Michael Reagan, who argued that his brother just was being used by the Democrats. Michael went on to say that Ron, Jr., "is a typical liberal; he hates George Bush."[112]

The Reagans became an undercurrent in the 2004 presidential campaign. In his appearance at the Democratic convention, Ron, Jr., all but endorsed the Democratic presidential candidate, John Kerry. Michael spoke at the Republican convention and in his remarks both honored his father and rebuked his brother: "I am Michael Reagan, and I consider myself the luckiest man in the world. My mother and father and birth-mother were pro-life and pro-adoption. Because they were, my father made me a Reagan. I've come to honor my father, not to politicize him."[113] Much to the disappointment of the White House, Mrs. Reagan declined to appear at the Republican convention. However, after President Bush paid a visit to Mrs. Reagan at her Bel Air home, she endorsed him, issuing a statement expressing the hope that "everyone will join" in supporting the Bush campaign.[114]

Throughout her tenure as first lady, the press and public alike roundly criticized Mrs. Reagan's involvement in her husband's presidency. During her ten years of caring for President Reagan and especially during the week of the state funeral, attitudes toward Mrs. Reagan seemed to change. The obsessive manipulation that brought her so much criticism in the White House now seemed merely her way of protecting her husband. The praise for Mrs. Reagan nearly equaled that of her husband. An editorial in the *Boston Herald* read in part, "To a nation which did not always show kindness to her, Nancy Reagan was incredibly kind and generous this week. She cradled our grief and treasured our memories, and showed us that a beloved leader's loss could be borne, even by one who loved him most."[115] Former White House correspondent Danny Romine Powell, speaking for a generation of female writers, wrote "we—my female contemporaries and female members of the press—were unforgiving. Nancy wasn't the role model many of us wanted or needed in the 1980s. But she more than made up for it in the 1990s and I think she understood something that many of us are yet to learn: that love and devotion are not just sappy, sentimental greeting card words. Sometimes, those words empty the bedpan. Sometimes they hang in there until death do us part."[116]

The period in which Nancy Reagan was first lady was historically important in helping define that institution. While Mrs. Reagan was in the White House, a debate was carried out in the press and in the minds of the public as to the role of first ladies. Should they be vocal about issues and play a public role in their husband's administration, or should their primary role be to support their husband, host state dinners, and champion safe causes? That debate has, of course, not centered on Mrs. Reagan alone. However, her success as first lady has often been evaluated based on one's position in this debate.

Nancy Reagan's ranking among first ladies in history will doubtless rise considerably from her rating in the 1994 Sienna poll of first ladies. Then, Mrs. Reagan ranked next to last, just above Mary Todd Lincoln and below Florence Harding.[117] As awareness of Mrs. Reagan's involvement in both personnel and policy decisions grows, she will be perceived as a stronger and more influential figure. Ironically, she may also benefit from the worsening drug problem. The "just say no" approach may not be the solution, but Mrs. Reagan will be remembered as someone who spoke out vigorously against drug use. Former President Reagan's battle with Alzheimer's disease might also help Mrs. Reagan's image and thus her place in history. The picture of a loving caretaker—which, in fact, Mrs. Reagan always was to her husband—may come to overshadow the image of Queen Nancy.

Nancy Reagan will probably never reach the top echelon of first ladies, as she neither fundamentally changed the institution nor had a profound and lasting impact on the country. She does, however, belong in group next to the top. She was strong, forceful, and protective of her husband, President Reagan, and she was committed to making his presidency a success. If there were an Academy Award for best supporting first lady, Mrs. Reagan might not win, but she would surely be a strong contender.

INTRODUCTION

1. An exception would be Garry Wills, *Reagan's America: Innocents at Home* (New York: Doubleday and Co., 1987), who writes briefly but with great insight about the transfer of Mrs. Reagan's gifts and skills as an actress to the White House.

2. Laurence Leaner, *Make-Believe: The Story of Nancy and Ronald Reagan* (New York: Harper and Row, 1983), p. 28.

3. Wills, *Reagan's America*, p. 190.

4. On the topic of gender roles in the late 1940s and 1950s, see Eugenia Kaledin, *Mothers and More: American Women in the 1950s* (Boston: Twayne Publishers, 1984); Stephanie Coontz, *The Way We Never Were: American Families and the Nostalgia Trap* (New York: Basic Books, 1992); and Stephen Mintz and Susan B. Kellog, *Domestic Revolutions: A Social History of the American Family* (New York: Free Press, 1988).

5. Nancy Reagan with Bill Libby, *Nancy* (New York: William Morrow and Co., 1980) p. 21.

1. A SUPPORTING ACTOR COMES OF AGE

1. Surprisingly little material is available on the role of supporting/character actors. There are books describing the careers of various supporting/character actors—for example, Jordan R. Young, *Reel Characters: Great Movie Character Actors* (Beverly Hills: Past Time Publishing Company, 1986); and there are some excellent autobiographies of actors who have played supporting roles—for example, Hume Cronyn, *A Terrible Liar: A Memoir* (New York: William Morrow and Co., 1991); but most either discuss acting methods and techniques or provide overviews of the history of acting. There are, however, some publications that discuss the importance of supporting/character actors in film and theater, including Terrence Rafferty, "Who *Is* That Guy?" *Gentleman's Quarterly* 71, no. 8 (August 2001); Coral Andrews-Leslie, "Unsung Heroes: The Supporting Players," *Performing Arts and Entertainment in Canada* 34, no. 1 (Autumn 2002);

Noland Bell, "Character Actors," *The Projector Booth,* http://www.projector booth.com/topics/topic.asp?topic=29; and Jordan McKay, "Whereabouts Unknown," *Texas Monthly* 26, no. 11 (November 1998).

2. Rafferty, "Who *Is* That Guy?" p. 81.

3. Bell, "Character Actors."

4. Her date of birth is often given as 6 July 1923, but her birth certificate and high school and college records indicate the actual year of her birth to be 1921. The discrepancy arose when Nancy subtracted two years from her age on the paperwork for her MGM contract. Although Nancy was christened Anne Frances after her grandmothers, her mother soon nicknamed her Nancy. Anne Edwards, *The Reagans: Portrait of a Marriage* (New York: St. Martin's Press, 2003), p. 3. Nancy is an unusual nickname for Anne Frances, yet not even Mrs. Reagan seems to know why her mother chose it. Michael K. Deaver, *Nancy: An Intimate Portrait of My Years with Nancy Reagan* (New York: William Morrow and Co., 2004), p. 17.

5. Nancy Reagan with Bill Libby, *Nancy* (New York: William Morrow and Co., 1980), p. 21.

6. There are numerous accounts of the loneliness Nancy experienced while staying with the Galbraiths. For example, see Frances Spatz Leighton, *The Search for the Real Nancy Reagan* (New York: Macmillan Publishing Co., 1987), p. 7; and Laurence Leamer, *Make-Believe: The Story of Nancy and Ronald Reagan* (New York: Harper and Row, 1983), p. 26.

7. Nancy Reagan with William Novak, *My Turn: The Memoirs of Nancy Reagan* (New York: Random House, 1989), p. 71.

8. Carole Chandler Waldrop, *Presidents' Wives: The Lives of Forty-Four Women of Strength* (Jefferson, N.C.: McFarland and Co., 1989), p. 363. The impression obviously stuck with Mrs. Reagan, as she also mentions it (in less detail) in *My Turn,* p. 71.

9. Reagan, *Nancy,* p. 23.

10. Bob Colacello, *Ronnie and Nancy: Their Path to the White House, 1911 to 1980* (New York: Warner Books, 2004), p. 48.

11. Leighton, *The Search for the Real Nancy Reagan,* p. 8.

12. Garry Wills, *Reagan's America: Innocents at Home* (New York: Doubleday and Co., 1987), pp. 182–83.

13. Reagan, *Nancy,* p. 27.

14. Leighton, *The Search for the Real Nancy Reagan,* p. 17.

15. Ibid., pp. 12–14.

16. Leamer, *Make-Believe,* p. 36.

17. Ibid.

18. Program, *First Lady,* author's collection.

19. Leamer, *Make-Believe,* pp. 44–53.

20. The life and work of Hallie Flanagan Davis are discussed in a number of sources. Among the most significant are Pauline Hahn, "Hallie Flanagan: Practical Visionary," in Helen Krich Chinoy and Linda Walsh Jenkins, eds., *Women in American Theatre* (New York: Theatre Communications Group, 1987); and Rachel A. France, ed., *A Century of Plays by American Women* (New York: Richards Rosen Press, 1979). For Hallie Flanagan Davis's impact on Nancy Reagan, see Leamer, *Make-Believe,* pp. 52–53.

21. Leamer, *Make-Believe,* p. 50.

22. Ibid., p. 51.

23. Paul Boller, Jr., *Presidential Wives* (New York: Oxford University Press, 1999), p. 453.

24. Leighton, *The Search for the Real Nancy Reagan,* p. 28.

25. Both ibid. and Wills, *Reagan's America,* p. 182, discuss the importance of Nancy's connections in her securing the MGM contract. Others, including Edmund Morris, suggest that Nancy received her screen test as repayment to her father for medical favors; see Edmund Morris, *Dutch: A Memoir of Ronald Reagan* (New York: Random House, 1999), p. 280.

26. Weiler and Shearer quoted in James G. Benze, Jr., "Nancy (Anne Frances Robbins Davis) Reagan," in Lewis L. Gould, ed., *American First Ladies: Their Lives and Their Legacy,* 2nd ed. (New York: Routledge Press, 2001), p. 395.

27. Leamer, *Make-Believe,* p. 158.

28. Quoted in ibid., p. 65.

29. Reagan, *Nancy,* p. 90.

30. Wills, *Reagan's America,* pp. 187–88, discusses the significance of Nancy Reagan's eyes for both her acting and her political career. He concludes that her eyes were her best physical asset.

31. Quoted in Lou Cannon, *Governor Reagan: His Rise to Power* (Boulder: Perseus Books, 2003), pp. 75–76.

32. Ronald Reagan with Richard G. Hubler, *Where's the Rest of Me?* (New York: Duell, Sloan and Pearce, 1965), pp. 233–35; and Reagan, *My Turn,* pp. 94–95.

33. In fact, some authors note that the Reagans probably met at a dinner party several weeks earlier: see Morris, *Dutch,* pp. 280–81, and Boller, *Presidential Wives,* p. 455. Given Nancy's insistence that they meet for dinner, it's likely that she was more interested in their meeting than was her future husband.

34. Leamer, *Make-Believe*, pp. 133–51.

35. Ibid., p. 147.

36. Reagan biographer Lou Cannon describes his aloofness and its effect on his relationship with Mrs. Reagan. Cannon, *Governor Reagan*, pp. 76–81.

37. Reagan, *Nancy,* p. 107.

38. Morris, *Dutch,* p. 596.

39. Quoted in Bob Colacello, "Ronnie and Nancy," *Vanity Fair,* August 2004, p. 222.

40. Morris, *Dutch,* p. 292.

41. Quoted in Leamer, *Make-Believe,* p. 158.

42. Tichi Wilkerson, *Hollywood Reporter: The Golden Years* (New York: Coward-McCann, 1984), p. 240.

43. Mrs. Reagan is not shy in admitting that Patti was conceived out of wedlock. In her biography, she encourages the reader to "go ahead" and count the weeks between her wedding and Patti's birth: Reagan, *My Turn,* p. 103.

44. Ibid., p. 98.

45. Leamer, *Make-Believe,* p. 160.

46. Mrs. Reagan has admitted that while her husband's persistent optimism is one of his best features, it can sometimes be wearing to live with someone who is so relentlessly upbeat. Reagan, *My Turn,* p. 98.

47. Ibid., p. 125.

48. Although President Reagan was truly an optimist, like most people he had his moments of doubt—for example, after the first 1984 presidential debate. It was during times like these that Mrs. Reagan would intervene to lift his spirits.

49. Leamer, *Make-Believe,* p. 185.

50. Quoted in Anne Edwards, *The Reagans,* p. 49.

51. Leamer, *Make-Believe,* p. 173.

52. Ibid.

53. Ibid., p. 181.

54. Morris, *Dutch,* p. 596.

55. Edwards, *The Reagans,* p. 65.

56. Reagan, *My Turn,* p. 128.

57. Ronnie Dugger, *On Reagan: The Man and His Presidency* (New York: McGraw-Hill Book Co., 1983), p. 12.

58. Ibid., pp. 15–16.

59. Bill Adler, *Ronnie and Nancy: A Very Special Love Story* (New York: Crown Publishers, 1985), p. 118.

60. Ibid., p. 119.

61. Morris, *Dutch*, pp. 331–33.

62. Reagan, *My Turn*, p. 121.

63. Ibid., p. 124.

64. Ibid., p. 133.

65. Ibid.

66. Leamer, *Make-Believe*, p. 198.

67. "Field Poll Record in Measuring Candidate Election Trends," http://field.com/fieldpoll/candidates.html.

68. Leamer, *Make-Believe*, p. 208.

69. Cannon, *Governor Reagan*, p. 237.

70. Deaver, *Nancy*, p. 15.

71. Lou Cannon, *Reagan* (New York: G. P. Putnam and Sons, 1982), p. 144.

72. Quoted in Adler, *Ronnie and Nancy*, p. 134.

73. Edwards, *The Reagans: Portrait of a Marriage*, p. 104.

74. Brown quoted in Adler, *Ronnie and Nancy*, p. 129.

75. Deaver, *Nancy*, p. 51.

76. Lou Cannon, *President Reagan: The Role of a Lifetime* (New York: Simon and Schuster, 1991), p. 504.

77. Leighton, *The Search for the Real Nancy Reagan*, p. 104.

78. Wills, *Reagan's America*, p. 188,

79. Reagan, *Nancy*, p. 57. Also quoted in Wills, *Reagan's America*, p. 187.

80. Deaver, *Nancy*, p. 56

81. Joan Didion, "Pretty Nancy," *Saturday Evening Post*, 1 June 1968, p. 20.

82. Mrs. Reagan was so upset by the way she was portrayed that years later, when writing her autobiography, she cited the interview as the first of many examples of how she was treated unfairly by the press. Reagan, *My Turn*, p. 34.

83. Kitty Kelley, *Nancy Reagan: The Unauthorized Biography* (New York: Simon and Schuster, 1991), p. 162.

84. Leighton, *The Search for the Real Nancy Reagan*, p. 115.

85. Office of the First Lady's Press Secretary, "The Foster Grandparent Program—Dear to the Heart of Nancy Reagan," 10 Nov. 1981, p. 1, author's collection.

86. Ibid., p. 3.

87. In his autobiography, Ronald Reagan insists that his only goal in 1968 was to gather enough support as a favorite son candidate to keep Nixon from gaining the Republican nomination. Ronald Reagan, *An American Life* (New York: Simon and Schuster, 1990), pp. 176–78.

88. Steven Hayward, *The Age of Reagan: The Fall of the Liberal Order, 1964–1980* (Roseville, Calif.: Prima Books, 2001), p. 380.

89. Leighton, *The Search for the Real Nancy Reagan*, p. 136.

90. Reagan, *My Turn*, p. 179.

91. Leamer, *Make-Believe*, p. 250.

92. Nofziger convinced Governor Reagan that his chief of staff was a leader of a homosexual ring and that he should be fired. The dismissal ultimately came back to haunt both the governor and Nofziger when columnist Drew Pearson broke the story, which led to speculation as to whether Reagan could survive the scandal of a homosexual ring operating out of the governor's office. Colacello, *Ronnie and Nancy: Their Path*, p. 366.

93. Wills, *Reagan's America*, pp. 302–3.

94. Leamer, *Make-Believe*, p. 251.

95. Dugger, *On Reagan*, p. 21.

96. Adler, *Ronnie and Nancy*, p. 150.

97. Cannon, *President Reagan*, p. 68.

98. Leighton, *The Search for the Real Nancy Reagan*, p. 278.

99. Quoted in Leamer, *Make-Believe*, p. 273.

2. LEARNING THE ROLE OF FIRST LADY

1. Michael K. Deaver with Mickey Herskowitz, *Behind the Scenes* (New York: William Morrow and Co., 1987), p. 111.

2. Anne Edwards, *The Reagans: Portrait of a Marriage* (New York: St. Martin's Press, 2003), p. 165. Mrs. Reagan's press secretary, Robin Orr, denied that Mrs. Reagan had suggested that the Carters move out early, although Mrs. Reagan's designer was anxious to get started on redecorating as soon as possible. "Mrs. Reagan Said to Drop a Gentle Hint," *New York Times*, 13 Dec. 1980, p. 12. The reaction of the Carter camp comes from an interview with Mary Hoyt, Mrs. Carter's press secretary, conducted on 7 Aug. 2004.

3. In her memoirs, Mrs. Reagan even claims that when they eventually moved in, they found soda cans and half-eaten sandwiches in the drawers of White House desks. Nancy Reagan with William Novak, *My Turn: The Memoirs of Nancy Reagan* (New York: Random House, 1989), p. 24.

4. Enid Nemy, "Word from Friends: A New White House Style Is on the Way," *New York Times*, 9 Nov. 1980, p. 80.

5. Interview with Mary Hoyt, 7 Aug. 2004.

6. Reagan, *My Turn*, p. 228.

7. Carl Sferrazza Anthony, *First Ladies,* vol. 2 (New York: William Morrow and Co., 1990), p. 357.

8. James S. Rosebush, *First Lady, Public Wife: A Behind-the-Scenes History of the Evolving Role of First Ladies in American Political Life* (Lanham, Md.: Madison Books, 1988), p. 35.

9. Carla Hall and Donnie Radcliffe, "Lenore Annenberg Named Protocol Chief," *Washington Post,* 12 Feb. 1981, p. F1.

10. Elisabeth Bumiller, "The First Lady's First Lady: As a Firm Voice from the East Wing, Sheila Tate Helps Remold an Image," *Washington Post,* 24 Oct. 1983, p. C1.

11. Ibid.

12. Ibid.

13. Interview with Sheila Tate, 12 July 2004.

14. Laurence Leamer, *Make-Believe: The Story of Nancy and Ronald Reagan* (New York: Harper and Row, 1983), p. 332.

15. Ibid.

16. Barbara Gamarekian, "Smoothing Mrs. Reagan's Way into the White House," *New York Times.* 5 Dec. 1980, p. B12.

17. Sara Fitzgerald and T. R. Reid, "Women's Rep," *Washington Post,* 10 Sept. 1981, p. A25.

18. Donnie Radcliffe, "Social Secretary Selected; Linda Faulkner to Rejoin Reagans," *Washington Post,* 12 July 1985, p. D1.

19. Steven V. Roberts, "Twilight Light for the 'Day One' Loyalists," *New York Times,* 6 Dec. 1988, p. 14.

20. Ibid.

21. Rosebush, *First Lady, Public Wife,* p. 33.

22. Anthony, *First Ladies,* p. 356.

23. Eric Schmertz, Natalie Datlof, and Alexej Ugrinsky, eds., *Ronald Reagan's America,* vol. 2 (Westport, Conn.: Greenwood Press, 1997), p. 680.

24. Interview with James Rosebush, 17 June 2004.

25. Interview with Sheila Tate, 12 July 2004.

26. Mary Battiata, "Reagan Maid Cleared in Smuggling Case; Return to White House Expected," *Washington Post,* 4 Nov. 1986, p. A1.

27. Quoted in Lynn Darling, "A New Staff Director Waits in the Wings," *Washington Post,* 16 Aug. 1979, p. D1.

28. Rosebush, *First Lady, Public Wife,* p. 38.

29. Anthony, *First Ladies,* p. 357; and Darling, "A New Staff Director Waits in the Wings."

30. Interview with Sheila Tate, 12 July 2004.

31. Rosebush, *First Lady, Public Wife*, p. 38.

32. Office of the First Lady's Press Secretary, "The Foster Grandparent Program—Dear to the Heart of Nancy Reagan," 10 Nov. 1981, p. 3, author's collection.

33. Pauken quoted in Office of the First Lady's Press Secretary, "Mrs. Reagan's First Nine Months as First Lady," 8 Oct. 1981, p. 5, author's collection.

34. Memo, Peter J. Rusthoven to Fred F. Fielding, re Proposed Establishment of a Foster Grandparents Foundation, 15 Dec. 1982, Office of the First Lady, PJR/Nancy Reagan—Foster Grandparents Book, OA9978, Reagan Library, Simi Valley, California.

35. James G. Benze, Jr., "Nancy (Anne Frances Robbins Davis) Reagan," in Lewis L. Gould, ed., *American First Ladies: Their Lives and Their Legacy*, 2nd ed. (New York: Routledge Press, 2001), p. 400.

36. The expenses (some called them excesses) of the Reagan inauguration are enumerated in many sources. For example, see Frances Spatz Leighton, *The Search for the Real Nancy Reagan* (New York: Macmillan Publishing Co., 1987), pp. 192–93, and Anthony, *First Ladies*, p. 321.

37. Leamer, *Make-Believe*, p. 283.

38. Elisabeth Bumiller and Elizabeth Kastor, "Dinner Deluxe for the Duke; the Reagans Toast Luxembourg's Royalty," *Washington Post*, 14 Nov. 1984, p. D1.

39. Stephen B. Bauer with Frances Spatz Leighton, *At Ease at the White House: The Uninhibited Memoirs of a White House Aide* (New York: Carol Publishing Group, 1991), p. 265.

40. Jane O'Reilly, "And the Ladies of the Club," http://www.time.com/time/archive/preview/0.10987.951274.00.html.

41. Anthony, *First Ladies*, p. 329.

42. Leighton, *The Search for the Real Nancy Reagan*, p. 231. According to Sheila Tate, Mrs. Reagan's press secretary, the first lady knew that she would be criticized for redecorating the White House, but proceeded anyway because she felt it was needed. Interview with Sheila Tate, 12 July 2004.

43. Anthony, *First Ladies*, p. 324.

44. Leighton, *The Search for the Real Nancy Reagan*, p. 266.

45. Ibid.

46. Office of the First Lady's Press Secretary, "White House China—An Historical Perspective," 3 Feb. 1982, p. 1, author's collection.

47. E-mail correspondence with Sheila Tate, 16 Aug. 2004.

48. Transcript, *Deborah Norville Tonight*, 8 June 2004, http://msnbc.msn. com/id/5174205, p. 9. Tate feels that to this day, people still do not understand that the china was paid for with private, rather than public, funds. Interview with Sheila Tate, 12 July 2004.

49. Memo, Peter Roussell to James A. Baker III, China and Mrs. Reagan, 13 Oct. 1981, Canzeri Files, China Presentation Folder, CFOA 152, Reagan Library, Simi Valley, California.

50. Memo, Sheila Tate to Mrs. Reagan, re Unveiling the China, Canzeri Files, China Presentation Folder, CFOA 152. See also Memo, Sheila Tate via Joe Canzeri to Mike Deaver, re Unveiling the New China, Canzeri Files, China Presentation Folder, CFOA 152.

51. E-mail correspondence with Sheila Tate, 16 Aug. 2004.

52. "Breaking in the New White House China," Currents in the News, *U.S. News and World Report*, 15 Feb. 1982, p. 7.

53. Anthony, *First Ladies*, p. 351.

54. Lynn Langway et al., "Mrs. Reagan's Free Clothes," *Newsweek*, 1 Feb. 1982, p. 59.

55. Michael K. Deaver, *Nancy: An Intimate Portrait of My Years with Nancy Reagan* (New York: William Morrow and Co., 2004), p. 82.

56. Ethics in Government Act, Title I, http://www.house.gov/ethics/Ethics_in Government_Act_link_page. htm.

57. Langway et al., "Mrs. Reagan's Free Clothes," p. 59.

58. Cohen quoted in Nina Hyde, "The Great Clothes Furor," *Washington Post*, 22 Jan. 1982, p. C1.

59. Memo, Fred F. Fielding to Michael Deaver, re Winston offer, 8 Sept. 1981, Office of the First Lady, OA11421, Peter J. Rusthoven Files, Reagan Library, Simi Valley, California.

60. Ibid., p. 2.

61. Reagan, *My Turn*, p. 32.

62. David Bird and Dorothy J. Gaiter, "Despite Criticism, Nancy Reagan Ranks No. 1," *New York Times*, 24 Dec. 1981, p. C13.

63. Donnie Radcliffe and Kenneth E. John, "Down in the Polls: 23% Give Mrs. Reagan 'Unfavorable' Rating," *Washington Post*, 25 Nov. 1981, p. C1.

64. Lynn Rosellini, "The First Lady Tells Critics: 'I Am Just Being Myself,'" *New York Times*, 13 Oct. 1981, p. A20.

65. Quoted in memo from Ann Keagy, Chairman, Department of Fashion Design, Parsons School of Design, to Sheila Tate, Press Secretary to the First

Lady, 18 Feb. 1982, p. 3, author's collection. For the complete list of gowns to be donated, when they were worn, and who they were designed by, see "First Lady— Clothing Items to Be Donated to Museums," 16 Jan. 1982, Records, Mrs. Reagan, OA10872, Michael K. Deaver Files, Reagan Library, Simi Valley, California.

66. Quoted in Anthony, *First Ladies,* p. 343.

67. Cynthia Z. Rachlin, "The World of Nancy Reagan," *Newsweek,* 21 Dec. 1981, p. 25.

68. Bird and Gaiter, "Despite Criticism, Nancy Reagan Ranks No. 1," p. C13.

69. Memo from Ann Keagy to Sheila Tate, p. 1.

70. Langway et al., "Mrs. Reagan's Free Clothes," p. 59.

71. "Remarks for the Associated Press Publishers' Luncheon," Monday, May 4, 1987, Mrs. Reagan's 1987 Speeches, OA 18721, Office of the First Lady: Records, Projects, and Events, p. 3.

72. Lewis Gould, Foreword, in Mary Finch Hoyt, *East Wing: Politics, the Press, and a First Lady* (Philadelphia: Xlibris Corp., 2001), p. 8.

73. Tom Nicholson, "Echoes of a Day of Terror," *Newsweek,* 27 April 1981, p. 21.

74. Reagan, *My Turn,* pp. 4–5. According to Donald Regan, the same type of confusion existed at the White House, where cabinet members could not even agree who was in charge. According to Regan, in his book *For the Record: From Wall Street to Washington* (New York: Harcourt Brace Jovanovich, 1988), pp. 163–70, the major problem was that the administration had been in place for only seventy days and the president's men were new to their jobs and to each other. Therefore, until the Vice President returned to the White House, no one was sure who was in charge or how they should act. The confusion led to Secretary of State Alexander Haig's announcing on television that he was in control.

75. Anthony, *First Ladies,* p. 331.

76. Tony Schwartz, "TV Networks Quickly Supply Vivid Documentation of Assassination Attempt," *New York Times,* 31 March 1981, p. 6.

77. Ibid.

78. Fay Willey, "A Father-in-Law's Complaint," *Newsweek,* 4 May 1981, p. 21.

79. Nicholson, "Echoes of a Day of Terror," p. 21.

80. Fred Barnes, "The Remaking of Nancy Reagan," *The New Republic,* 16 and 23 Sept. 1985, pp. 16–21.

81. Ibid.

82. Reagan, *My Turn,* p. 42.

83. Although Sheila Tate is generally credited for the "Second Hand Rose" performance, she contends that the basic idea was hers but that Mrs. Reagan

also deserves some of the credit. She not only agreed to do the number, she also assembled her own "wardrobe" and practiced rigorously to get the routine down right. Interview with Sheila Tate, 12 July 2004.

84. Memorandum from Sheila Tate to East Wing Scheduling Committee regarding media interview requests, 29 Dec. 1981, Joseph Canzeri files, OFOA 152, Mrs. Reagan's File.

85. Memo from Sheila Tate to Ginny Frizzi, Collection PR016, Folder 054525–058799, Casefile, 056054, Box 2.

86. Mrs. Reagan was aware of the unusual nature of her relationship with Mrs. Graham, and years later, in eulogizing her friend, remarked, "I'm certain, over the years, someone has asked, 'Kay Graham and Nancy Reagan—friends?' After all, Kay owned the paper that wasn't very friendly to Republicans and I was the wife of a man who many thought could be the next Republican president. . . . I can't explain the magic or chemistry, but with great friendships, you don't try to figure them out, you simply enjoy them, because they are so rare in life." Special Report, "The Kay We Loved," *Newsweek,* 30 July 2001, p. 54.

87. In hindsight, some East Wing staffers thought that keeping the meetings closed was a mistake and contributed to the general perception that Mrs. Reagan was interested only in fabric swatches and china patterns. Interview with Sheila Tate, 12 July 2004.

88. For an idea of the many different approaches considered for Mrs. Reagan's antidrug campaign, see Memo, Ann Wrobleski to Mrs. Reagan, re Drugs/Alcohol 1981, 24 March 1981, Michael E. Baroody Files, Drugs/Alcohol, Mrs. Reagan, OA 11221, Reagan Library, Simi Valley, California. See also Briefing Outline, re Mrs. Reagan Drug Program, [n.d.]; and Memo, Ann to Sheila, re NDR Alcohol/Drug PSA's, 1981, 24 March 1981, Michael E. Baroody Files, Drugs/Alcohol, Mrs. Reagan, OA 11221, Reagan Library, Simi Valley, California.

89. Memo, Peter Roussel to Michael K. Deaver, re proposal, 2 Dec. 1981, Office of the First Lady: Project Office, Records 1981–89, OA 18721, Michael K. Deaver Files, Reagan Library, Simi Valley, California.

90. Memo, Sheila Tate to Joe Canzeri, re Peter Roussel's proposal, 8 Dec. 1981, Office of the First Lady: Project Office, Records 1981–89, OA 18721, Michael K. Deaver Files, Reagan Library, Simi Valley, California.

91. Barnes, "Remaking of Nancy Reagan," pp. 16–21.

92. Note, Ann Wrobleski to Joe Canzeri, re Drug Abuse, [n.d.], Joseph Canzeri Files, First Lady General, CTOA 152, Reagan Library, Simi Valley, California.

93. Edwards, *The Reagans,* p. 236.

94. Rosebush, *First Lady, Public Wife,* p. 89.

95. The White House Office of the First Lady's Press Secretary, "Drug and Alcohol Abuse: Mrs. Reagan's Genuine Concern," 10 Nov. 1981, pp. 1–3, author's collection.

96. "$45 Billion Yearly Drug Traffic Hits Main Street," *U.S. News and World Report,* 19 Feb. 1979, pp. 28–32.

97. The White House Office of the First Lady's Press Secretary, "Drug and Alcohol Abuse: Mrs. Reagan's Genuine Concern," p. 1.

98. "Drug Users—1 in 3 in U.S. Military," *U.S. News and World Report,* 29 June 1981, pp. 10–11.

99. Ibid.

100. Editorial, "The Drug Carnival," *Washington Post,* 10 Aug. 1981, p. A16.

101. "$45 Billion Yearly Drug Traffic Hits Main Street."

102. Elisabeth Bumiller, "Peter McCoy Moves On," *Washington Post,* 11 Dec. 1981, p. C14.

103. Cass Peterson and Pete Early, "Verstandig Expected to Get Liaison Post," *Washington Post,* 25 May 1983, p. A23.

104. In fact, James Rosebush and Sheila Tate were both instrumental in developing the "Second Hand Rose" routine and, together with Michael Deaver, felt that Mrs. Reagan's focus on drug abuse should emphasize children (lots of good visuals), not just government agencies. After all, one of the important goals of the project was to humanize the first lady. Edwards, *The Reagans,* p. 249. Rosebush feels that in addition to being successful on its own merits, Mrs. Reagan's "Just Say No" program did more to improve her relations with the press that any other single factor. Interview with James Rosebush, 17 June 2004.

105. Interview with James Rosebush, 17 June 2004.

106. Anthony, *First Ladies,* p. 345.

107. Enid Nemy, "First Lady Finds a Cause," *New York Times,* 19 Feb. 1982, p. B5. See also the discussion of Mrs. Reagan's trip in Anthony, *First Ladies,* p. 345. In thanking Ross Perot for his efforts, the first lady noted not just his financial contribution, but also his solicitation of funds from other corporate sponsors. Letter from Nancy Reagan to Ross Perot; re drug issue, 29 March 1981, WHORM: Alpha File, H. Ross Perot, Reagan Library, Simi Valley, California.

108. Edwards, *The Reagans,* p. 250. Edwards points out that there is no small irony in the phrase "Just say no," as no one in the Reagan White House ever said no to Mrs. Reagan. For a discussion of the "Drugs are dumb" phrase, see Memo, Sheila Tate to Michael Deaver and Jim Rosebush, re Mrs. Reagan's first trip concerning drugs, 2 Feb. 1982, Michael K. Deaver Files, Mrs. Reagan, OA 10872, Reagan Library, Simi Valley, California.

109. Anthony, *First Ladies,* p. 364.

110. Office of the First Lady's Press Secretary, "Remarks of the First Lady in Meeting with National Federation of Parents for Drug Free Youth," 9 Nov. 1981, p. 1, author's collection.

111. The White House Office of the First Lady's Press Secretary, "Summary of Mrs. Reagan's Activities against Drug and Alcohol Abuse," 31 March 1985, p. 1, author's collection.

112. White House Press Guide, "The First Ladies Conference on Drug Abuse," 24–25 April 1985, p. 2, author's collection.

113. Legal counsel assured the White House that such a fund could be established without violating existing laws or regulations, but cautioned that Mrs. Reagan should separate her role as first lady from the fund and that neither she nor the president should take governmental action on behalf of the fund. The question of who would legally control the funds after the first lady left office was not addressed. Memo, Ralph W. Tarr to Richard Hauser, re Charitable Fund, 27 Feb. 1982, H. Lawrence Garret Files, Office of Counsel to the President, Reagan Library, Simi Valley, California.

114. See, for example, the efforts of congressman Dennis Smith on behalf of White Oaks, an alcohol and drug treatment center. Memo, C. Christopher Cox, re Nancy Reagan Drug Abuse Fund, 5 Sept. 1986, Office of the First Lady, Records, OA 19256, Folder PMB Nancy Reagan Drug Abuse Foundation, Reagan Library, Simi Valley, California.

115. Peter Kerr, "The American Drug Problem Takes on Two Faces," *New York Times,* 10 July 1988, Section 4, p. 5.

116. Memo, Jack L. Courtemache, Review of Staff Meeting, 1986, Office of the First Lady, Records, OA 13637, Folder, "First Lady's Staff Meetings."

117. Barnes, "The Remaking of Nancy Reagan," pp. 19–20.

118. Rosebush, *First Lady, Public Wife,* p. 44.

119. Ibid.

120. So much so that by 1986, there would be serious discussion of naming a chair in medicine at the East Carolina University School of Medicine after Mrs. Reagan in honor of her crusade against drug abuse. Memo, C. Christopher Cox to Peter J. Wallinson, re Nancy Reagan Chair at East Carolina University School of Medicine, 21 Oct. 1986, First Lady: Various Matters, OAS 15526: Christopher C. Cox Files, Reagan Library, Simi Valley, California. That same year, the Dana Foundation, a private philanthropic foundation, provided Mrs. Reagan with an honorary award, which included a $50,000 donation to a drug abuse charity of her choice. "East Wing Staff Meeting with the First Lady," 29 Jan.

1986, Office of the First Lady, Records OA 13637, Folder "East Wing Staff Meeting," Reagan Library, Simi Valley, California.

121. Garry Wills, *Reagan's America: Innocents at Home* (New York: Doubleday and Co., 1987), pp. 187–90, provides an excellent analysis of Mrs. Reagan's use of acting techniques.

122. Jane Mayer and Doyle McManus, *Landslide: The Unmaking of the President, 1984–1988* (Boston: Houghton Mifflin, 1988), pp. 35–36.

123. Memo from Muffie Brandon to George Stevens and Ann Wrobleski, 10 Dec. 1982, Mabel Brandon, OA 7176, Mrs. Reagan Taping for NBC Special—10 Dec. Blue Room, 2:30 p.m., Reagan Library, Simi Valley, California.

3. NANCY REAGAN, CASTING DIRECTOR

1. Mrs. Reagan never had any formal experience as a casting director. However, given her familiarity with stage and screen, she certainly realized the importance of having a good cast and knew that getting the right players into position did not just happen, whether in the theater, the movies, or in a Presidential administration; and Mrs. Reagan was willing to take the necessary steps to ensure that her husband had the supporting cast he needed.

2. Garry Wills, *Reagan's America: Innocents at Home* (New York: Doubleday and Co., 1987), p. 192.

3. Ibid., p. 195.

4. Michael K. Deaver with Mickey Herskowitz, *Behind the Scenes* (New York: William Morrow and Co., 1987), p. 39. To emphasize his point, Deaver goes on to say that "if Ronald Reagan had owned a shoe store, Nancy would have been pushing shoes and working the register. And she would have been happy" (p. 115).

5. Stewart quoted in Jane Mayer and Doyle McManus, *Landslide: The Unmaking of the President, 1984–1988* (Boston: Houghton Mifflin, 1988), p. 8.

6. Helene Von Damm, *At Reagan's Side* (New York: Doubleday and Co., 1989), p. 227.

7. Ronald Brownstein and Nina Easton, *Reagan's Ruling Class: Portraits of the President's Top 100 Officials* (Washington, D.C.: Presidential Accountability Group, 1982), p. 645.

8. Ibid., p. 649.

9. Quoted in Carl Sferrazza Anthony, *First Ladies*, vol. 2 (New York: William Morrow and Co., 1990), p. 319.

10. Ibid.

11. Von Damm, *At Reagan's Side*, p. 260. Mrs. Reagan did not win all of her personnel battles. She tried for years to get Caspar Weinberger removed from the Department of Defense, but never succeeded. Lou Cannon, "A Protector, Not Policymaker," *New York Times,* 9 March 1987, p. A2. According to Donald Regan, she also wanted William Casey, head of the Central Intelligence Agency, removed (even though he was terminally ill) because of his involvement in Iran-contra. However, his illness, rather than Mrs. Reagan's influence, was what finally forced Casey to step down. Donald Regan, *For the Record: From Wall Street to Washington* (New York: Harcourt Brace Jovanovich, 1988), pp. 66–67.

12. Von Damm, *At Reagan's Side*, p. 233.

13. Bob Schieffer and Gary Gates, *The Acting President* (New York: Dutton, 1989), p. 192.

14. Nancy Reagan with William Novak, *My Turn: The Memoirs of Nancy Reagan* (New York: Random House, 1989), pp. 242–43.

15. Ibid., p. 243. According to James Rosebush, that was quite a compliment: Mrs. Reagan rarely took anyone's word about the weather; she preferred to check herself. Interview with James Rosebush, 17 June 2004.

16. Quoted in Schieffer and Gates, *The Acting President,* pp. 49–50.

17. Shultz quoted in William E. Pemberton, *Exit with Honor: The Life and Presidency of Ronald Reagan* (New York: M. E. Sharpe, 1998), p. 164.

18. Edwin Meese III, *With Reagan: The Inside Story* (Washington, D.C.: Regnery Publishing, 1992), pp. 111–14.

19. Reagan quoted in Mayer and McManus, *Landslide,* p. 60.

20. Wrek quoted in Anthony, *First Ladies,* p. 355.

21. Anne Edwards, *The Reagans: Portrait of a Marriage* (New York: St. Martin's Press, 2003), p. 281.

22. Anthony, *First Ladies,* p. 376.

23. Ibid., p. 355.

24. The "Morning in America" tag line became the theme for the television advertising campaign used by the Reagan campaign in 1984. The ad campaign was structured around a song by Lee Greenwood, "God Bless the USA," and showed "houses built, flags raised, couples married, flags raised, autos purchased, and more flags raised." Kathleen Hall Jamieson, *Packaging the Presidency: A History and Criticism of Presidential Campaign Advertising,* 2nd ed. (New York: Oxford University Press, 1992), p. 449.

25. Lou Cannon, *President Reagan: The Role of a Lifetime* (New York: Simon and Schuster, 1991), p. 343.

26. The first lady was aware of her husband's limitations as a debater, but thought that those who coached him should also have been aware of them and should have taken them into account in preparing him for the debates. Ibid.

27. Wills, *Reagan's America,* p. 195.

28. Paul Boller, Jr., *Presidential Wives* (New York: Oxford University Press, 1988), p. 469.

29. Jamieson, *Packaging the Presidency,* p. 456.

30. Wills, *Reagan's America,* p. 192.

31. Ibid.

32. Marlin Fitzwater, *Call the Briefing!* (New York: Random House, 1995), p. 140.

33. Anthony, *First Ladies,* pp. 368–69.

34. Mayer and McManus, *Landslide,* p. 22.

35. Ibid.

36. Mrs. Reagan was a devoted follower of polls (much more so than her husband). She kept in close consultation with Richard Wirthlin, the president's pollster, especially through the 1984 election.

37. Schieffer and Gates, *The Acting President,* p. 279.

38. Ibid.

39. Anthony, *First Ladies,* p. 385.

40. Quoted in Cannon, *President Reagan,* p. 567.

41. Quoted in Schieffer and Gates, *The Acting President,* p. 279.

42. Regan, *For the Record,* p. 292.

43. Schieffer and Gates, *The Acting President,* p. 298.

44. Regan, *For the Record,* p. 291.

45. In fairness to Michael Deaver, who himself assumes all the blame for the fiasco, there were mitigating circumstances. The German government was asked if anything at the cemetery might embarrass the president, and their response was no. In addition, when the White House advance team inspected the cemetery, they literally could not see the problem—because of snow covering the tombstones. Deaver, *Behind the Scenes,* pp. 180–81.

46. Reagan quoted in ibid., p. 184.

47. Ibid.

48. Deaver suggests that the best way to "handle" the first lady in such circumstances was simply to admit you had made a mistake and were trying to fix things. Unless something catastrophic happened to the president, Mrs. Reagan would overlook your mistake—but she would never forget it. Ibid., pp. 183–84.

49. At the time, few within the administration fully appreciated the role that Deaver played as the first lady's handler. As Schieffer and Gates, *The Acting President,* pp. 93–95, point out, every minute the first lady was on the phone with Deaver meant a minute she was not on the phone with someone else.

50. Mayer and McManus, *Landslide,* p. 617.

51. Ibid.

52. Reagan, *My Turn,* p. 314.

53. Mayer and McManus, *Landslide,* p. 619.

54. Regan, *For the Record,* pp. 366–69. Regan was so upset by the process that led to his dismissal that his book's final chapter dealing with his resignation is entitled "A Public Burning."

55. Edwards, *The Reagans,* p. 274.

56. Quoted in Mayer and McManus, *Landslide,* p. 619. There are numerous accounts of the meeting and, although the exact wording varies, they are very close in tone. For example, see also Edwards, *The Reagans,* p. 322, and Cannon, *President Reagan,* p. 722.

57. Schieffer and Gates, *The Acting President,* p. 300.

58. Ibid.

59. David Hoffman and David Broder, "Outside Advisers Urge Reagan to Act on Crisis; Ability to Govern Effectively Said at Risk," *Washington Post,* 12 Dec. 1986, p. A1.

60. Schieffer and Gates, *The Acting President,* p. 301.

61. Donnie Radcliffe, "Nancy Reagan's Private Obsession: A Tenacious Struggle to Oust Donald Regan from the President's Team," *Washington Post,* 27 Feb. 1987, p. C1.

62. Anthony, *First Ladies,* p. 397.

63. Quoted in ibid., p. 399.

64. Regan's rationalization was soon recognized as such, and he was heavily criticized not only for Iran-contra, but also for his attempt to escape blame.

65. Regan, *For the Record,* p. 364.

66. Although the East Wing maintained that the story's leak was accidental, others in the administration didn't see things the same way. Marlin Fitzwater, President Reagan's deputy press secretary, viewed the leaking of Regan's resignation as a classic effort to "seal the deal" so that the resignation could not be rescinded. Fitzwater, *Call the Briefing!,* pp. 167–69.

67. Mayer and McManus, *Landslide,* p. 380.

68. Anthony, *First Ladies,* p. 400.

69. Mayer and McManus, *Landslide,* p. 387.

70. By this time, staff members had learned to dread Mrs. Reagan's phone calls. Larry Speakes told Marlin Fitzwater when he went to Camp David for the first time as the president's deputy press secretary that a successful weekend would be one in which Mrs. Reagan never learned Speakes's name. Fitzwater, *Call the Briefing!,* pp. 167–69.

71. Mayer and McManus, *Landslide,* p. 387.

72. William Safire, "The First Lady Stages a Coup," *New York Times,* 2 March 1987, p. A17.

73. Bernard Weinraub, "Nancy Reagan's Power Is Considered at Peak," *New York Times,* 3 March 1987, p. A1.

74. Richardson quoted in Amy Wilentz, "Just Say GoodBye, Don," *Time,* 9 March 1987, p. 30.

75. Joseph C. Hersch, "In Defense of Nancy Reagan," *Christian Science Monitor,* 17 March 1987, p. 15.

76. Anna Quindlen, "In Praise of Nancy Reagan's Drive," *New York Times,* 11 March 1987, p. 22.

77. Nancy Reynolds, "In Defense of Mrs. Reagan," *New York Times,* 5 March 1987, p. 27.

78. This is the position taken by James Rosebush, Mrs. Reagan's chief of staff, in a phone interview. Rosebush suggested that in many ways Mrs. Reagan was more successful in promoting individuals (such as James Baker and George Shultz) than in having individuals demoted. James Rosebush interview, 17 June 2004.

4. LIVING UNDER THE LIGHTS

1. Betty Boyd Caroli, *First Ladies* (New York: Oxford University Press, 1987), details the rise of the first lady as celebrity during the late 1800s with the growth of mass media (pp. 84–166) and explains that by the 1920s, first ladies such as Florence Harding were involved in the "intentional management" of the press (p. 163).

2. Harold W. Stanley and Richard G. Niemi, *Vital Statistics on American Politics* (Washington, D.C.: Congressional Quarterly, 1994), pp. 53–79.

3. James McGregor Burns et al., *Government by the People* (Upper Saddle River, N.J.: Prentice Hall, 2000), pp. 321–22.

4. Ethan Mordden, *The Hollywood Studios* (New York: Alfred A. Knopf, 1988), p. 136.

5. Lou Cannon, *Governor Reagan* (New York: Public Affairs, 2003), p. 236. Michael Deaver, in *Behind the Scenes* (New York: William Morrow, 1987), p. 109, also notes Mrs. Reagan's thin skin while first lady of California, suggesting that

even Lou Cannon's description of her as "formidable" was remembered even years later.

6. Nancy Reagan with William Novak, *My Turn: The Memoirs of Nancy Reagan* (New York: Random House, 1989), p. 56.

7. Ibid., p. 338.

8. Ibid., p. 364.

9. Carl Sferrazza Anthony, *First Ladies,* vol. 2 (New York: William Morrow and Co., 1990), p. 347.

10. Anne Edwards, *The Reagans,* pp. 269–70.

11. Lou Cannon, *Reagan* (New York: G. P. Putnam and Sons, 1982), p. 144.

12. Reagan, *My Turn,* p. 74.

13. Cannon, *Reagan,* p. 142.

14. The two would later settle their differences, and Mrs. Reagan would be able to rely on her stepbrother's support during the president's illnesses and her own bout with breast cancer. Edwards, *The Reagans,* p. 271.

15. Ronnie Dugger, *On Reagan: The Man and His Presidency* (New York: McGraw-Hill Book Co., 1983), p. 12.

16. Michael K. Deaver with Mickey Herskowitz, *Behind the Scenes* (New York: William Morrow and Co., 1987), pp. 13–14.

17. Reagan, *My Turn,* p. 56.

18. Michael Deaver, *Nancy: A Portrait of My Years with Nancy Reagan* (New York: William Morrow and Co., 2004), p. 70.

19. Maureen Reagan, *First Father, First Daughter* (Boston: Little, Brown and Co., 1989), pp. 95–97, and Michael Reagan with Joe Hymans, *Michael Reagan: On the Outside Looking In* (New York: Kensington Publishing Corp., 1988), pp. 74–77.

20. Donnie Radcliffe, "Michael Reagan: 'It's Been Tough to Connect,'" *Washington Post,* 28 Oct. 1984, p. K6.

21. Reagan, *My Turn,* p. 148.

22. Stephanie Mansfield, "Reagan's Son Asks Apology; 'Hurt and Stunned' by First Lady, Michael Says," *Washington Post,* 23 Nov. 1984, p. C1. See also Michael Reagan, *Michael Reagan,* p. 244.

23. Michael Reagan, *Michael Reagan,* p. 244.

24. Ibid.

25. Ibid., pp. 43–45.

26. In 1976, after Ronald Reagan won the Republican California primary, Ron, Jr., and Patti, neither of whom had campaigned, were invited into their father's waiting room, while the campaign staff made Maureen, Michael, and

Michael's wife wait outside. In 1980, Michael campaigned for his father for months before his father was even aware of Michael's efforts on his behalf.

27. At the time, both Michael and Maureen were feuding with Michael Deaver, who they felt wanted them involved in the campaign, but kept in the background, out of the media's sight (Edwards, *The Reagans*, p. 326). However, it was Deaver who arranged a reconciliation between Michael and his parents at the second inauguration. Deaver was motivated primarily by the thought that it would be good for the president's image (Edwards, *The Reagans*, p. 298).

28. Michael Reagan, *Michael Reagan*, pp. 41–48.

29. Maureen Reagan, *First Father, First Daughter*, pp. 90–94.

30. Reagan, *My Turn*, pp. 149–50.

31. Maureen Reagan, *First Father, First Daughter*, p. 382.

32. According to Maureen Reagan, *Newsweek* seemed particularly anxious to interpret the president's response in this fashion, and even suggested that a rift in the family had been opened as a result of Maureen's campaign and her father's reaction. Maureen felt strongly that her old staff nemesis, Michael Deaver, was the likely source of the *Newsweek* story. Reagan, *First Father, First Daughter*, p. 383.

33. Reagan, *My Turn*, p. 177.

34. Copy of letter sent from Nancy Reagan to W. Ernest Minor, 14 July 1987, author's collection.

35. Elisabeth Bumiller, "Keeping on His Toes: Warm Words and Presidential Pride at Ron Reagan Jr.'s Met Debut," *Washington Post*, 16 March 1981, p. C1.

36. Carole Krucoff, "Stepping Out: Tight Security among the President's People," *Washington Post*, 19 May 1981, p. C1.

37. Ibid.

38. According to Mrs. Reagan, Ron, Jr., and his wife, Doria, were married the same day that they applied for a marriage license in order to avoid the mob scene that was sure to accompany a public wedding. Reagan, *My Turn*, p. 174.

39. Reagan, *My Turn*, p. 161.

40. Merle Rubin, "Typical First Novel from an Atypical Writer: Home Front," *Christian Science Monitor*, 3 April 1986, p. 24.

41. Patti Davis, *The Way I See It* (New York: G. P. Putnam's Sons, 1992), pp. 40–41.

42. 1980 Acceptance Speech at the Republican Convention, http://www. nationalcenter.org/ReaganConvention1980.html. The language used was vintage Reagan, and was largely his own: he sat down with a few notes from Ken

Khachigian, one of his favorite speechwriters, and wrote the address out in longhand. David Gergen, *Eyewitness to Power: The Essence of Leadership: Nixon to Clinton* (New York: Simon and Schuster, 2001), p. 236.

43. Judith Mann, "When It Comes to Living Out Family Values," *Washington Post,* 27 July 1988, p. B3.

44. Thomas quoted in Conconi, "More on the Reagan Squabbles," *Washington Post,* 3 Dec. 1984, p. C3.

45. Donnie Radcliffe, "The Dark Year of Nancy Reagan: Cancer Surgery, Her Mother's Death, Estrangement from Patti—The First Lady Looks Back," *Washington Post,* 4 Dec. 1987, p. D1.

46. Larry Speakes, "Memorandum for Donald T. Regan; Attachment—Press Briefing on the President's Health," 6 Aug. 1985, p. 16, Collection, PR016-04, Folder 264872–367000, Case file, 354610, Reagan Library, Simi Valley, California. See also Anthony, *First Ladies,* pp. 384–388, for an overview of Mrs. Reagan's role during her husband's illnesses.

47. Donald Regan, *For the Record: From Wall Street to Washington* (New York: Harcourt Brace Jovanovich, 1988), p. 68.

48. Radcliffe, "The Dark Year of Nancy Reagan," p. D1.

49. Edwards, *The Reagans,* p. 326.

50. Reagan, *First Father, First Daughter,* p. 383.

51. Gina Kolata, "Mastectomy Seen as Extreme for Small Tumor," *New York Times,* 18 Oct. 1987, p. 1.

52. Lawrence K. Altman, "Surgeons Remove Cancerous Breast of Nancy Reagan," *New York Times,* 18 Oct. 1987, p. 1.

53. Reagan, *My Turn,* pp. 287–88.

54. Nora Underwood and Larry Black, "Nature against Cancer," *Maclean's,* 2. Nov. 1987, p. 60.

55. Ibid.

56. Reagan, *My Turn,* p. 302.

57. Ibid., p. 307.

58. Edwards, *The Reagans,* p. 327.

59. Regan, *For the Record,* pp. 70–74, 367.

60. Ibid., pp. 3–5 and p. 344. The impact of Mrs. Reagan's astrologer on the signing of the INF treaty is also noted by Anthony, *First Ladies,* p. 406.

61. Regan, *For the Record,* pp. 70–74.

62. Joan Quigley, *What Does Joan Say?* (New York: Carol Publishing, 1990), p. 180.

63. See ibid., pp. 58–66, for Quigley's description of her input into the 1980 campaign, especially the timing of debates. In her memoirs, Mrs. Reagan acknowledges the astrologer's involvement in that campaign. Reagan, *My Turn*, p. 49.

64. Laura Sessions Step, "Astrology Reports Disturb Some Evangelical Leaders; Interest in Zodiac at Odds with the Bible," *Washington Post*, 5 May 1988, p. A3.

65. "Reagan Is Asked to Eschew Astrology," *Washington Post*, 25 June 1988, p. B6.

66. Reagan, *My Turn*, p. 51.

67. Ibid., p. 49.

68. Garry Wills, *Reagan's America: Innocents at Home* (New York: Doubleday and Co., 1987), p. 192.

69. For a discussion of the origins of various theater superstitions, see "Theater Superstitions," Defying McBeth, http://www.angelfire.com/fl3/Defy mcbeth/Super3.html.

70. Anthony, *First Ladies*, p. 330.

71. See Wills, *Reagan's America*, p. 192, for a more detailed discussion of so why many actors become dependent on astrologers.

5. NANCY REAGAN, SCREENWRITER

1. Lawrence Konner, "On Screenwriting," http://www.screen writer.com/ Lawrence Konnerw.html.

2. Reynolds quoted in Sidney Blumenthal, "The Mommy Track: In Defense of Nancy," *New Republic*, 13 May 1991, p. 3.

3. Richard Neustadt, *Presidential Power and the Modern Presidency: The Politics of Leadership from Roosevelt to Reagan* (New York: Free Press, 1990), p. 312. Neustadt feels that every president should have an advisor such as Mrs. Reagan, who was devoted solely to the president's interests. He argues that Iran-contra most likely occurred because Donald Regan had removed from the policy loop the one advisor who could have alerted President Reagan to the dangers involved. Neustadt suggests that future presidents take special care to not "let your Nancy be immobilized" (p. 316).

4. Quoted in Anne Edwards, *The Reagans: Portrait of a Marriage* (New York: St. Martins Press, 2003), pp. 273–74.

5. Michael K. Deaver with Mickey Herskowitz, *Behind the Scenes* (New York: William Morrow and Co., 1987), p. 39.

6. Carl Sferrazza Anthony, *First Ladies*, vol. 2 (New York: William Morrow and Co., 1990), p. 311.

7. Enid Nemy, "The First Lady Finds a Cause," *New York Times,* 19 Feb. 1982, p. 5; and Howard Jacob Karger and David Stoesz, *American Social Welfare Policy* (Boston: Allyn and Bacon, 2002), p. 275. For a discussion that places the drug treatment cuts in the context of the larger Reagan budget cuts, see Ronnie Dugger, *On Reagan: The Man and His Presidency* (New York: McGraw-Hill Book Co., 1983), pp. 285–312. The rationale for the "zero tolerance" policy adopted by the administration can be found in Edwin Meese III, *With Reagan: The Inside Story* (Washington, D.C.: Regnery Publishing, 1992), pp. 307–12. For a contrasting view, see "Annual Report of the Select Committee on Narcotics Abuse and Control," House of Representatives, 98th Congress (Washington, D.C.: U.S. Printing Office, 1985) (author's collection), p. 45, which noted the positive effects of the first lady's personal involvement in raising awareness about the dangers of drug abuse and expressed serious concern that federal leadership in drug abuse treatment had seriously eroded under the Reagan administration.

8. Kurt Anderson, "Co-Starring at the White House," *Time,* 14 Jan. 1985, p. 30. Michael Deaver supports Anderson's premise about Mrs. Reagan's involvement in both domestic and foreign policy issues: Deaver, *Behind the Scenes,* pp. 110–17. Another female voice urging Ronald Reagan to begin talks with the Soviets was Margaret Thatcher: Edwards, *The Reagans,* p. 313.

9. James Rosebush feels that the focus on the Donald Regan affair obscured the most important impact Mrs. Reagan had on her husband's administration: the ability to promote the people she wanted to the positions she wanted them in. Interview with James Rosebush, 16 June 2004.

10. Eric J. Schmertz, Natalie Datlof, and Alexej Ugrinsky, eds., *Ronald Reagan's America,* vol. 2 (Westport, Conn.: Greenwood Press, 1997), pp. 652–53.

11. Quoted in John W. Sloan, *The Reagan Effect: Economics and Presidential Leadership* (Lawrence: University Press of Kansas, 1999), p. 93. Edwards, *The Reagans,* pp. 239–40, points out that in the early 1980s a powerful woman in Washington, D.C., was very rare, that Washington was almost exclusively a men's club, with only one really powerful woman—Katharine Graham, the publisher of the *Washington Post.*

12. Reynolds quoted in Sloan, *The Reagan Effect,* p. 93.

13. Martin Anderson, *Revolution* (New York: Harcourt Brace Jovanovich, 1988), pp. 293–94. Anderson feels strongly that Mrs. Reagan has not gotten enough credit for her political astuteness, which he feels was equal to the best of the Reagan aides. See also Peggy Noonan, *What I Saw at the Revolution: A Political Life in the Reagan Era* (New York: Random House. 1990), p. 163.

14. Donnie Radcliffe, "Nancy Reagan on the Role of Presidential Spouse," *Washington Post*, 5 May 1987, p. D1.

15. Helene Von Damm, *At Reagan's Side* (New York: Doubleday and Co., 1989), p. 227.

16. David Broder, "The Social Agenda Could Spoil the Party," *Washington Post*, 23 Nov. 1980, p. C7. See also Sloan, *The Reagan Effect*, pp. 66–67, 104.

17. World Politics and Current Affairs, "New Right: Moral Minority," *The Economist*, 19 Sept. 1981, p. 21.

18. Bill Peterson, "American Public, by Wide Majority, Supports Legalized Abortion," *Washington Post*, 8 June 1981, p. A1. See also Broder, "The Social Agenda," p. C7; and David A. Stockman, *The Triumph of Politics: Why the Reagan Revolution Failed* (New York: Harper and Row, 1986), pp. 83–84.

19. The National Republican Party Platform Language on Abortion Rights, 1980, http://www.presidency.uscb.edu/showplatforms.php?platindex=80; see also "The Platform Reagan Will Run On," *U.S. News and World Report*, 28 July 1980, p. 72.

20. "Text of Reagan's Speech Accepting the Republican Nomination," *New York Times*, 18 July 1980, p. 8.

21. Lou Cannon, *President Reagan: The Role of a Lifetime* (New York: Simon and Schuster, 1991), p. 812.

22. Schmertz, Datlof, and Ugrinsky, *Ronald Reagan's America*, pp. 86–87.

23. Ibid.

24. Cannon, *President Reagan*, p. 812.

25. Michael Reese, "Reagan's First Defeat," *Newsweek*, 20 Sept. 1982, p. 24. William Crotty, *American Parties in Decline*, 2nd ed. (Boston: Little, Brown and Co., 1984), p. 74, also notes the new right's disenchantment with the Reagan administration's limited efforts on a constitutional amendment banning abortion. Robert Shogan suggests that in 1980 the evangelicals had hitched a ride on Reagan's bandwagon by working hard for his election, but ended up with little to show for their efforts. Robert Shogan, *War without End: Cultural Conflict and the Struggle for America's Political Future* (Boulder, Colo.: Westview Press, 2002), p. 198. Also see Clyde Wilcox, *Onward Christian Soldiers? The Religious Right in American Politics* (Boulder, Colo.: Westview Press, 1996), p. 85. For an argument that the conservative right actually did quite well under the Reagan administration, see William E. Pemberton, *Exit with Honor: The Life and Presidency of Ronald Reagan* (New York: M. E. Sharpe, 1997), pp. 147–48.

26. Melina Beck, "The Issue That Won't Go Away," *Newsweek*, 31 Jan. 1981, p. 31.

27. Ibid. See also Shogan, *War without End,* pp. 179–86, and Lawrence Barrett, *Gambling with History: Ronald Reagan in the White House* (New York: Doubleday and Co., 1983), pp. 61–63.

28. Blumenthal, "The Mommy Track: In Defense of Nancy," p. 19.

29. Letter from President Ronald Reagan to the Members of the National Right to Life Committee, 7 Jan. 1986, author's collection.

30. "Nancy Reagan Issues Abortion Clarification," *New York Times,* 10 Sept. 1984, p. B12.

31. Ibid.

32. Christine Russell, "Some at FDA Fear Politics Tainting Science," *Washington Post,* 8 June 1982, p. A1.

33. James McGregor Burns et al., *Government by the People* (Upper Saddle River, N.J.: Pearson/Prentice-Hall, 2004), p. 387.

34. Michael Kramer, "Reagan's Backdoor War on Abortion," *U.S. News and World Report,* 17 Aug. 1987, p. 14.

35. Dugger, *On Reagan,* p. 229.

36. Ibid.

37. Viguerie quoted in "A Setback for School Prayer," *Newsweek,* 2 April 1984, p. 37.

38. Lou Cannon, "Reagan Renews Appeal for Antiabortion Action," *Washington Post,* 31 Jan. 1984, p. A1.

39. The National Republican Party Platform Language on Abortion Rights, 1984, http://www.presidency.uscb.edu/showplatforms.php?platindex=1984.

40. Noonan, *What I Saw at the Revolution,* p. 163.

41. "Remarks Accepting the Presidential Nomination at the Republican National Convention in Dallas, Texas," http://www.reagan.utexas.edu/resources/speeches/1984/82384f.htm, 23 Aug. 1984.

42. Donald Regan, *For the Record: From Wall Street to Washington* (New York: Harcourt Brace Jovanovich, 1988), p. 77.

43. Cannon, *President Reagan,* p. 814.

44. Ibid., p. 815; see pp. 814–19 for a larger discussion of Dr. Koop's determined leadership in combating the AIDS epidemic. Also see Edwards, *The Reagans,* p, 339; and Pemberton, *Exit with Honor,* pp. 137–38.

45. Cannon, *President Reagan,* p. 816.

46. John S. Lang, "For the First Lady, a Role That Keeps Growing," *U.S. News and World Report,* 29 July 1985, p. 24. See also Pemberton, *Exit with Honor,* p. 124.

47. Cannon, *President Reagan,* p. 306.

48. Pemberton, *Exit with Honor*, p. 162; Deaver quoted in Lang, "For the First Lady, a Role That Keeps Growing," p. 24.

49. Quoted in Anthony, *First Ladies*, p. 389.

50. Nancy Reagan with William Novak, *My Turn: The Memoirs of Nancy Reagan* (New York: Random House, 1989), p. 64.

51. Ibid.

52. "Remarks Accepting the Presidential Nomination at the Republican National Convention in Dallas."

53. Republican Party Platform, "America Secure and the World at Peace," http://www.cnn.com/ALLPOLITICS/1996/conventions/san.diego/facts/past. platforms/gop84/index.shtml.

54. Bernard Weintraub, "The Washingtonization of Nancy Reagan," *New York Times*, 26 March 1985, p. 20.

55. Quoted in Cannon, *President Reagan*, p. 289.

56. Ibid.

57. John Herbers, "Religious Leaders Tell of Worry on Armageddon View Ascribed to Reagan," *New York Times*, 21 Oct. 1984, p. 1.

58. McFarlane quoted in Cannon, *President Reagan*, p. 290. Anderson, *Revolution*, p. 99, agrees that Reagan saw the SDI initiative as the moral alternative to the strategic policy of mutually assured destruction. Caspar Weinberger, *Fighting for Peace: Seven Critical Years in the Pentagon* (New York: Warner Books, 1990), p. 309, strongly argues that the Strategic Defense Initiative was President Reagan's own proposal, not one pressed upon him by staff. The same point is made in Pemberton, *Exit with Honor*, p. 131. Pemberton quotes Strobe Talbot as saying that Reagan "was a romantic, a radical, a nuclear abolitionist."

59. In Schmertz, Datalof, and Ugrinsky, *Ronald Reagan's America*, p. 656, James Rosebush argues that rather than claiming that Mrs. Reagan moderated the president's view on the Soviet Union, it would be more accurate to state that she deserves credit for appealing to that part of the president's nature that wanted to make peace with the Soviets.

60. Henry Trewitt, "Testing Time for Shultz," *U.S. News and World Report*, 11 May 1987, p. 14. See George Shultz, *Turmoil and Triumph: My Years as Secretary of State* (New York: Charles Scribner and Sons, 1993), pp. 533–36 and pp. 752–59 for his views on arms control and the preparations for the Geneva and Reykjavik summits, respectively.

61. Reagan, *My Turn*, p. 243.

62. Edwards, *The Reagans*, p. 313.

63. Reagan, *My Turn*, p. 345.

64. Blumenthal, "The Mommy Track: In Defense of Nancy," p. 3.

65. Julie Johnson, "Washington Talk: The First Lady; Strong Opinions with No Apologies," *New York Times*, 25 May 1988, p. 22.

66. W. Dale Nelson, "Books on the Reagans Reveal Powerful First Lady," *Austin American-Statesman*, 14 April 1991, p. A5. In his memoirs, Wright was not quite as direct about Mrs. Reagan's involvement, though he does say his staff members told him that Ronald Reagan was interested in making peace in Central America primarily because Mrs. Reagan wanted it. Jim Wright, *Balance of Power* (Atlanta: Turner Publishing, 1996), p. 460.

67. Schmertz, Datlof, and Ugrinsky, *Ronald Reagan's America*, pp. 647–648.

68. Ibid., p. 647.

69. Lee Wlczak, "Ed Meese Is Beginning to Make the White House Nervous," *Business Week*, 16 Sept. 1985, p. 41. Barbara Hickson Craig and David M. O'Brien, *Abortion and American Politics* (Chatham, N.J.: Chatham House Publishers, 1993), pp. 173–74, describes the shift in the Justice Department when Edwin Meese replaced William French Smith as the new attorney general and began to push the administration's conservative agenda through litigation and judicial appointees.

70. Michael Stachell, "A Divisive Issue Starts to Heat Up Again," *U.S. News and World Report*, 7 Sept. 1987, p. 16. See also Pemberton, *Exit with Honor*, p. 139.

71. Stachell, "A Divisive Issue Starts to Heat Up Again," p. 16.

72. Editorial, "Back to the Back Alley?" *St. Petersburg Times*, 3 Feb. 1988, p. 16a.

73. Johnson, "Washington Talk: The First Lady," p. 22.

74. Craig and O'Brien, *Abortion and American Politics*, p. 184.

75. Blumenthal, "The Mommy Track: In Defense of Nancy," p. 3.

76. Lynn Nofziger, *Nofziger* (Washington: Regnery Publishing, 1992), pp. 302–4.

77. Donnie Radcliffe, "Poll Gives First Lady 63 Percent Mark," *Washington Post*, 11 March 1987, p. C1.

78. Reagan, *My Turn*, p. 64.

6. THE CURTAIN FALLS

1. In 1980 Rona Jaffe published a survey of her 1951 Radcliffe classmates in *Ladies Home Journal* in which she concluded, "We married what we wanted to be. If we wanted to be a doctor or a lawyer, we married one." She added that a great many of her classmates expected to find their identities in their husband's. Eugenia Kaledin, *Mothers and More: American Women in the 1950s* (Boston: Twayne Publishers, 1984), p. 43.

2. Nancy Reagan with William Novak, *My Turn: The Memoirs of Nancy Reagan* (New York: Random House, 1989), p. 76.

3. Much later, President Reagan was asked how he would like to be remembered. His response was seemingly rather modest: "What I'd really like to do is go down in history as the president who made Americans believe in themselves." Carl Sferrazza Anthony, *First Ladies,* vol. 2 (New York: William Morrow and Co., 1990), p. 416. In other words, he would do for the country what Mrs. Reagan so often did for him.

4. Reagan, *My Turn,* p. 322.

5. Ibid., p. 314.

6. Lou Cannon, *President Reagan: The Role of a Lifetime* (New York: Simon and Schuster, 1991), p. 719.

7. Reagan, *My Turn,* p. 315.

8. Michael Deaver, *Behind the Scenes* (New York: William Morrow and Co., 1987), p. 39.

9. Nofziger quoted in Deborah Hart Strober and Gerald S. Strober, *Reagan: The Man and His Presidency* (New York: Houghton Mifflin, 1998), pp. 49–50.

10. John B. Roberts II, *Rating the First Ladies* (New York: Kensington Publishing Company, 2003), p. 326.

11. Cannon, *President Reagan,* pp. 507–8.

12. Edmund Morris, *Dutch: A Memoir of Ronald Reagan* (New York: Random House, 1999), p. 613.

13. Interview with Sheila Tate, 12 July 2004.

14. Interview with James Rosebush, 17 June 2004.

15. Joan Didion, "Pretty Nancy," *Saturday Evening Post,* 1 June 1968, p. 20. Also quoted in Lou Cannon, *Governor Reagan* (New York: Public Affairs, 2003), p. 235.

16. Graham quoted in Reagan, *My Turn,* p. 314. See also William E. Pemberton, *Exit with Honor: The Life and Presidency of Ronald Reagan* (New York: M. E. Sharpe, 1997), pp. 122–23.

17. Reagan, *My Turn,* p. 314.

18. Quoted in Betty Boyd Caroli, *First Ladies* (New York: Oxford University Press, 1987), p. 327.

19. For more on the various "waves" of feminism, see Linda Nelson, ed., *The Second Wave: A Reader in Feminist Theory* (New York: Routledge Press, 1997); Wendy Kolmar and Frances Bartkowski, *Feminist Theory: A Reader* (Toronto: Mayfield Press, 2000); and Catherine Orr, "Charting the Currents of the Third Wave," *Hypatia* 12, no. 3 (Summer 1997).

20. Alan Abramowitz, *Voice of the People: Elections and Voting in the United States* (Boston: McGraw-Hill Book Co., 2004), p. 86.

21. Ronnie Dugger, *On Reagan: The Man and His Presidency* (New York: McGraw-Hill Book Co., 1983), pp. 229–30.

22. See Susan Faludi, *Backlash: The Undeclared War against American Women* (New York: Random House, 1995), in which Faludi argues that during the 1980s the successes of the feminist movement of the late 1960s and 1970s came under an attack that was part political and part cultural.

23. Dugger, *On Reagan*, p. 221.

24. Elizabeth Dole, "Women's Strategy: A Two Year Plan," Elizabeth Dole Files, Box 6411, File Folder Women's Strategy, pp. 1, 2, Reagan Library, Simi Valley, California.

25. Elizabeth Dole, issue paper, "The 52% Solution—Issues of Importance to Women and the Gender Gap," Elizabeth Dole Files, Box 6411, File Folder Women's Strategy, pp. 1–2.

26. Elizabeth Dole, memo to Baker, Deaver re "Women's Strategy: Anticipating the Defeat of the Era," Elizabeth Dole Files, Box 6511, File Folder Women's Strategy, January–June 1982, p. 2, Reagan Library, Simi Valley, California.

27. Faith Ryan Whittlesey, memo to Michael Deaver re Communications—President's Programs for Women, 24 May 1983, Faith Ryan Whittlesy Files, OA 9002, p. 2, Reagan Library, Simi Valley, California.

28. Report, "Women's Issues Meeting," 6 March 1983, Edwin Meese III Files, File Folder, "Women's Issues" OA 946, p. 1, Reagan Library, Simi Valley, California.

29. Memo: Michael Uhlman to Edwin Harper re: "Status Report," Edwin Meese III Files, File Folder, "Women's Issues," OA 946, p. 2.

30. Abramowitz, *Voice of the People*, p. 86.

31. Germaine Greer, "Abolish Her: The Feminist Case against First Ladies," *The New Republic*, 26 June 1994, pp. 20–26.

32. Rita J. Simon and Jean Landis, "Women's and Men's Attitudes about a Woman's Place and Role," *Public Opinion Quarterly*, Summer 1989: 268, quoted in James G. Benze, Jr., "Nancy Reagan: China Doll or Dragon Lady?" *Presidential Studies Quarterly* 20, no. 4 (Fall 1990): 777.

33. I am indebted to Gil Troy, *Mr. and Mrs. President* (Lawrence: University Press of Kansas, 2000), for the analysis of Mrs. Reagan's challenge to feminism.

34. For a more complete articulation of this newer feminism, see Naomi Wolf, *Fire with Fire: The New Female Power and How It Will Change the*

Twenty-first Century (New York: Random House, 1993); Katie Roiphe, *The Morning After: Sex, Fear, and Feminism* (Boston: Little, Brown and Co., 1993); and Rene Denfeld, *The New Victorians: A Young Woman's Challenge to the Old Feminist Order* (New York: Warner Books, 1995).

35. Anthony, *First Ladies*, p. 407.

36. "Mrs. Reagan's Remarks: Address to the United Nations," White House Office of the Press Secretary, author's personal collection.

37. Kristen A. Conover, "How DARE Began and Spread," *Christian Science Monitor*, 22 Jan. 1990, p. 14.

38. Brian Bailker, "Just Say No: An Advocate of Drug Law Reform Says DARE Is Twenty-Year Failure," http://drugpolicy.org/library/newsweek_4_15_03.cfm, p. 7.

39. GAO-03-172R, "Youth Illicit Drug Use Prevention," http://www.GAO.gov, p. 2.

40. Bailker, "Just Say No," p. 8.

41. Memo: Ann Wrobleski and Sheila Tate to Mrs. Reagan, re Drug Q&A for AMA and *Good Morning America*, 24 March 1981, p. 5. First Lady's Press Office, Joseph Canzeri Files, CFOA152, Reagan Library, Simi Valley, California.

42. Michael K. Deaver, *Nancy: An Intimate Portrait of My Years with Nancy Reagan* (New York: William Morrow and Co., 2004), p. 94.

43. GAO-03-172R, "Youth Illicit Drug Use Prevention," p. 9.

44. "Remarks for the Associated Press Publishers' Luncheon," 4 May 1987, Office of the First Lady: Records, Projects and Events, Mrs. Reagan's 1987 Speeches, OA 187221, p. 1.

45. Ibid., p. 13.

46. Crispin quoted in "Borrowed Rags," *Financial Times* (London), 20 Oct. 1988, p. 28.

47. Ibid.

48. John Robinson, "Nancy Reagan's Dress Blues," *Boston Globe*, 19 Oct. 1988, p. 29.

49. Jay Peterzell, "Designing Woman: The IRS vs. Nancy Reagan," *The New Republic*, 10 Feb. 1992, pp. 12–13.

50. Reagan quoted in Lionel Barber, "Reagan Rules Out Pardon for North," *Financial Times* (London), 20 Jan. 1989, p. 4.

51. Phil Gailey, "Reagan Balks at Helping His Hero, Oliver North," *St. Petersburg Times*, 2 April 1989, p. 7D.

52. On the friction between the Reagans and the Bushes, see Anne Edwards, *The Reagans: Portrait of a Marriage* (New York: St. Martin's Press, 2003),

pp. 337–38. Other authors characterized the transition as a "friendly takeover" marked by "harmonious relations between transition planners and campaign staff." John P. Burke, "A Tale of Two Transitions: 1980 and 1988," *Congress and the Presidency* 28, no. 1 (Spring 2001): 7.

53. Barbara Bush quoted in Anthony, *First Ladies,* p. 414.

54. "Revlon Elects Nancy Reagan to Board of Directors," *PR Newswire,* 1 June 1989.

55. James G. Benze, Jr., "Nancy (Anne Frances Robbins Davis) Reagan," in Lewis L. Gould, ed., *American First Ladies: Their Lives and Their Legacy,* 2nd ed. (New York: Routledge Press, 2001), pp. 604–5.

56. Retha Hill, "Drug Program Reprieved: P.G. Center Gets Reagan Foundation Help," *Washington Post,* 19 March 1992, p. B3.

57. "Keeping Score 1998," http://www.drugstrategies.org/ks1998/p_preven.html.

58. Jill Taylor, "Professor's Program Honored," *Florida Times Union,* 17 June 2000, p. L5.

59. Ronald Reagan, "Speech at 1992 Republican Convention," http://www.townhall.com/halloffame/reagan/speech/92conv.html.

60. Nancy Reagan, *I Love You, Ronnie: The Letters of Ronald Reagan to Nancy Reagan* (New York: Random House, 2000), p. 188.

61. Ibid., pp. 179–80.

62. Alzheimer's Association, Ronald and Nancy Reagan Research Institute, http://www.alz.org/Research/reagan/overview.asp.

63. Edwards, *The Reagans,* pp. 337–38.

64. William E. Pemberton, *Exit with Honor: The Life and Presidency of Ronald Reagan* (New York: M.E. Sharpe, 1997), pp. 199–201.

65. Michael Wines, "Reagan Friends Reflect on the Fading of a Giant," *New York Times,* 6 Nov. 1994, p. A1.

66. Although all presidents undergo yearly physicals, they are not tested for Alzheimer's disease. Therefore, it is impossible to draw a definitive conclusion about Reagan's condition in his last years as president.

67. William Plummer, "Endless Love: Once Considered Cold and Controlling, Nancy Reagan Emerges as a Selfless Care Giver," *People,* 13 March 2000, p. 133.

68. Reagan, *I Love You, Ronnie,* p. 184.

69. Carla Koehl, "Nancy Makes a Sad Choice," *Newsweek,* 2 Sept. 1996, p. 6.

70. Larry Lipman, "Senate Panel Hears Alzheimer's Plea: Boost Research Funding, Reagan Daughter Asks," *Atlanta Journal and Constitution,* 22 March 2000, p. 2E.

71. Enid Nemy, "Maureen Reagan, 60, Activist and President's Daughter," *New York Times,* 9 Aug. 2001, p. B8.

72. Deaver, *Nancy: An Intimate Portrait,* p. 200.

73. Nancy Reagan, "Statement by Nancy Reagan Regarding the Death of Maureen Reagan," Office of Ronald Reagan, http://www.reagan.utexas.edu/maureenorr.htm.

74. James Ivey, "Patti Davis Says That Relationship with Dad Has Grown Deeper," *Omaha World Herald,* 26 May 2000, p. 42.

75. George Rush, "As Ron Ails, Family's Cold War Thaws," *New York Daily News,* 25 Sept. 2002, p. 22.

76. Patti Davis, *Angels Don't Die: My Father's Gift of Faith* (New York: HarperCollins, 1995), pp. 35, 7.

77. Sarah Baxter, "Reagan's Family Awaits Merciful Release," *Can West Interactive,* 29 Sept. 2002, p. A7.

78. "Reagan Doing Well, Says Son," *Sunday Herald Sun,* 11 May 2003, p. 45.

79. Kent Jenkins, Jr., "North Refuses Fight with Nancy Reagan, Who Calls Him a Liar," *Houston Chronicle,* 29 Oct. 1994, p. 5.

80. Eleanor Clift, "Nancy with the Centrist Face: Derided as an Elitist, Mrs. Reagan's Impact Was Unequaled," *Washington Post,* 8 Jan. 1995, p. C5.

81. Jenkins, "North Refuses Fight with Nancy Reagan," p. 4.

82. Newsmakers, "First Ladies Sway Few in Abortion Debate," *Chicago Sun Times,* 25 Sept. 1994, p. 29.

83. Periscope, "Nancy Scores Some Points," *Newsweek,* 20 March 1995, p. 6.

84. David Maranis, "Where the Past Meets the Present: Reagan Is Absent from San Diego but Remains Star of the Show," *Washington Post,* 13 Aug. 1996, p. A13.

85. Ibid.

86. Mrs. Reagan had clearly come a long way as a speaker. Sheila Tate noticed the change, describing Mrs. Reagan in the early days of the administration as being so nervous that she would tremble when she had to give a speech. By the end of Tate's tenure at the White House, however, she and Mrs. Reagan would often hold conversations right up to the moment the first lady had to walk to the podium to deliver her speech. Interview with Sheila Tate, 12 July 2004.

87. Roxanne Roberts, "Carrying on for the Gipper," *Washington Post,* 16. May 2002, p. C01.

88. Libby Copeland, "Mister Rogers' Honored Neighbors," *Washington Post,* 10 July 2002, p. C01.

89. Reuters News Service, "Nancy Reagan Makes Appeal for Stem-Cell Research Funding," *Houston Chronicle,* 15 July 2001, p. 8.

90. Editorial, "Mrs. Reagan Backs Stem Cell Research," *San Antonio Express,* 6 Oct. 2002, p. 2G.

91. Ceci Connolly, "Nancy Reagan Backs Cloning for Research," *Washington Post,* 7 Feb. 2003, p. A10.

92. Deaver, *Nancy: An Intimate Portrait,* p. 161.

93. Bill Hutchison, "Nancy Reagan Backs Stem Cell Research," *New York Daily News* (10 May 2004), p. 14.

94. Philip M. Boffy, "Using Fetal Tissue as a Cure Debated," *New York Times,* 15 Sept. 1988, p. 31.

95. Frank Bruni, "Bush Says He Will Veto Any Bill Broadening His Stem Cell Policy," *New York Times,* 14 Aug. 2001, p. 1.

96. When asked by Larry King whether she would place her husband in a hospital that specialized in treating Alzheimer's patients, Mrs. Reagan responded, "Oh, no. Oh, no. Never. Never. No, no. He is going to stay at home." Corky Siemaszko, "Nancy's Pledge on Ron," *New York Daily News,* 6 Feb. 2001, p. 6.

97. Reagan, *I Love You, Ronnie,* p. 184.

98. Baxter, "Reagan's Family Awaits Merciful Release," p. A7.

99. Pamela Warrick, "Former First Lady Struggles to Deal with Heavy Emotional Toll," *Chicago Sun Times,* 10 Aug. 1997, p. 8. Some longtime Reagan associates stopped visiting because they found it too difficult to deal with the former president's condition. Michael Deaver describes a visit in which it was clear that Reagan no longer remembered his former aide. It was at that point that Deaver ended his visits. Michael Deaver, *A Different Drummer: My Thirty Years with Ronald Reagan* (New York: Harper Collins, 2001), p. 29.

100. Warrick, "Former First Lady Struggles to Deal," p. 9.

101. Scott Shepard, "Reagan Dies at 93: Nation Mourns 'Great Communicator,' " *Atlanta Journal Constitution,* 8 June 2004, p. 1A.

102. Patti Davis, "Waiting and the End," *People,* 21 June 2004, p. 104.

103. Quoted in Michelle Caruso, Bill Hutchison, and Corky Siemaszko, "One Last Look: Patti Says Ron, Nancy Shared a Final Glance," *New York Daily News,* 8 June 2004, p. 4.

104. Julian Conan, "Nancy's Time for Tears as Sun Sets on Reagan," *London Sunday Telegraph,* 13 June 2004, p. 9.

105. Faye Fiore, Vicki Kemper, and Daryl Kelley, "Reagan Buried at Cemetery: His Children Reflect on the Father They Knew," *Los Angeles Times,* 12 June 2004, p. 1.

106. Adam Nagourney and Bernard Weintraub, "For a Frail Mrs. Reagan, a Week of Great Resolve," *New York Times,* 12 June 2004, p. 1.

107. Quoted in Bob Colacello, *Ronnie and Nancy: Their Path to the White House, 1911 to 1980* (New York: Warner Books, 2004), p. 13.

108. Patti Davis, "The Gemstones of Our Years," *Newsweek*, 14 June 2004, p. 42.

109. Fiore, Kemper, and Kelley, "Reagan Buried at Cemetery," p. 1.

110. Ann E. Donlan, "Democratic National Convention: Beantown Blowout; Politics Aside, Reagan Pitches for Stem Cell Research," *Boston Herald*, 28 July 2004, p. C6.

111. Richard Cohen, "Ron Reagan's Pere Pressure," *Washington Post*, 15 July 2004, p. A21.

112. Helen Kennedy, "Reagan Sib Spears Ron," *New York Daily News*, 29 July 2004, p. 24.

113. John Sawyer, "Cheney Says Kerry Is Unfit to Lead," *St. Louis Post-Dispatch*, 2 Sept. 2004, p. A1.

114. Maura Reynolds and Mark Z. Barabak, "The Race to the White House: Bush, Kerry Try to Stir Up Support in the Los Angeles Area," *Los Angeles Times*, 13 Aug. 2004, p. A1.

115. "A Gift from Nancy Reagan," *Boston Herald*, 12 June 2004, p. 16.

116. Quoted in Caroline Overton, "How Nancy Went from Being an Object of Ridicule to Sainthood," *Melbourne Age*, 19 June 2004, p. 3.

117. "Eleanor Roosevelt, Hillary Clinton Top First Ladies Poll," Siena Research Institute, Siena College, 10 Jan. 1994, http://www.siena.edu/sri/results/First%20Ladies.htm.

BIBLIOGRAPHIC ESSAY

MANUSCRIPTS

Nancy Reagan's personal papers and the diary she kept during her White House years are not yet open to researchers. A significant amount of other relevant material is available through the Ronald Reagan Library at 40 Presidential Drive, Simi Valley, California 03605. This includes about 65 percent of the materials related to Mrs. Reagan's official duties as first lady. Among the most valuable are the First Lady Press Office Records, particularly OA 13312 and OA 13313, which contain much of the material on Mrs. Reagan's "Just Say No" program. The records from the Office of the First Lady, which contain Mrs. Reagan's official correspondence, are now about 60 percent open, as is the material from the Office of the First Lady, Projects. Information about the availability of specific materials is available through the Reagan Library web page at www.reagan.utexas.edu.

Despite these limitations, I was able to consult over forty documents—over two hundred pages in all—of primary source material, primarily from the First Lady Press Office Records and from the Office of the First Lady. These included interoffice memos, travel itineraries, handwritten thank-you notes, and position papers.

During the early years of my research, when much less material was available from the Reagan Library, other authors kindly forwarded copies of documents pertaining to the former first lady that they had found in their research. Numbering approximately a dozen, these primary sources are referred to as being from the author's own collection.

The Reagan Library has opened the files of a number of Mrs. Reagan's closest aides, including Elaine Crispen, James Rosebush, and Sheila Tate. Because Mrs. Reagan also worked closely with several of President Reagan's advisors, the papers of White House aides also are useful sources. Particularly important are the files of James Baker, Michael Deaver, and Donald Regan, all of whose papers are now open. In addition, Donald Regan's private papers are available at the Library of

Congress. An excellent introduction to the first lady's papers is Carl Sferrazza Anthony, "She Saves Everything: The Papers of Nancy Reagan," in Nancy Kegan Smith and Mary C. Ryan, ed., *Modern First Ladies: Their Documentary Legacy* (New York: Dimension, 1989).

BIOGRAPHIES AND SECONDARY WORKS

Mrs. Reagan has published two autobiographies. *Nancy,* with Bill Libby (New York: William Morrow and Co., 1980), deals primarily with her life before Ronald Reagan ran for governor of California. Her second autobiography, *My Turn: The Memoirs of Nancy Reagan* (New York: Random House, 1989), written with William Novak, while sometimes not completely accurate factually, contains Mrs. Reagan's perspective on such areas as her image and relationship with the press, her relations with her children, her interest in astrology, and her overall role in the Reagan presidency. In the process, Mrs. Reagan settles a few scores, most notably with Donald Regan and Raisa Gorbachev.

Biographies of Nancy Reagan (none based on her personal papers) include Chris Wallace's *First Lady: A Portrait of Nancy Reagan* (New York: St. Martin's Press, 1986), Frances Spatz Leighton's *The Search for the Real Nancy Reagan* (New York: Macmillan Publishing Co., 1987), and Kitty Kelley's *Nancy Reagan: The Unauthorized Biography* (New York: Simon and Schuster, 1991). Kelley's book appears to be exhaustively researched, but many of her most controversial claims are loosely sourced, resulting in an impression of author bias against Mrs. Reagan. More recently, Michael K. Deaver has written *Nancy: An Intimate Portrait of My Years with Nancy Reagan* (New York: William Morrow and Co., 2004). For a brief biography of Mrs. Reagan, see James G. Benze, Jr., "Nancy (Anne Frances Robbins Davis) Reagan" in Lewis L. Gould, ed., *American First Ladies: Their Lives and Legacy* (New York: Routledge Press, 2001).

Joint biographies of President and Mrs. Reagan include Laurence Leamer's *Make-Believe: The Story of Nancy and Ronald Reagan* (New York: Harper and Row, 1983) and Bill Adler's *Ronnie and Nancy: A Very Special Love Story* (New York: Crown Publishers, 1985), both of which provide interesting detail about the Reagans prior to their years in the White House. Anne Edwards, *The Reagans: Portrait of a Marriage* (New York: St. Martin's Press, 2003), is the most recent biography. While Edwards' biography is not as thorough on the Reagans' early lives as those by Leamer and Adler, it offers many interesting details about their time as president and first lady, and touches upon the post–White House years. Garry Wills, *Reagan's America: Innocents at Home* (New York: Doubleday and Co., 1987), analyzes the significance of Mrs. Reagan's acting background more thoroughly than the other biographies. The most recent biography of the Reagans is Bob Colacello, *Ronnie and Nancy: Their Path to the White House, 1911 to 1980* (New York: Warner Books, 2004). Colacello is one of the few biographers to have received Mrs. Reagan's cooperation, which resulted in his having access not only to her thoughts but also to the personal papers of the Davis and Reagan families. Colacello's work (the first of a planned two volumes) helps clarify important points of the Reagans' lives together, but does not encompass Mrs. Reagan's tenure as first lady.

President Reagan's own memoir, *An American Life* (New York: Simon and Schuster, 1990), details the extraordinarily close relationship between the president and first lady, but provides little insight into her influence on political decisions. His earlier autobiography, *Where's the Rest of Me?* (New York: Duell, Sloan, and Pierce, 1965), describes their early lives together.

The memoirs of various members of the Reagan administration are useful sources of information about the first lady and her influence. Michael Deaver's *Behind the Scenes* (New York: William Morrow and Co., 1987) and *A Different Drummer: My Thirty Years with Ronald Reagan* (New York: Harper Collins, 2001) provide insight into the Reagans' relationship; based on his over twenty years with Ronald Reagan, Deaver argues that the first lady was one of her husband's most trusted political advisors. Donald T. Regan's *For the Record: From Wall Street to Washington* (New York: Harcourt Brace Jovanovich, 1988) also documents Mrs. Reagan's influence, although not always in a flattering light. Regan was the first to discuss the impact of Mrs. Reagan's astrological beliefs on the scheduling of the administration's business. Helene Von Damm, who worked for the president from the beginning of his political career, provides a conservative interpretation of Mrs. Reagan's involvement in her husband's political affairs in *At Reagan's Side* (New York: Doubleday and Co., 1989). Von Damm suggests that the first lady's influence generally worked to favor moderate over conservative interests within the administration.

Other memoirs, such as Larry Speakes, *Speaking Out* (New York: Charles Scribner and Sons, 1988); Lynn Nofziger, *Nofziger* (Washington:

Regnery Publishing, 1992); Marlin Fitzwater, *Call the Briefing!* (New York: Random House, 1995); Edwin Meese III, *With Reagan: The Inside Story* (Washington: Regnery Publishing, 1992); Martin Anderson, *Revolution* (New York: Harcourt Brace Jovanovich, 1988); David Gergen, *Eyewitness to Power: The Essence of Leadership from Nixon to Clinton* (New York: Simon and Schuster, 2001); Peggy Noonan, *What I Saw at the Revolution: A Political Life in the Reagan Era* (New York: Random House, 1990) and *When Character Was King: A Story of Ronald Reagan* (New York: Viking Press, 2001); Caspar Weinberger, *Fighting for Peace: Seven Critical Years in the Pentagon* (New York: Warner Books, 1990); and George Shultz, *Turmoil and Triumph: My Years as Secretary of State* (New York: Charles Scribner and Sons, 1993), describe Mrs. Reagan's role in both foreign and domestic policy.

Eric J. Schmertz, Natalie Datlof, and Alexej Ugrinsky, eds., *Ronald Reagan's America* (Westport: Greenwood Press, 1997), is one of the many works on the Reagan presidency that pays particular attention to Mrs. Reagan's effect on both personnel and policy in her husband's administration. Others include John W. Sloan, *The Reagan Effect: Economics and Presidential Leadership* (Lawrence: University Press of Kansas, 1999); Lawrence Barrett, *Gambling with History: Ronald Reagan in the White House* (New York: Doubleday and Co., 1983); Ronnie Dugger, *On Reagan: The Man and His Presidency* (New York: McGraw-Hill Book Co., 1983); Steven Hayward, *The Age of Reagan: The Fall of the Liberal Order, 1964–1980* (Roseville, Calif.: Prima Books, 2001); Bob Schieffer and Gary Gates, *The Acting President* (New York: Dutton, 1989); and Jane Mayer and Doyle McManus, *Landslide: The Unmaking of a President* (Boston: Houghton Mifflin, 1988).

General biographies of Ronald Reagan discuss Mrs. Reagan's impact on her husband's life and presidency. President Reagan's official biographer, Edmund Morris, in *Dutch: A Memoir of Ronald Reagan* (New York: Random House, 1999), portrays Mrs. Reagan as having a much less substantial policy impact than have other authors. Lou Cannon, in both *Governor Reagan: His Rise to Power* (Boulder: Perseus Books, 2003) and *President Reagan: The Role of a Lifetime* (New York: Simon and Schuster, 1991), and William E. Pemberton, *Exit with Honor: The Life and Presidency of Ronald Reagan* (New York: M. E. Sharpe, 1997), portray the first lady as an active participant in all aspects of her husband's presidency.

Some of the general texts in the growing scholarship on first ladies shed considerable light on Mrs. Reagan's role in her husband's administration. James Rosebush, Mrs. Reagan's chief of staff, in *First Lady, Public Wife: A Behind-the-Scenes History of the Evolving Role of First Ladies in American Political Life* (Lanham, Md.: Madison Books, 1988), offers numerous insights into Mrs. Reagan's influence and provides a wealth of information about the structure and responsibilities of her staff. Gil Troy, *Mr. and Mrs. President* (Lawrence: University Press of Kansas, 2000); Carole Chandler Waldrop, *Presidents' Wives: The Lives of Forty-Four Women of Strength* (Jefferson, N.C.: McFarland and Co., 1989); Paul Boller, Jr., *Presidential Wives* (New York: Oxford University Press, 1999); and especially Anthony, *First Ladies,* vol. 2 (New York: William Morrow and Co., 1990), provide interesting detail on Mrs. Reagan's involvement in personnel and policy matters.

Three of the Reagan children—Patti Davis in *Homefront* (New York: Crown Publishing, 1986), Michael Reagan in *Michael Reagan: On the Outside Looking In* (New York: Kensington Publishing Corp., 1988), and Maureen Reagan in *First Father, First Daughter* (Boston: Little, Brown and Co., 1989)—have written about their lives growing up with well-known parents. The common theme running throughout the books is that Ronald and Nancy Reagan were so strongly committed to each other that their children often felt excluded from their parents' love.

While the final verdict has not been passed on Mrs. Reagan's "Just Say No" program, there is a growing body of literature that questions its effectiveness. Jeff Elliot, "America's 'Just Say No' Addiction," *Albion Monitor,* http://www.monitor.net/12–3-95/dare.html; Brian Bailker, "Just Say No: An Advocate of Drug Law Reform Says DARE Is Twenty-Year Failure," http://drugpolicy.org/library/newsweek_4_15_03.cfm; and a General Accounting Office Report, GAO-03–172R, "Youth Illicit Drug Use Prevention," http://www.GAO.gov, all question the effectiveness of antidrug programs built around the "Just Say No" approach.

A number of interesting articles have also been written about Mrs. Reagan. Joan Didion's "Pretty Nancy," *Saturday Evening Post,* 1 June 1968, is a devastating critique of Mrs. Reagan, who was then first lady of California. Much later Germaine Greer, in "Abolish Her: The Feminist Case against First Ladies," *The New Republic,* 26 June 1994, critiqued both Mrs. Reagan and the position of first lady in general from a feminist perspective. My own "Nancy Reagan: China Doll or Dragon Lady,"

Presidential Studies Quarterly 20, no. 4 (Fall 1990) uses Mrs. Reagan's term as first lady to illustrate the conflicting roles that first ladies are expected to play. Sidney Blumenthal, "The Mommy Track: In Defense of Nancy," *The New Republic*, 13 May 1991, offers a defense of Mrs. Reagan's involvement in the Reagan administration's policies.

To gain greater insight into Mrs. Reagan's influence on policy and personnel decisions, her staff system and its relationship to the West Wing staff, and her relation with the press, I interviewed Mrs. Reagan's former chief of staff, James Rosebush, and her press secretary, Sheila Tate. An interview with Rosalynn Carter's press secretary, Mary Hoyt, gave me additional details about the controversial transition from the Carter to the Reagan administrations. Each of the interviews was conducted by phone, taped to insure accuracy, and lasted about one hour.

INDEX

Portland Community College